MY TIME

My Time

WHAT LIFE IN RETIREMENT CAN BE

Jeffrey Golland

Charleston, SC
www.PalmettoPublishing.com

My Time
Copyright © 2021 by Jeffrey Golland

First Edition

ISBN: 978-1-63837-234-9

To my wondrous grandchildren, Owen, Myles, Oliver and Charlie.
For whenever you're ready.....

Introduction

As I was approaching retirement, now more than a decade ago, I found myself among the many in this category wondering what comes next. I knew, after a career as an attorney that spanned 37 years, that enough is enough even though I was perfectly happy in my work environment. As they say, the world is a big place out there; there is much to learn, much to explore, much to experience. But, these are largely intellectual challenges, understood in the brain but not necessarily in the heart. Or, you might say these are abstractions not visceral calculations. For example, I would find myself muttering to myself, "well, what are you going to do next... Tuesday?" What happens when you don't have those so well established rhythms of the work life and, instead, face seemingly unending hours of I don't know what? Of course, there are many who would describe this unstructured, open ended life as "freedom." Again, this is an easy word to say, but, in those moments of angst, you wonder whether you're ready to be freed.

Facing these uncertainties, I vividly recall having a conversation with friend and work colleague, Arathi, who suggested to me that I start writing a blog. In response, I said, "what's a blog?" Arathi patiently explained to me what a blog is and gave me a specific format that I might pursue. I thanked her not realizing in that moment how meaningful, how inspiring, this suggestion would turn out to be. In the course of the years that followed, as Lily and I traveled the world from Africa to Europe to South America to Southeast Asia and elsewhere, the blog would become my way of memorializing my life as I drew away from the professional sphere and into the uncharted territory of freedom. Some of our most enjoyable experiences overseas were those we shared with our amazing sons, Jesse and Alex, and our fabulous daughters-in-law, Laura and Katie. But, even apart from our travel experiences, what a wondrous adventure retirement life has turned out to be, where it became so much easier to stop, look around, take a deep breath, and smile knowing how lucky we have been. And, I would like to think that my accounts of these adventures and life experience have gotten better over the years.

Not that we're done with our life adventures, but at some point my thinking became influenced by the grandchildren in our lives. They are so young now and, while they know their Meme and Poppy at some level now, they are hardly at an age that they would have the depth of understanding of what it is to live a life and, in particular, the lives of their grandparents. And, so I thought why not collect my stories and put them in book form so that one day many years from now, probably long after we have left the scene, they might pick up this book and learn about Lily and me in terms they had never considered? Let them see from at least one person's perspective what freedom can mean from someone close to them in their lives. My hope is not just that they will find a new appreciation for us, but, far more importantly, that they will learn about the kinds of things that life has to offer that can enrich their own personal life experience. And, with that, bring a happier and more fulfilling life of their own.

Randomly Speaking

So, what's this? What self-focused, fatuous, self-indulgent, narcissistic fantasy is this? As if someone other than I would have any interest in hearing what I have to say. Ridiculous. First, it was Facebook, now a blog. have I any dignity left? Unlikely. but, it could be fun, right?

Let me begin with a few casual observations, of interest perhaps only to me.

1. As a recent emigre to Charleston, I have noticed how incredibly friendly the locals are. First, there was the guy, a total stranger, who offered to help me tote my new huge TV from the store to my house even though we had met 9 seconds earlier. This volunteerism included helping me tote this huge box up a flight of steps and into the living room. Then, there's the very nice lady at the Piggly Wiggly who blesses me every time I check out on her line. My path to heaven is absolutely insured. and, there's the local postmistress who asked me just the other day to come over and cook dinner for her family on the strength only of a t-shirt I was wearing indicating I might know something about food.

2. The median age of the folks who live in my immediate community full-time appears to be 109. Very nice, friendly folks, but not a lot of mountain climbers here.

3. I find it a bit unsettling that the "experts" do not appear to agree on whether it's "butt naked" or "buck naked." Shouldn't we be sure about this?

4. I discovered the other night how incredibly tasty a tilapia is when it is marinated in a chipotle sauce and, after a good saute, it is topped with sliced kiwi and banana that have been caramelized a bit in a pan with toasted sesame oil. try it.

5. I do believe there are more religious radio stations here than places where you can get shrimp and grits, and that's saying something. You've got your religious music stations (traditional and rock), your fire and brimstone stations, your sermon-laden stations, and your chatty moral advice shows. It's all there, and it's a bit of a challenge to find stations to fill up those auto pre-set positions for the car radio, believe me.

The Artwalk

I always knew that Charleston has a thriving art community, but I had no idea how user friendly it could be made for relative cultural neanderthals like me. take the Charleston Artwalk, for example, a divine inspiration. So simple in design, so enjoyable in the execution. the premise is that many of the city's galleries, linked together within blocks of one another, form a sort of hedonistic chain as they entice passers by to come inside and not just enjoy their wares, but drink their wine and eat their food as well. They got my attention. And so began my early education in, and introduction to, the low country art universe. Sometimes stacked 3 or 4 in a row, these galleries -- now morphed into cocktail party mode -- opened my eyes into a truly entertaining, and sometimes inspiring, creative surrounding. To see this region depicted in so many wildly diverse perspectives is to find new appreciation for the area we now call home. From watercolors to oils to etchings to mixed media to photography, they all reflect a true melange of color and ideas. if you close your eyes and try to synthesize all the different impressions you've just been exposed to, it really does create a sort of 3-D impression of this part of the world. Sure, there were moments when gallery owners would drone on long enough to make you want to say, "yes, but are you serving any wine?" But, the show they put on was worth the occasional extended tutorial. And, we won't mention the one gallery where I mortifyingly tripped into one room throwing all of the red wine in my cup against a wall that just moments before was a perfect white. Thankfully, my profuse apologies were quickly accepted although I have suspicions they deleted me from their mailing list the moment I walked out the door.

The Charleston Food & Wine Show

With the possible exception of New Orleans, no city in this country defines itself through its food more than Charleston. So -- when the city hosts its annual Food & Wine Festival, you drop everything and go. No excuses. And so I went.

I had a plan. I would be disciplined. I would start with appetizers and salads, work through the heartier offerings, and then do a dessert round (or rounds). Well, that plan lasted about 9 seconds as I began with a microbrew beer followed almost immediately by a caramel gelato. From that point on, it was essentially pure, random chaos. The gloves were off; all normal dietary rules were abandoned. Prepare yourself for what follows: pig head remoulade, tomato basil soup, couscous with leeks and shrimp, artichoke relish, praline pecans, banana pudding, catfish stew, sweet tea vodka bloody mary, coconut jasmine rice pudding (getting dizzy yet?), pinots run amok: noir, gris, and grigio. Double duck salad of confit and breast, blueberries, strawberries, and a vanilla bean vinaigrette; chilled Yukon potato soup with leeks and pickled crab salad, sauvignon blancs and malbecs, dark chocolate toffee crunch, pizza on flatbread with prosciutto, arugula and sliced parmesan. And, as they say, so much more. After two full hours of what had long since stopped being a casual grazing but had become instead a food frenzy worthy of your typically ravenous shark, I waddled semi-consciously to my car, hung out the "wide load" sign and got home so I could fall down.

It's good these events only come once a year.

Hell of a Meal

Amazing dinner tonight. Inspired totally by my new cooking environment: new oven, microwave, cooktop, and sink. How could that not be inspiring, right? Sooo, here's what I did. Sashimi-grade tuna, marinated in a mix of soy sauce, wasabi mustard, and fresh lime juice. Seared in a hot pan so that the tuna is crusty on the outside and raw on the inside. sliced fairly thin and arrayed on a bed of sauted leeks and shallots. Additionally, I roast some broccolini lightly doused in olive oil, balsamic vinegar and sprinkled with freshly ground pepper. Lastly, I do some sweet potato slices enhanced with olive oil, curry powder, cumin, paprika, and ground pepper and roasted to a crisp perfection. These three parts of the dinner have absolutely nothing to do with one another. No harmony here at all, no scheme, no theme except that each part is delicious and each is what I want to eat. Think of it as Italian-Indian-Japanese fusion if you're looking for a label. No rules here, after all. Be governed only by what you want. They call that hedonism, don't they?

Deep Seated or Deep Seeded?

Thought you knew, didn't you? I did too. But, when Lily raised to me the other day the notion that it was not "deep seated" at all but "deep seeded," well, I won't say I was rocked to my foundation, but I was taken aback that there was even another option. You would think that when you've been saying something all your life and you've never been corrected, you feel you're pretty safe that whatever you're saying you are saying correctly, right? The funny thing is that both versions of this phrase are virtually indistinguishable from one another to the naked ear, as it were. So - I had to acknowledge that it could have been the case over the years that other folks hearing me say this phrase may well have been thinking to themselves that I was, in fact, saying "deep seeded." and, when you get to think about it, a solid case could be made for both. "Deep seated" meaning, of course, felt down to your very crotch -- to where it all began, the source of all things, down to one's true core. But, "deep seeded" evokes a very similar sentiment: a primeval thought, present almost at the creation. Naturally, the "experts" are all over the place although it does give me some comfort that dictionaries are solidly in my corner. one of life's enduring mysteries? Probably not. But still….

Riding an Ostrich vs. a 4x4: Compare and Contrast

All kidding aside, surmounting an ostrich who has other plans is no mean feat. They may be incredibly stupid, but they know what they don't like, and that includes having homo sapiens on their backs. First, ostriches do not provide the same level of comfort as most other modes of transport, such as the 4x4. Instead of the nice wide soft seat in the 4x4, the ostrich offers a bony, narrow "saddle" area. In the case of the ostrich, I seriously underestimated its ability to accelerate. While I similarly underestimated the power behind the throttle of the 4x4, I never sensed its desire to throw me from the vehicle. Rather, I felt firmly astride a very grounded machine with a low center of gravity and which had many fewer feathers. I was tossed almost immediately by the ostrich. He quite literally zoomed out from under me. I had no chance. With the 4x4 I couldn't fall off except with great effort on my part even as we flew up deeply rutted hills and down steep embankments occasionally pocked with hub-cap high water hazards.

When riding an ostrich, one must grab hold of its wings and lean back, almost like water skiing. with the 4x4, you grab the much more user friendly handle bars around which one can easily wrap one's fingers without wondering if you're choking the bejesus out of it as was the case with the understandably stressed ostrich. With the 4x4, you gently hit the throttle and easily control your rate of speed. In contrast, the ostrich simply can't wait to get you off his back.

But, in the end, there's no denying that the 4x4 just doesn't have those long eyelashes so prominently visible on the ostrich. It's tough not to like these critters even if they do want to kill you.

The Jump

Thirteen years ago, when we were in New Zealand, we permitted a 13 year old, Jesse, to bungee jump. It was his driving ambition (to the extent someone of that age can have such a thing) and we, caught up in the moment, the so-called adults (Lily and me), permitted this insanity. I recall that after our return, people whose judgment we normally trusted looked at us agog and muttered that Family Services or the ASPCA or someone in authority should know about this.

We flash forward now to 2009. Alex is 22, hoping to see 23. In front of us looms the allegedly highest bungy jump on earth. This would put it at about 216 meters, or roughly the same as jumping off a 65 story building. It's located in Bloukrans along the southern coast of South Africa. Let me tell you, it is one thing to contemplate a jump like this, and quite another to stare into the maw of the endless descent that awaits you. Yet, here we are and Alex's bravado is now tinged with a trace of "oh, my god. what was I thinking?" Charlie, Alex's traveling buddy, who joins in on the mayhem, appears to be preternaturally calm, but admits to an elevated pulse rate.

Lily and I join the two masochists as sane holdout witnesses. The jumping off point is the underside of a bridge that spans a deep-cut gorge. It is the largest bridge in South Africa. To get to the jump, one must first traverse a walkway that inconveniently has only a widely spaced metal grate for a floor, so that with each passing step, if you look down, you see the increasing depths, both literal and figurative, that both Alex and Charlie are about to jump into. I unconsciously find myself holding on too much to the mesh "walls" of the walkway.

As the moment arrives, Alex and Charlie are bound up with harnesses, braces, ropes and pads. The similarities to an execution are too numerous to ignore. With their legs bound together, they must literally hop to the precipice where they await the mercifully short countdown. Alex, unconsciously grasps the sleeve of a staff member who instantly orders him in no uncertain terms to let go. Alex holds his arms wide and, in his best effort to replicate a swan dive, he steps off into the nothingness. My stomach flip flops.

We watch a live video feed of his descent and hold our breath as he recoils several times with skyward bounces each time the bungee cord is fully stretched. I am aware that I am breathing again. When he is back on the bridge, his grin could not be wider. You know, the kind of grin one can only have when you feel you have cheated death.

Later that day, I am introduced to a wonderful Cuban rum. I conclude that the two events are not entirely unrelated.

End Points

I do not believe myself to be an obsessive person, but I do own up to one obsession: end points of land. Those are the spots beyond which you cannot step on terra firma and which constitute the most western or southern point, etc. of a land mass. There's an allure in it for me -- the ability to say at that moment no man is further south, east, north or west of me. It's a bit silly, I know, and most definitely self-congratulatory, but I persist. Key West was one of these; Cabo de la Roca in Portugal another (western most point in Europe). and, this trip has delightfully provided two. the first was a few days ago on the trip down to the Cape of Good Hope at the bottom of the peninsula stretching south from Capetown. Its spectacular setting of craggy mountains and crashing waves only enhanced the fact that you could stand on a spot and claim in that moment that no man could stand more southwest than you and still be on the African continent.

A few minutes ago, we had a similar experience at Cape Agulhas. It is here that you can stand on the absolute southernmost point of the African continent, and also where you can figuratively have one foot in the Atlantic Ocean and one on the Indian Ocean. Perfection!

Next, I want to straddle the equator, but that's for another time.

How to Greet a Cheetah

It's somewhat more elaborate than you might think. First, our "handlers" at the cheetah sanctuary we visited outside Stellenbosch advised us not to approach these beasts from the front. Apparently, they consider this way too threatening, so this is a good thing to know. Second, you should stroke them only with a flat hand, and, for God's sake, stay away from the groin area. Third, do not reach for their heads. I don't know what the problem is with that, but I considered it sage advice nevertheless. Fourth, stay in a crouched position with one knee on the ground so you can jump back fairly quickly should the big guy get a sudden hunger pang.

It appears that while sitting next to a grown cheetah is really quite safe, they can get "boisterous" (their term, not mine). And, you don't want a boisterous cheetah whose claws are maybe 18 inches from your jugular, if you get my drift. In this case, it was Hemingway, a 4 year old male. Hemingway seemed calm enough, but when there's no fence between you and a cheetah, your imagination can become very vivid, if you know what I mean. We learned that cheetahs sleep about 22 hours per day -- the consummate 4 legged couch potato -- but when they want to hunt (which, oddly, is solely a day-time activity for them), they earn their title as fastest animal on the planet.

I'll bet you didn't know that the hair where a cheetah's black spots are of a different consistency than the rest of its coat, giving the black spots a slightly raised appearance to better camouflage them. Yeah, it was new to me too.

THURSDAY, APRIL 30, 2009

So it Begins With the Animals

We were headed south to the Cape of Good Hope. You know -- the point of land immortalized by Vasco de Gama a half millennium ago. The peninsula leading down to the Cape is now park land, mile after mile of breathtaking emptiness. Not barrenness, mind you, just endless miles of dramatic land and seascapes with absolutely no hint that humans walk the earth. Fabulous.

Apparently, a lot of animals think so too since they pop up like "whack-a-moles" when you least expect them. On today's program, we had the pleasure of meeting up with baboons, penguins, ostriches, and dassies (more on these particular creatures later). First, the baboons. They are fearless. We came upon them first on the open road -- and I mean literally on the road -- where they nonchalantly occupied the center of the roadway causing something of a traffic back-up. I'm not thinking "cute" or "adorable" when in their presence. These guys are big, let me tell you. And, as the phrase goes, if looks could kill, these guys would be doing jail time. Their laser-like stare would cause the most hardened mafia hit man to blink. People, such as myself, would get within a couple of feet of them, and we might as well have been invisible. They just didn't care. The signs in the area promised that baboons were dangerous and so we discretely ceded them the right of way until they would let us pass.

Then came the penguins. Not your regal emperor bird found in Antarctica, but the South African penguin. Much smaller, but again, almost fearless. We came upon them on a path to the beach and allowed us to come within inches of them. I touched one and found

13

how surprised I was at how feathery they are, like birds. (Oh, right, they are birds.) What was more amazing, however, was a scene in which penguins and people shared a beach together. I'm talking sunbathers and their kids, with people playing paddleball. The penguins, while not exactly dodging beach blankets, would literally swim around splashing kids and scolding parents as if they were some sort of fixture, like a tree. Amazing.

In a somewhat more secluded spot, we watched one penguin come up from taking a dip in the water to where his or her spouse was sitting on a couple of babies. While I couldn't be entirely sure of this, it appeared that the squawking going on between them was in the manner of one saying to the other, "where the hell have you been? I've been sitting on these guys for hours while you're out joyriding!" Male and female penguins are very hard to distinguish -- at least for me they are -- so, it was hard to know who was griping at who. As if it matters.

A final word about dassies. I had never heard of these creatures before, but have been told they are genetically linked to elephants. This comes as a bit of a surprise to me since dassies look like small groundhogs and weigh about two tons less than their alleged partners-in-evolution, the elephant. Additionally, the dassie's ears are tiny while we all know the elephant's ear to be the size of a small station wagon. With some skepticism, I cross examine a park person about this, and she assures me the organic structure and skeletal design of the two creatures are very similar. To my ear, this is like saying that I am biologically linked to a redwood tree. I'm not getting it.

Driving on the Left....

is serious business. What a challenge to your senses. Everything is so thoroughly counter intuitive. Steering wheel on the right, turn signal and lights on the right side of the wheel, manual shift on the left! Clockwise moving traffic circles! You must suppress every driving instinct you have because the alternative is not good, my friend. So - to repeat the mantra my friend, marcus, left me with, "left is right and right is wrong." I know he meant to be helpful with this, but given the split seconds in which some driving decisions must be made, I've reduced this most essential guidance to "left!!" Can't wait to get out of Capetown to make this mental and physical effort simpler. My advice: do not multi-task while attempting this fretful activity. This means no music, talking, maybe even no gum chewing. And, never, I repeat, never do this when jet lagged. I am at red alert all the time.

(Yes, it does get better. But, that's much later.)

Capetown

As Alex said to me, Capetown is one of those few places on the planet that exceeds already unrealistically high expectations. What a vibrant mix this place is! It is, first, beautiful; a jewel of a city nestled into the protective shadow of Table Mountain, an enormous, awe-inspiring colossus of a stone formation that provides a backdrop from almost any sight line in the city. Capetown is chic; it is tropical; it is cosmopolitan; it is diverse, and, at least for our visit, offers air that is crisp and fresh while still managing to bask in almost 90 degree temperatures. As is true for many of the world's great cities, Capetown's diverse population is not so much a source of tension as it is a promoter of energy. Its mix of Muslims, whites, blacks and Indians has produced for us in our short stay thus far a visual and cultural vitality that you just don't see every day.

After the hearty and tempting feast offered to us at breakfast at our B&B (De Tafelberg Guest House), Alex literally appeared at my shoulder as I chatted with our host, Kris. Not having seen Alex for 3 months, and having lived vicariously through his vivid emails of his not-so-safe exploits in South America, he was a sight for sore eyes, now with a nicely developing beard. (To add to his colorful bag of exploits -- like skydiving and trekking for days through glaciers and mountains -- he informed us he had spent his time in South Africa getting dropped into the cold waters off Gainsbaai in cages while ravenous great white sharks banged up against the bars looking for dessert. Not my idea of a restful morning, but who am I to argue?) Since he had been in town a few days, Alex served as tour guide as he led us through city neighborhoods and parks. We visited the 6th

District Museum, a poignant testimonial to the many who suffered under apartheid and, specifically, the thousands who were forcibly evicted from their downtown homes and forced into townships to make way for urban development. I spoke to the man who established the museum, and marveled at the museum's (and his) upbeat message about hope and perseverance.

With a wonderful lunch under our belts at an outdoor cafe, we discovered the city's open air market, an intricate maze filled with a dizzying array of local art, artifacts, clothing and junk. I particularly loved the awesome tribal masks carved from wood that I wish I had room for in my suitcase. All this came complete, of course, with a laughingly funny array of hawkers who would charm, cajole, plead and arm twist any possible sale -- a negotiator's smorgasbord.

This is a very cool place.

An Unending Transit

Those of you who have traveled long distances by air know the weird transformation that takes hold of one's psyche during these encounters. In my case, the current episode is the numbingly long flight from Washington, D.C. to Johannesburg, non stop, which, according to Wikipedia, is the third longest such flight on planet earth. Up here, at 39,000 feet, the notion of day and night evaporates. You sit, watch movies, read, sleep, eat, listen to music, talk. and, repeat and repeat and repeat. In this case, 16 hours' worth of this sedentary dance. (Kudos, by the way, to South African Airways: touch screens with a bevy of movies, TV shows, music options, and games. and, free wine. not bad.) The joy for me came moments ago when it became socially acceptable to open the window shades and below lay Africa. Namibia, to be precise. A vast brownness of the likes I know I've never seen. Africa! Vast stretches of sand dunes, crusty lunar-scapes with widely scattered strands of snake-like roads leading absolutely nowhere. No, Toto, we're definitely not in Kansas anymore.

To be honest, notwithstanding the difficulties of such unending transits, they do add something to the experience other than a sore butt. The charm of distance, for one thing, and the palpable feel of the exotic would be diminshed without this "labor." You know you have come a long way to experience something special. And, so it is with me.

Meeting Up With The King

I was about 8 or 9 feet from two 400 pound lions today. They were sound asleep...at first. But, when one of them raised his head, turned, and looked me straight in the eye, my fight or flight impulses raged out of control. It was exhilarating and unnerving all at the same time. I don't recall an event that so focused my senses. While I took the lion's stare with all the gravity owing in such encounters, I must say that the king of beasts was at best bored, and at worst absolutely oblivious. As much as I cared about where I found myself, he could not have cared less. Total insouciance! Shaun, our guide, was as calm and unconcerned as "big boy," as they called him. He assured us that as long as we didn't approach them head on (which they perceive as a threat), and as long as we didn't stand up or make sudden movements we would be fine. By staying seated, Shaun said, the lions would not distinguish us from the land rover, which I guess is not threatening to them. Standing up, however, would be a game changer. Then, we would be perceived as humans and the rules would change instantly. I must have asked shaun several times about how these "rules of engagement" were agreed to. Was there some memo that set all this out that the lions confirmed in some regal signing ceremony? How could he be absolutely certain it would work like this in all cases? In any event, as I sat in the very open and exposed land rover, I tried to become physically and psychically merged with my seat.

Shaun stopped the rover and we watched these huge lions for about 20 minutes. I prayed the car would start when it was time to go.

How To Have Fun And Be Nervous At The Same Time

We experienced today what they call a "walking" safari. Sounds simple enough but, then again, maybe not. we are met by our guide, Samson, a local tribesman who doubles as our tracker on our morning and evening safaris. I cannot help but notice the large weapon he is shouldering. I begin to appreciate the earnestness of the threat out there when he shows us his bullets which are larger than most toes. We are about to walk out into the bush and Samson is our first and last line of defense. On today's walk, it's just Samson, Lily, Alex and me.

Samson tells us to walk single file behind him. When I ask why, he calmly tells me it's so he has a better field of vision should he need to shoot an attacking animal. My breathing becomes a bit shallower. Alex and I jostle for position to see who can adhere as closely as possible to the back of Samson's shirt. Lily, however, thinking she's out for a walk on the beach -- head down, looking for the perfect seashell -- lags behind apparently content to become an amuse bouche for a lurking predator.

Samson is delightful as he introduces us to his wide ranging knowledge of all things flora and fauna in the bush. Under any other circumstance, this would be a joyful experience, but I get a stiff neck craning it in every possible direction checking to see if there might be a 4 legged beast tagging along, stalking. We are told that under no circumstances are we to run if we see one of the big guys: lion, cheetah, leopard, buffalo. apparently, that act rings their dinner bell. Thanks for the heads up, Samson.

Game On!

You gotta be kidding me! We're still on the airplane doing a slow taxi to the terminal in Hoedspruit when we spot 3 warthogs in the tall grass next to the runway. And, get this. They're being stalked by a cheetah! We see the tail of the cheetah as it makes its move -- a nano-glimpse of a high arching jump that we know to be the attack -- only to have the plane continue on toward the terminal, leaving the fate of the warthogs.....uncertain.

We leave our porcine friends to head out to the Pondoro Game Lodge, some miles north. On the 10 mile dirt, and heavily rutted, road to this private reserve we see giraffes by the side of the road, impala, wildebeast, and zebra. crazy. And, we have yet to go on our first game drive.

A word about the lodge: outrageous! Check it out online (http://www.pondoro.co.za/). Canopied beds in their 6 mini-lodges; a bath tub out on a deck overlooking the Oliphants River; a shower with a full glass wall revealing another nice view of the river; a shower head reminiscent of the one that almost killed Kramer in an epic Seinfeld episode; 3 gourmet meals a day; 2 4-hour driving safaris per day, one at 5:30 a.m., the other at 4 p.m.; a walking safari after breakfast; and a full menu of spa offerings. (Alex gets his first ever full body massage and a pedicure!)

On our first game drive the afternoon we arrive, the giraffes, zebras, wildebeast and impala show up in earnest. they are simply every-where. Oddly, though, the comic star of the afternoon is a quirky bird they call the helmeted guinea fowl. Apparently, these sorrowful birds are seriously contending for the honor of most stupid animal on planet earth. Unlike most flocks of birds who flee in a flash when one of their tribe is either threatened (or even thinks he's threatened), these bozos -- we are told -- actually are happy to sit on a branch while the friend immediately next to him or her is shot out of the tree, completely oblivious to the notion of danger. We take note that as our land rover approaches them, it doesn't occur to them to get out of the way. No, no, that wold be far too simple a solution. Instead, they run -- imagine what a bird on fire might run like -- skirting the front wheels of the rover as if a place squarely under the tires would be the safest place to be! Darwin is definitely scratching his head at these evolutionary outliers.

As darkness falls, we spot a leopard, not an easy sighting, we are told. it's a young male. about 15 feet away. he's wary at first at our presence, but soon enough emerges from the bush to continue his nocturnal hunt. Beautiful.

Enter Mojo

It was a difficult start. I mean, just imagine: you are separated from your family and friends; you are put to sleep and then awaken only to find that your balls have been cut off; you are in considerable pain; people come to greet you who are total strangers, but who act like they know you; you are whisked off to a strange place; you poop on the floor. Is this not the bottom, or what? And, so it was with Mojo the newest member of our family. Hello!

We should have seen it coming, but the next morning we saw a new dog: tail wagging, plainly happy to see us, eager to get outside to relieve himself there rather than re-enact his performance of the evening before. And, brandishing a furious appetite like any self-respecting lab puppy. We take him to the beach where he freaks out (although not really in a bad way) at the wave action at the shore-line, leaping straight up in the air as if the waves were electrically charged. Forty-eight hours later he is leaping into the waves, again, like any self-respecting lab. He is as black as night, his coat as shiny as a penguin's. We are told he was thrown out of a car in the back roads of South Carolina only to be rescued by a near-by hunter who sees this and who swoops him up and takes him to the local vet. He is fostered by a family and named Miller after the vet who saved him from a bout with parvo, deadly to most puppies.

A word on his name. No, he is not named as a cutsey salute to Austin Powers. "Mojo" in the local Gullah culture here means "black magic." Knowing what this little guy has been through – the abandonment, the parvo – how is it not a miracle that this little guy is still with us?

Mojitos R Us

People are funny when it comes to describing what their vision of heaven is. For some, it's the proverbial pearly gates, angels cooing, trumpets blaring. For others, it's whatever their personal vision of what peace and tranquility might be -- maybe a seductive, secluded beach or perhaps an inspiring and cooling mountain lake. My sense is a bit different. For me, it's an eternal Mojito Challenge of the type just served up here in Charleston, just as it is every year when one's thoughts turn to tropical drinks.

This year's affair was set at the Charleston Aquarium, a brilliant choice for a venue when you think about it: a fabulous array of all things aquatic from sharks to snakes to seahorses to jellyfish and all things in between. Plus, the totally pleasurable option of the outside verandas where one can seek refuge from the teeming and wonderfully boisterous crowds who have come to share in the exact pursuit that brought you here -- the perfect mojito. What was once a simple and pleasing concoction of rum, simple syrup and some muddled mint now becomes a feverish (and highly entertaining) smack down among the city's best bartenders to catch that special edge that will earn them the much sought after bragging rights of the best mojito maker in town.

And, make no mistake about it, these combatants will go to considerable lengths to get your attention. No fruit is left unexplored. You have your strawberry, kiwi, peach, watermelon, passion fruit, and banana, naturally. But, have you wondered what your mojito might taste like with a shot of elderberry, rosemary, cucumber, agave, dragonfruit, or --perhaps most exotic of all -- the yuzu? Really, the yuzu? You know -- a Japanese fruit somewhat resembling the grape-fruit. Somewhat. Introduce into this sublime ocean of vitamin C some ginger, a tannic lime meringue, or a poblano infused simple syrup or a simple splash of vanilla and you begin to see how demonic the pursuit of a prize winner can be. No stone is left unturned; no essence is left unexplored.

I concede my judgment may have become a bit clouded after sampling 14 different concoctions. My recollection is that they were all good. Some too sweet. Some too obviously gimmicky. Some bearing absolutely no resemblance to the mojito that inspired this event. But, what a fabulous evening.

Oh. The winner? A zesty concoction from "Coast," a restaurant that has experienced more than its share of success at this event in the past. This year's entry: a potion of strawberry, rhubarb and rosemary and -- the clincher -- a shot of strawberry pop rocks thrown in at the last moment that effervesce up your nose for a most memorable and sensory mojito experience. Ta da!

Lost and Found

All in all, it lasted only about an hour, but I swear in my heart it lasted much, much longer. I left Mojo on the deck, walled in (or so I thought) eliminating the possibility of escape. Lily was inside no more than 15 feet away. I ran off to hit some golf balls content that Mojo would be pleased to stay on the deck with a full bowl of water and lots of sunshine. Life is good, right? I returned to find the deck empty and then, to my horror, discovered he was not in the house either. Lily and I went to red alert (more frequently known as panic mode) as we frantically decided to scan the neighborhood and beach, she on foot, me in the car. And, here's where the stress really ramps up. Is he safe? Has he been taken? Has he left the area? Will he walk into oncoming traffic? Is he suffering in this heat without water? Has an alligator gotten to him -- not an idle worry in these parts. Then the thoughts turn to: Will we ever see him again? He's such a great dog. How can we lose him so quickly, just as he's hitting his stride as a member of our family and as part of the larger community here. Can he just disappear into thin air?

After driving the neighborhoods and asking every living soul if they've seen a wayward black lab, I head back to the house certain he must be there. It has to be a mistake. There's no logical explanation for his escape. Nothing but empty, quiet space. He is truly gone. I head to the Community Association which alerts the area security and the local police. I am aware that my mind is working much faster than my consciousness can keep up with it. I am reacting, not really thinking, at least not analytically.

Then the break comes. Lily picks up a phone message from a voice belonging to a young girl who asks that we pick up Mojo as quickly as possible. The problem is the call is from a cell phone and is so garbled we really can't decipher the words to make out an address or phone number. Infuriating! So frustrating! As I head back to the Community Association for a look at the Directory, Lily calls me and thinks she has figured out the name and address of our rescuers. I call them and a young girl tells me her sister is working her way on foot toward our house. I don't wait. I get in the car and head in their direction only to spot the rogue Mojo and his ever so young rescuer. She apologizes for allowing him to follow her dogs (an Irish setter and a golden retriever) and for allowing Mojo to roll in the mud. She has cleaned him up the best she can. I spend the next minute falling all over myself to assure her there's nothing for her to apologize about; that we are very, very grateful for her efforts. I ask her for her name and in an instant forget it. Maybe we will see her again, maybe not. Mojo jumps into the car. I believe he looks guilty, but I might have been reading a bit too much into it.

And Mojo? He's in the dog house. Big time.

THURSDAY, JULY 23, 2009

Corkie and Frank

Corkie and Frank are sweet guys, really. They may seem like they're 109, but they're not. Retired military guys: a bit salty but, as they say, true as the day is long. These guys meet every morning at 7 a.m. sharp, and I mean every morning like since the Coolidge Adminstration where they proceed to stroll to the beach figuratively arm in arm (although they'd be embarrassed by that notion). Not only can you set your watch by these guys, but they always wear the same thing: Corkie is in his khaki shorts, white polo and green cap while Frank is partial to his faded U.S. Open t-shirt and blue swim trunks. Every day. Corkie and Frank are notable for a number of reasons, but in my world, they are noteworthy because of their love for Mojo. They take great delight in seeing my somewhat unruly pup, maybe because as former dog owners they miss their own companions, or maybe because they are just smitten with Mojo.

It has become a ritual, this daily early morning meeting. Mojo knows they're lurking about because his sense of anticipation is acute. This may be because Mojo likes these guys as they like him, or (as is more likely) it is because Corkie and Frank bring dog treats every day which Mojo looks forward to the way you and I look forward to breathing. If the guys have reached the beach before us, I spend all my efforts in trying to keep my arm from being torn out of its socket as Mojo urges us forward to the beach in much the same way you and I would run if free $100 bills were being given away fifty feet in front of us. To avoid unnecessary surgery, I simply let Mojo off the leash and watch him tear off like the proverbial bat out of hell as he heads for the sand in search of what apparently is the world's most heavenly and delicious tasty tidbits available to canines. I mean, how good can they be? When Mojo reaches the guys, he sits dutifully -- closer than a shadow -- and waits in frantic anticipation of what comes out of the old guys' pockets. I hear their laughter as I slowly catch up to this truly comical and endearing scene, and then -- once his dog treat habit has been satisfied -- brace myself for Mojo's totally predictable fixation on the tennis balls I bring that will exercise his virtually endless desire to chase moving objects.

Not a bad way to start the morning

No, that wasn't Michael Phelps

I've taken to the pool. It was a reluctant embrace. I'm a runner, not a swimmer. But, an assortment of back and hamstring ills drove me to do whatever I could to fulfill my need for exercise in the morning. The problem is I am very slow. I imagine a visit by the folks from the Guinness Book of World Records informing me that I am the third slowest swimmer on the planet, faster only than a 96 year old woman in Brooklyn and an Argentine amputee. There are leaves floating in the pool that, shockingly, seem to keep up with my less than torrid pace.

The thing about swimming laps is that there may be almost no other human endeavor that forces you to be alone with your thoughts for so long. There is truly nothing to distract you unless you consider watching the black tile line on the bottom of the pool a "distraction." Running is a solitary sport, but at least then your eyes can scan the scenery or, if on the treadmill, you can lose yourself in sports highlights, the news, or the latest culinary concoction from the Food Network. No, the closest things to this experience are those sleepless nights when you lay in bed in the dark and let your brain do somersaults making you crazy with irrational thoughts. So - I'm learning that to be a successful lap swimmer you need to be comfortable in your own skin and okay to be alone with your thoughts. So far, so good.

To keep track of where I am in this monotonous wet universe, I have strangely adopted a system of remembering my lap count by labeling them with a uniform number of a Yankee of ages gone by. Thus, lap 3 is Babe Ruth; lap 7, Mickey Mantle; lap 14, "Moose" Skowren; lap 25, Joe Pepitone, and so on. Yes, I know it's a bit embarrassing, but it is effective, if juvenile.

I started out doing 10 laps (Tony Kubek). Then got to 19 ("Bullet" Bob Turley), and last week, the much sought after lap 33 (David Wells) which denotes 66 times up and back -- a full mile! Of course, it took me almost an hour and a half to do it. That's enough time for some empires to rise and fall. But, I was stoked hitting that magical mark. Now, I'm thinking of going for two miles, but the folks here had better turn on the flood lights for that adventure.

Dinner Tonight (and, yes, I'm talking to you)

Here's what you need: some shrimp, some red chili linguini (although, frankly, any pasta will do), a shallot, as many garlic cloves as your mate will tolerate, a scallion or two, white wine you like, the juice of maybe half a lemon, a nice handful of pine nuts, some fresh basil, olive oil, shredded romano cheese, and the obligatory freshly ground pepper.

Here's what you do:

1. boil your shrimp erring perhaps on undercooking them a bit. Shouldn't take more than a minute.
2. chop your shallot and garlic and saute in a bit of olive oil until they become translucent. When they do, add in a nice soaking of the white wine and allow the mixture to reduce. When reduced, add to this mixture some chopped scallion.
3. separately toast the pine nuts either dry or in a bit of olive oil. Be careful not to burn -- use a low heat.
4. cook your pasta. In the case of the chili linguini I used, it took 3 minutes. Drain the pasta.
5. If you haven't done it already, chop your basil leaves.
6. after you've shelled the cooked shrimp, add the shrimp to the saute mixture for maybe a minute. No more. Sprinkle liberally with the ground pepper. Add in the pasta and stir.
7. to this shrimp and pasta mix, add in the toasted pine nuts and chopped basil. Squeeze in the lemon juice, and, if you like, drizzle some more olive oil over the mix.

8. top the whole shebang with as much shredded romano cheese as you like. (Yes, yes, I know. Italians would frown and mumble not so subdued expletives at adding cheese to a seafood pasta dish, but folks this isn't Italy.)

Be prepared to chow down on a multi-textured, tasty melange of flavors.

You got better plans?

Now I know Why They Call Them Fire Ants

Because they hurt like hell, that's why. We've just spent a kingly sum on fixing up the "estate." Let's just say, we spent enough to keep a small third world economy afloat for a bit. So, as you might imagine, when the landscaper encouraged us to give extra water to the newly planted trees, shrubs, and flowers, we were more than willing. And, mind you, this does not come naturally to us. Our idea of gardening is watching someone else do it. There is no Plan B. The trouble with gardening in the semi-tropics, as you have here, is that you have the constant company of scorching heat and humidity that can peel any man-made substance off any surface exposed to the atmosphere. Plus, there are the bugs. For example, the mosquitoes here are required to have drivers' licenses. The palmetto bugs are so large they can be drafted to pull small carts, if you have that need. No one warned me about the fire ants though.

So there I was trying to be manly about ignoring the pothole sized mosquito bites I was actively collecting on my shins and back when I could not help but notice that my feet were on fire even though I couldn't see the flames. I looked down to see a populous nation of black ants literally covering my feet. If it was human flesh they sought, they had hit the mother lode. The yelp I emitted got Mojo's attention, although only for a moment as he turned over on the driveway to continue his mid-day snooze. I did what any fire department would do -- I hosed down my feet, but the burning would now have to run its course.

I mentioned this experience to the guys who were finishing up with the landscaping and their eyes and mine simultaneously gazed down at their feet: combat boots that would make Attila the Hun proud. Impenetrable.

I'm off to the shoe store.

Bruschetta, American Style

Everyone loves bruschetta, right? Crunchy bread with ample flavors of garlic and tomatoes and basil. The Italians have perfected it, and I am not at all inclined to mess with a formula that has had a successful run pretty much since Julius Caeser. Ok, so maybe I am. I can't help myself. I'm calling my version.... bruschetta, American style.

What you need: all the things you normally need -- a good, crunchy bread. Personally, I like a fresh ciabatta, but, really, there are so many freshly baked loaves that will do. Plenty of fresh basil, several cloves of garlic, a package of grape tomatoes. (stay away from large tomatoes -- they get too mushy when you saute them.) add in some sliced up sun dried tomatoes, shallots, maybe two scallion, and -- for the American wrinkle -- get a package of chicken tenders and a ripe avocado.

To prepare: marinate your chicken in whatever prepared marinade you like. Truly, it hardly matters. In my case, I used Mrs. Dash's Lemon Herb Peppercorn, but knock yourself out here. Use whatever you like. Saute the marinated chicken in a little olive oil. While the chicken is getting happy, chop your garlic cloves and shallots and place in a pan with some olive oil. Chop up your grape tomatoes and add those to the mix along with the chopped scallion and sundried tomatoes. Chop your basil and add to the saute mix. Cut the avocado into small squares.

When the chicken is almost fully cooked, remove the tenders from the pan and cut into small pieces. For maybe a minute or so, add the chicken to the saute mix of tomatoes, garlic, shallots, etc. Throw the whole mix into a large bowl and add in the chopped avocado. Cut your bread into thin slices and toast. When the toast is done, rub with a garlic clove and spread with a bit of olive oil. Top with the chicken, garlic, tomato mix piling it as high as you dare. If you're a cheesy kind of guy, feel free to sprinkle some shredded romano cheese over the this gorgeous creation. Understand that this will provide you with a messy dining experience, so don't wear your Sunday finest when enjoying this.

Wine is a must with this. Amazing how either red or white will do the trick. You decide.

The French would say, "bon apetit." I don't know what the Italians would say.

Comfort Food, Jeff Style

For some people it's oatmeal. For others it's clam chowder. And, for others still it's meat loaf and mashed potatoes or maybe some brownies. For me, though, it's something much closer to what I prepared last night. A sumptuous bed of Israeli couscous laced with sautéed peppers, toasted pine nuts, and some chopped scallion. Atop this mouth watering base sit some sautéed shrimp which have just shared a pan with shallots and garlic. As a side, I roasted some leeks and grape tomatoes, and added the always welcome crusty bread that's been sprinkled with olive oil. Oh yeah, this is good. And, really, not hard to put together. You will want to do this, I'm telling you. Well, that is if you like to eat.

Ok, here's what you need: a box of Israeli couscous (sometimes called toasted pasta pearls -- it's larger and rounder than the more standard couscous you tend to see), maybe a pound of shrimp, one leek, chopped, a good handful of grape tomatoes, a chopped shallot, a couple of chopped garlic cloves, one red pepper, chopped, 2 cups of chicken or vegetable broth, maybe three scallions, a nice chopped chunk from a seedless cucumber, some chopped chives, a healthy handful of pine nuts, course ground pepper, and the ever-popular olive oil and balsamic vinegar.

As I am wont to do, I did all my chopping first, and so should you. You'll be glad you did. That means your chives, shallot, garlic, red pepper, cucumber, and scallions. Shell and de-vein the shrimp (or, better yet, have a kindly friend do this). Pre-heat your oven to 450 degrees, and on a tinfoil covered pan, array your chopped leek and your grape tomatoes. Sprinkle the leeks and tomatoes with olive oil and balsamic vinegar and top with some ground black pepper and salt (if you like). Then, roast the leeks and tomatoes for maybe 10 minutes. Cook the couscous using the broth instead of water, following the directions on the box. Sauté the chopped red pepper in a pan with some olive oil until it starts turning dark. When the peppers are done, add into the couscous, and add in as well the chopped cucumber and scallion. In a pan, sauté the chopped shallot and garlic in some olive oil until nicely translucent. At the same time, separately toast the pine nuts in a little olive oil and add them to the couscous mix. (These little guys can burn easily so keep an eye on them.) Add in the shelled shrimp to your shallot and garlic mix and top with a healthy coating of ground pepper. The shrimp shouldn't take long to cook -- maybe 2 minutes. While you're turning the shrimp, heat up that crusty bread.

Place a nice mound of the couscous mix on the plate (next to the leeks and tomatoes) and top with as many shrimp as you dare to eat, and, finally, top the shrimp with your chopped chives.

That's how you spell comfort!

I love thee not!

The legend grows. Mojo has by now firmly established himself as a force of nature on the beach during our early morning romps, but every now and then he accentuates his reputation with an exclamation point that is as large and black as he is. This morning was such a time. It is not unusual, especially over holiday weekends, for families having re-unions here to gather at the beach for an early morning photo shoot. Everyone is dressed to the nines; the kids are scrubbed; the photographer is restless to get the job done before the sunlight becomes too bright. Today, Mojo and I spotted what appeared to be one of these groups arrayed near the shore line, and we headed in that direction up the beach, as we always do. Unfortunately, Mojo took off to get closer to what he hoped would be "new friends" and he frantically dove into the mix. What I did not realize was that this group was a wedding party, and they were in the midst of the ceremony when Mojo crashed it! Naturally, he shook off all the loose water on him in the space between him and the bride and pastor, and he deftly dropped his tennis ball at the bride's feet with clearly great expectations for further play. Some were amused; others were not. The bride's maid and best man, in particular, were doing whatever they could to unceremoniously and forcibly usher Mojo to the exit.

As I approached the assembled wedding party, I knew I could not pretend to feign ignorance of the ownership of this beast. The ball launcher in my hand and a sandy leash were pretty much a smoking gun, if you know what I mean. So, I did my best sheepish routine but did not slow my pace. I will say that the bride -- in the midst of the ongoing ceremony -- gave me a furtive wave as if to allay my horror at the poor etiquette of my very own wedding crasher.

On the return trip down the beach, the wedding group was breaking up giving me an opportunity to apologize in a more personal way. Most everyone assured me it was all copacetic, except, that is, for the bride's maid. I don't know that she thought my apology was all that sincere.

Maybe it was the two bags of dog shit I was toting that dampened the mood.

Hell on Wheels

Why do they say -- when referring to a long lost skill -- it's "like riding a bike," as if this is something you never forget? Well, I forgot. It had been 35 years since I rode a bike. I guess the statute of limitations had run because this was an alien form of movement to me. When I was a kid I never had a bike. My mother made no bones about it. She had lost a younger brother to a bike accident when he was a late teen, and so I was not to have one. She fully confessed that this was irrational, but this was to be the law of the land in the Golland household. As a young lawyer I actually bought a bike in an effort to self-teach, but that was 35 years ago, and it was not a smashing success.

A couple of weeks ago, Lily bought a bike and encouraged me to do the same so we could share this activity. I asked her why she was in such a hurry to get her hands on the proceeds of my life insurance policy. She assured me she harbored no such thoughts. This morning, with our friend Maggie in town, the three of us set out on bikes --Maggie and I on rentals -- to explore the Isle of Palms. Why the bike rental folks let me have this contraption is beyond me. I took off in a style that can only be described most generously as "wobbly." Madly over-correcting, and otherwise displaying the kind of erratic behavior that most sane folks steer clear of like the plague, I tried to make my way out of the small parking lot.

Allow me to get the bad news out of the way right away. Over the course of the next three hours, I fell four times. Once when I simply could not negotiate a left turn in the time allotted and spilled over into someone's front yard. A second time when I ran headlong into an oncoming cyclist because of my paralyzing indecision of whether to stop or turn. This one was on concrete and left me suitably blood-ied. It is a tribute to the other cyclist that he didn't flatten me. The third and fourth spills were on the beach where diabolically placed pools of water appeared out of nowhere causing me to exit my bike as if it were fitted with an ejection seat.

I will say that once I got my sea legs, I loved seeing what was for me previously unseen parts of Wild Dunes and other parts of the Isle of Palms. Some pretty gorgeous neighborhoods, great views of the marshlands, and the picturesque intracoastal waterway and local marina.

I also came away with a vastly higher level of respect for Lance Armstrong.

When Necessity is the Mother of Invention

Alex loves all things sports. As whacked out as he is in this very specialized domain of human pursuit, his love for NFL football dwarfs all other passions. It makes his love of basketball, which is almost unsurpassed, seem passive by comparison. When he left on his year long sojourn around the globe, his abiding concern was how he would get to watch football games from the other side of the planet. He got edgy when asked about it. And, here we are at the onset of the 2009 NFL schedule and Alex finds himself in Perth, Australia -- perhaps better known for its kangaroo steaks than its opinions on how to run the wildcat offense. Alex's feverish pursuit of football mania included his recent all-nighter when he participated in not one, but two, fantasy league drafts that were actually taking place in far more civilized time frames in the western hemisphere.

Opening day: Sunday, September 13. Alex is so pumped because he has discovered a website that will enable him to watch any and all NFL games online, and in hi-def to boot. The fact that, for him, these contests will take place in the dark of Perth nights when most normal Aussies are sound asleep is irrelevant. Alex has taken long naps during the day to prepare himself for his night-long, pass-happy vigil.

And then, disaster strikes: the website crashes leaving him -- in a football sense -- deaf, blind and mute. He stalks the streets of Perth, a pilgrim in search of answers and none are forthcoming. In a desperate "fourth and long" attempt to salvage a fighting chance to watch his beloved Washington Redskins, he reaches me on Skype knowing that in Charleston the Skins game is being televised locally. He asks whether he can watch the game with me by me arranging my laptop in front of the TV so he can watch on his computer screen Down Under. I oblige. I wrangle a crude platform about two feet in front of my very large TV, turn up the volume, adjust the laptop so it is taking in the full TV picture, and sit down "with" Alex to watch the game.

It is an odd experience. I am in Charleston; Alex is in the lobby of a sketchy hostel in Perth about as far away as one human can be from another and still inhabit the same planet. And yet, we are reacting to the same event -- which is taking place in New York -- as if we are in the same room. Which we are, sort of. Alex yells and so do I. We react to the same incident on the field and confer although when I catch myself I realize I am speaking to some disembodied voice coming out of a small computer sitting oddly in the middle of my living room.

We stick with this arrangement until the end of the first quarter when his sorely missed NFL website comes back online. I say good-bye to the voice coming from the computer, and put my laptop back on the dining room table from whence it came.

I confess for the rest of the game, when I hurled some epithet at the screen I would sometimes look over to the dormant laptop looking for a reaction.

Bringing Back a Memory

When I was a kid -- maybe 9 or 10, my family used to take weekend day trips from White Plains to Atlantic Beach out on Long Island. A real schlep, but my folks had the ocean in their veins, a character trait that would soon be hard-wired in me as well. The place we went had a pool, and while I was apt to spend my time on the beach, one weekend we found ourselves at the pool with the intent of swimming laps. I was not a swimmer, but my sister, Susan, was. She was a wonderful swimmer having done some time swimming competitively. A natural. Baseball was more my thing. Susan took to the pool and effortlessly did her laps. I got in and with some labor made it up and back several times, but I was clearly tiring. My father did not want me to quit. He kept urging me to do "just one more" and he walked alongside the pool as I swam cajoling, encouraging, and cheerleading to get me to finish 10 laps. I was getting exhausted; my body felt like lead. I thought there was a distinct chance I would sink. Why I kept going, I really will never know. But, I do know I will never forget that moment in my life. When I amazingly finished my 10 laps, I fell like a wet noodle into my father's arms who gave me a big hug and then bought me a toasted bagel. Nothing ever tasted so good.

We flash forward a half century. I have been swimming laps of late, but I always have alternated the crawl with the breast stroke, mostly so I would have the lasting power to swim about an hour. But, part of me felt that I was in some way "cheating" in not swimming the crawl for all, not just half, my laps. This morning, alone in the pool, I set out to do only the crawl hoping to go as long as I could, but clearly understanding that I might not have the stamina to do very much.

The laps floated by. After the first few, I was in a zone, a rhythm. Some might have called it a kind of zen-like state of mind. It was wonderful. I just kept rolling. I swam fifty laps and by the time I had gone maybe 20 my mind was full of the memories of that day long ago bringing back, as best I could, the emotions and sensations of that day. It has been years since I've thought so much of my father, but, in a way, he was there this morning.

This one's for you, Dad.

It's a Good Thing They Weren't Served Drinks

Imagine you're attending a cocktail party. Everyone around you is dressed nicely. Not to the nines, but definitely cleaned up for the occasion. You're in a nice sized room; people are mingling with cabernets in hand and nibbling on a nice array of finger food like roasted pork crostini with raspberry mustard, shrimp, meatballs, and black bean and corn salsa. You get the picture. Now -- introduce into this lovely atmosphere thirty dogs... running free! Changes your image a bit, doesn't it? Civility gives way to chaos. Wine refills occur at higher than normal intervals to replace the cups unhanded from folks who think they're dodging bullets or freight trains. Dogs ricochet off legs, human legs that is. "Keep your knees bent" is the advice of the moment.

This was the scene I found myself in the other evening at "Planet Bark," the place we board Mojo when we're out of town. The irrepressible new owner, Mary, wants to more actively market Planet Bark in what has become a fairly competitive market for such places in suburban Charleston. When I arrive, I applaud her bravery. She acknowledges that she's not sure the event might spin out of control, but she's all smiles. And, she's right. A good time will be had by all. Or, almost all.

And, the dogs? My God -- so many butts to sniff, so many legs to bite, so much rolling on the floor to be done! So much humping to be had! Mojo, not -- how you say -- calm when in the company of other canines, bursts at warp speed from one corner of the room to another as if he is on the receiving end of a life sentence to cease and desist from any butt sniffing except what he can take in over the next hour or so. Many are willing. Sunny, a lab mix and Sanford, an English bulldog apparently experience the same ecstasy Mojo has found as they roll around the floor in one undifferentiated hairy mass, teeth gnashing, tails wagging. Bliss doggy-style. Others are not so thrilled. Threading their way around and through the legs of the human guests, the more timid dogs -- with mixed success -- try to elude the more aggressive four-legged party animals (if I may use that term). They whine, sometimes growl in mock anger while their owners down their crostini hoping that it is not their dogs who are engaging in overly boorish behavior. Mojo assumes the always pleasing submissive legs-up position in wrestling bouts which appears to earn him a pass from most, if not all, party attendees. Mojo -- regardless of his many endearing traits -- earns me special attention from a couple of dog trainers in attendance who apparently believe my dog is -- shall we say-- a good candidate for behavior modification. Puppy exuberance, I assure them.

After almost two hours of this mayhem, I take my leave, probably to the relief of some. Mojo is wet from the absurd amount of saliva he's been smeared with from the other dogs. His tongue is hanging out the side of his mouth and his countenance is oddly similar to that of a mad bomber's. I get him into the back seat of my car. As I turn around to see where I'm backing out, I note he is dead asleep.

Richly earned, my friend.

Yes, Mojo, They Call This Rain

I slept in today. This can mean only one thing: it's raining. This is eventful on the Isle of Palms where rain seems to come as seldom as snow no matter how hard it may be raining inland. Something about the prevailing winds and ocean currents -- don't ask. For only the second time in about four months I did not pop out of bed at 7 a.m. so that Mojo and I could get to the beach for our early morning romp. How strange to turn over. Mojo, to his undying credit, was similarly hypnotized by the rain as he slept in his usual fashion - on his back, legs wide and spread in the air in a pose that suggests nothing short of complete surrender to Morpheus. Getting up at 8:30, which normally almost feels like lunch time to me, I felt not only the moist air, but the chill too. This is not good news. I know it's October, but in these parts there's plenty of "summer" left and I am not done with that season just yet. When I had completed drying off all the rain that had come through the windows, I found myself reaching for long pants and socks -- each for the first time in five months. And, a fleece! So depressing.

Soon, however, I would learn that these new climatic conditions could teach me new skills. Like how to balance an umbrella, a leash with a diabolically energetic dog at the far end, a cup of coffee, and a bag of dog poop -- all in a driving rain. This will take some practice if this morning's performance is any indicator. Mojo's penchant for diving between my legs as we walk caused me a couple of drops of both umbrella and poop bag. Not a pretty picture. There was no one in the streets, though. No witnesses. There aren't that many folks here at this stage of the season, and the rain certainly provided no incentive to venture outdoors. Wimps.

The downside of all this? As we returned, and Mojo inhaled his breakfast, he wasted not one moment in finding one of his favorite toys inviting me to chase him to wrest it away from him. It was the least I could do since the little guy was deprived of his normally exhausting expenditure of energy at the beach. And, so we spent our morning. Mojo, head cocked in a playful attempt at gamesmanship, ran laps through the house as I gamely (and futilely) chased him. Maybe I should wear my running shoes when I do this.

All Politics is Local, Right?

Health care reform wasn't on the table. Neither were troop levels in Afghanistan. Ditto for global warming. Other, more weighty, matters were in the forefront. Like, where to put the next cross walk. And, whether speed limits on local streets should be uniform. And, whether rental property signs announcing to renters rules on maximum occupancy should be conspicuously posted within 15 feet of the front door. And, most importantly to me, the issue of whether dogs might be allowed more off-leash time on the beach during the off-season. Such were the issues du jour for the intrepid members of the Isle of Palms City Council last night. For me, this would be my first glimpse into the local political arena, and judging from the healthy crowd in the hearing room, I knew I was not alone in my intense interest in something that would be of absolutely no consequence anywhere else on planet earth.

The councilmen, mostly white men with a smattering of women, plodded on trying to muster as much dignity as they could to offset the impossibly trivial matters they believed ruled their personal universes. Mostly, they wore suits -- a brave gesture in the overheated hearing room. Their body language was worth noting as well. Like the frustrated guy who never opened his mouth while all around him others were flapping theirs. Finally, in what I sensed was a spontaneous outburst to show he was a player to be reckoned with, his remarks were greeted by vacant stares from the semi-circular panel as if they were thinking, "Did he really say that?"

The measure on speed limits was tabled for want of more research on the matter. Why am I thinking the Brookings Institution will not be invited to opine on this one? The measure on posting maximum occupancy signs in rental properties was met with thinly veiled sarcasm by one Council guy who wondered whether the police ought to be fitted with new belts that would accommodate a tape measure so they could get into the business of measuring whether the signs were, in fact, posted within 15 feet of the front door. And, oh yes, the Council decided unanimously to approve a sole source contract to a guy who does the fireworks show for the July 4th celebration. What? Why? I'm thinking there may be an extra firecracker in these guys' stocking this Christmas, if you get my drift.

And, the dog measure? Passed in a breeze. "Island friendly, " they called it.

As for my future at local political events, I'm sensing a possible write-in campaign for me: "Golland for City Council. Maybe not the sharpest tool in the shed, but a guy who's likely to amuse us." Has a nice ring to it, doesn't it?

A New York Moment

We spent the weekend in New York and it was filled with the sensations you would want in such a visit: lots of bagels and lox, a smashing performance by Hugh Jackman and Daniel Craig in "A Steady Rain," French food, Cuban food, Italian food, and wonderfully visual (and tasty) jaunts through Soho and Chelsea. Through it all, you could not help but be so impressed by the diversity, energy, and sheer numbers of persons out on the streets soaking up all things New York. It truly is an amazing place. And, sharing it with our friends Maggie, Vernon, Leslie, Tom and Ellen only enhanced the pleasure.

While all of this sensory stimulation was exactly what we were looking for, I was not prepared for what appeared to be an inconsequential turn on Sunday. We had just parted company with our friends, Vernon and Leslie, and were headed over to Maggie's office near Bryant Park. As we headed up Broadway, I mentioned how a thousand years ago, my father's business was located at 1412 Broadway, on the corner of 39th Street. We decided to do a "drive-by" so I could peek into the lobby of the place that had once in my life been a very familiar haunt since it was not only my father's place of business, but a place where I had worked a few summers as a messenger boy in my early teens.

We tried the front doors of the building but they were all locked…. except one. We entered the lobby. Some of those old memories started reeling through my mind. At the elevator bank was the guard, a young fellow named Muhammad. I introduced myself and, when I told him how I worked there a half century ago, he leaned back, eyes widened, and looked at me as though he was talking to a living Civil War hero. I told him how way back then the elevators had human operators -- old guys who would spit on the floor if they could get away with it, and grumpy. When I asked Muhammad if we could take a peek at the old place -- up in the rooftop offices on the 25th floor -- he said that would not be permitted. But, a few moments later, he relented -- perhaps caught up in the moment. He locked the sole open door to the building and took us up the one elevator that went to the roof.

We emerged and there it was -- the old site of Victory Studios, Inc., the business that had paid for our family home, our college educations and the food on our table. Of course, the old business was long gone, now replaced by a beauty supply house. But, interestingly, a peek inside the door revealed essentially the same layout as the one I had known so many years ago. And, even better, there was actually someone working in there who spotted us and generously let us in to look around.

How weird. Now, all the old memories came flooding back. I noted the reception area where Helen, my father's old secretary, sat. To the right and rear was the space where the designers worked, punching out their designs for sale to the garment district's fabric firms. Then, the showroom where Oscar, Vic, and Paul would ply their skills in selling those designs. And, in the rear left, my father's office. I walked in there and was thrilled and moved. It had all been so very long ago.

What I didn't tell Muhammad was that so many years ago, I used to go out on the roof and look down on what was then the old site of the Metropolitan Opera House. Every now and then, they would host a posh roof top event at the Met -- an afternoon cocktail party for the cognoscenti of the city. My adolescent urges led me to make hundreds of paper airplanes with droll messages inscribed on them, like "I see what you're doing" or, "what are you drinking anyway?" I would toss these airborne missives off in droves hoping that just one would sail amid the swirling air currents above Broadway and land across the street on the rooftop garden many stories below. And, in rare but wonderful moments, a plane would land among the partyers who would cast semi-frantic glances skyward, aghast that they were being spied upon.

It doesn't get much better than that.

The Last Man on Earth (or so it seemed)

Around these parts, once the last suggestion of summer leaves for more southern climes, folks around here perform an exodus as if they were fully expecting an imminent, winter-long convention of mastodons and t-rex at Wild Dunes. To say this place becomes a ghost town is, in truth, doing a disservice to ghosts because this place would make even ghosts feel a tad lonely. We are told that one-quarter of property owners live here full-time, but I'm convinced either that this is a grotesque overstatement or these guys are most comfortable riding out winter in their basements, far from human view, madly at work on the great American novel or, perhaps, a challenging video game.

So -- tonight, as Mojo and I took our evening constitutional, I was struck by the notion that it would not be such a reach to play the role as last man on planet earth. We wandered empty street after empty street, and as the twilight gave way to darkness, I was reminded again how resoundingly black it gets here with street lights appearing maybe once every half mile. We ventured down to the ocean because from a block away you could hear the waves crashing, and this was most certainly worth a view. It was the kind of sound that made you think that something important was happening there. There was but one soul on the beach, a truly forlorn looking cyclist leaning into the wind, which was now just a bit shy of furious. He could not have been enjoying himself. Otherwise, the expanse was free of any life form. Just the waves, the sand, the full moon and Mojo and me. The day had played out in a way that invited this air of isolation as the weather gurus spoke of high winds, pounding rain, flooding, severe thunderstorms, and even some tornado warnings. It was a day best suited to browsing Amazon.com in search of a well-priced ark.

While the streets were empty, there were actually a few cars that ventured by, their lights an annoying distraction from my last man on earth fantasies. An intrusion, really. May I say that Mojo could not have been more pleased? Or, that he could not have been more oblivious to the encroaching darkness which made him all but invisible. As usual, he pranced through our entire human-free walk, leash firmly planted in his mouth as if to make sure I understood that it was he, not I, who was taking the other for a walk.

As serene and uncomplicated as this walk was, I would not wish for this experience every night. I am far too social for that. I enjoy the repartee with total strangers, some with dogs, some without. It doesn't matter.

I do not want to be the last man standing, thank you very much.

When Are We?

(Dec. 9, although possibly Dec. 8 or 10) Lily and I have had our fannies firmly planted in airline seats for 22 hours today. Count 'em: 22 -- Charleston to Dulles (1 hour), Dulles to Tokyo (13½ hours), Tokyo to Singapore (7½ hours). Trust me, our fannies are not pleased with this arrangement, and our backs aren't entirely thrilled either. Like so many others, we have experienced this before -- these long trips -- which tells you how strong the pull is of our chosen destination that we would endure this numbing, voluntary incarceration. We mentally wave out our window at Ontario, the Yukon, the Northern Slopes of Alaska, the Aleutians, Vladivostok, Okinawa, Guam, and Borneo. From 35,000 feet, it's all the same. We not only endure, but look forward to, the airline's less than elegant attempts at food service since, if nothing else, it provides a break in the otherwise totally stalled and bland action of air travel.

It is a matter of some hilarity that we attempt, futilely, to figure out what time it is, which is, of course, impossible. Time is a moving target up here. Do we look at our watches and say to ourselves it's 5 p.m. when that's eastern standard time, or do we keep track of the ever-changing time zones below? Like the intrepid, but confused, heroes in "Lost," it is far better not to ask "where are we?," but rather "when are we?"

Walking the aisles at "night" in our jumbo jet, it is amusing to see how others meet the challenge. There are, of course, the stubborn few with open books or laptops, and others watching, glazed over, their sixth movie. Mostly, folks try -- vainly, I believe -- to find a position where sleep will provide a much needed escape from this seemingly endless monotony. You have your folks with sleep masks, face masks, and many others with blankets pulled over their heads. Others appear as comfortable as one might when bracing for a head-on collision, but with their eyes closed, as if by jamming their eyelids shut they can force unconsciousness upon themselves. Some say you should set your watch to that of your destination and start adjusting to that when you take your seat. Yeah, good luck with that.

Oh, the joy! After a 6 hour layover in Singapore, we head out in the early a.m. again, only this time for another multi-hour aerial hike, this time to Phuket. I'm thinking even Cary Grant would look a bit disheveled after this, don't you?

Paradise Lost

There are few things as sweet as being reminded of a wonderful, but long ago, experience. Sometimes this is triggered by smells (maybe the cooking of some cherished comfort food), or sounds (like hearing a song that once had great meaning). But, most often, and most powerfully, the sensation is the greatest when you return to a place that holds some of your warmest memories. And, so it was yesterday with Lily and me. We found ourselves in the same exact spot we had not seen for 30 years: Patong Beach in Phuket, Thailand.

The interesting thing, I think, about these encounters is trying to resist re-living the experience since, after all, so many things have changed. You can "re-acquaint" but you cannot "re-live." Here, in Phuket, we knew things would be different. But, would it matter? What was once a relatively undiscovered backwater unknown to most of the western world, was now a bustling, crowded destination resort polka-dotted by high rises and replete with wave upon wave of European tourists, tattoo parlors, and the ubiquitous t-shirt shops. Hello civilization; goodbye paradise. This was a far cry from the place we once knew that promised on the beach bungalows for $6 a night and grilled fresh fish dinners for $3. But, when you looked seaward, out into the Andaman Sea, we could see what we loved so much: fluffy white sand, water as warm as a bath, and a succession of changing tints of blue -- like a blue rainbow -- from almost clear to turquoise to the deepest navy. The crescent-shaped bay was still guarded by green hills diving down to the shoreline. And, the hot sun served as an open invitation to spend the day submerged in that wonderful water.

We returned to the place that we had once stayed, Phuket Cabanas, now completely transformed into an upscale and beautiful hotel, and had cocktails at sunset and a fabulous alfresco Thai dinner. The starter was a soup so beautifully aromatic it could do well in a perfume competition. The catch? It was laced with paralyzingly hot chilies that, as they say, cures what ails you. Not for the timid, this soup. What followed was everything from red snapper to chicken to shrimp to a seafood salad of shrimp, octopus and ginger. All of it fabulously delicious.

So, it wasn't the old Phuket. So what? We're not the old Lily and Jeff either.

Island Life, Thai Style

Koh Phi Phi (pronounced "Pee Pee") is a small island about a 2 hour ferry ride from Phuket. What Disneyland is to 6 year olds, Phi Phi is to a slightly older population. There's no Donald or Goofy here, and no rides, but if you are, let's say, 25, all you want is right here. The village is a grid richly crowded with open-air bars with small tables and chairs spilling out onto the "street." Internet cafes, t-shirt shops, dive shops, massage venues, and an amazing array of eateries fight for your attention. It is an assault on your senses, but not an unpleasant one. As you make your way up the congested walkways, you are invited to all manner of evening parties and shows. All that's missing is a carnival barker. The streets -- some paved, some not -- give the appearance that Koh Phi Phi is crowded. But, I believe this impression is created only because the walkways -- there are no cars here -- are narrow forcing whoever's here to share limited walking space. The many locals who try to navigate this maze on bikes are, fittingly, candidates for cirque de soleil. They make 90 degree turns on a dime, routinely stop motionless while remaining upright and somehow (mostly) avoid pedestrians with magical consistency even though those on foot always seem mere centimeters from their front wheels. This task is complicated by the steady infusion of small children, running and biking with no apparent pattern, often without an adult in view. Cyclists gamely blurt out "beep beep" as they make their way through as if fair notice has been given. Really, we are all players in a life-sized video game here.

If there were a flag for Phi Phi it would most certainly feature a large flip flop since that is all you see here. They are not just ubiquitous;

they are universal. Ok, ok I did see a couple of guys in worn out running shoes and one eastern european dude wearing combat boots, but these were very much the exception.

Along the alleyways, there is almost always the strains of some music, but not the minor chords of thai music as you might expect. Rather, from somewhere, you hear the voices of Cat Stevens, Bob Marley and Janice Joplin. It's weird, but somehow it fits. This theme picks up at the Millie and Tia Sunflower Beach Bar on the sand on the other side of the island. It doesn't take too much imagination to picture this place in Key West, or maybe San Diego. You take a seat at one of the curved carved tables facing the ocean, Singha beer in hand, awaiting the sunset. Stray cats jump up on your table. The longboats are now dormant providing a picture postcard foreground for the sunset that is soon to appear painting the sky in the reddest reds and the bluest blues. The ambient music is all acoustic, naturally. My camera does not even remotely do justice to all this.

This is a beer commercial, right?

Scuba

After graduating from our rigorous and amusing introduction to breathing underwater in a pool, and having reviewed endless reams of dive instructions and instructional videos, we are now ready for our first open water dive. We go to Maya Bay, site of "The Beach" with Leonardo DiCaprio. Fantastically beautiful, the bay is surrounded by steep, green limestone cliffs evocative of what we imagine pre-historic times to have looked like. In that moment, as we enter the bay, an appearance by a t-rex does not seem utterly out of the realm of possibility. In our longboat, it is just Lily and me, our dive master, Keira, and our boatman. These long, narrow wooden craft you've seen a thousand times in movies set in this part of the world.

We submerge. It is hard to keep from smiling. A whole new world reveals itself. Within minutes, we find ourselves circling a sea turtle which is attacking a huge jellyfish from beneath, essentially trying to eat him alive. The jellyfish tries to move away as quickly as nature permits, but his throbbing hulk is no match for the sea turtle. I root for the jellyfish, the underdog, hoping he will miraculously find breakaway speed, but today is not his day.

I delight in new perspectives. Unlike the "horizontal" world where you pass someone either on the left or right, here you have an additional option. Go over or under. How novel! I find myself passing over Lily and a couple of other divers, all arrayed in a vertical plane. As I look down, I feel like I have the barest appreciation for what it's like to fly in formation with the Blue Angels. Swimming above Lily, I have the absolutely delightful experience of having her air bubbles drift up and past me. They appear as metallic, shiny invert-ed saucers, reflecting light as clearly as mirrors. I poke them and they break apart into fifty smaller saucers. This is, at heart, a psychedelic experience.

As part of the test for scuba certification, we are asked to jump out of the boat and swim 200 meters to shore. Forgive me, but I think of myself as Leonardo as he and his friends make the desperate swim ashore to "the beach," just as I am doing in that moment.

Really, I do apologize for this.

A Day in Full

Days can be memorable for so many reasons. The one we had today, I suspect, as wonderful as it was in the moment, will become mythic with the passage of time. The major ingredients were all there. It was the first day in virtually a year that Lily, Jesse, Alex and I had been together in one place. With Alex scampering around the globe and Jesse and Laura encamped in Denver, putting us all together in one place was all but impossible. Yet, here we were together again -- a huge delight without more. Add to this that we were all in Bali, and though we had not much more than a day there, it provided an exotic setting for our reunion.

Our day was hinged around a trip up to Ubud, a slow 2 hour journey up into the hills with our driver, Lele. Ubud is known for its crafts and, while we hoped to absorb as much as we could, our day's entertainment came from other pursuits. We stop first at Mandala Wisata Wanara Wana, a lengthy Sanskrit denomination for a monkey sanctuary. Here, the inmates (as it were) run the institution. The macaques who reside here run wild and free. If you're worried about not getting close enough, worry no more. They find you, believe me. All it takes is a bunch of small bananas in hand to bring them running, and they do like their bananas here. If you want one on your shoulder, no problem. You want a grandpa or maybe a baby, they're yours. What you realize after several minutes is that you've taken 900 pictures many of which you just know you'll want to delete before sharing. But, this is fun without a doubt.

We follow with a trek through rice paddies, a tougher task than we first realized. Our guide, Made (pronounced "Maddy") takes us down steep slopes through steamy jungle terrain with slippery rocks and dirt, a chore that us flipflop wearing touristas make more difficult than necessary. But, the beauty we witness is incomparable. What is revealed to us, we all agree, is what we had always believed to be the essence of Indonesia: greens so vivid they render the term "technicolor" woefully inadequate; terraced rice paddies that, taken together, provide a stunning landscape mosaic-- so utterly and exclusively Asian. We are dripping from our efforts after the long climb back up to where Lele is to meet us, but we are unanimous in our delight for what we have just come to see.

We stop for lunch at "Indus" recommended by Lele and this special day continues. Spicy calamari salads, an incredibly flavorful lemongrass chicken, and even a paella. All this served on an elevated open air terrace overlooking the rolling Bali countryside. Perfect.

Returning to our hotel, we can't wait to hit the pool and then have drinks as we watch sunset over the Indian Ocean. Lastly, again at Lele's suggestion, we are ferried to another part of the city for a grilled fish dinner on the beach at the Ganesha Café. He said it had the best seafood around, and it didn't disappoint. Grilled red snapper with garlic sauce, all washed down with Bintang beer.

We all regretted having just this one full day in Bali, but as our heads hit the pillow that night, we did not feel cheated.

Mayhem on Main Street

A word about the traffic here in Bali. Astounding. Beyond compre-hension. There is simply no analog in the western world for this par-ticular brand of hysteria. I grew up thinking that the mad dash urban traffic scenes of Paris and Rome were the benchmarks for madness -- where the rule of law evaporated in the no man's land beyond the city's sidewalks. What I didn't know then was that these traffic models would be mere child's play -- a stroll in the park -- compared to what southeast Asians engage in every day. To say the streets are crowded goes without saying, of course. The roads are blanketed by cars, trucks, buses, cyclists, and the ever-present scooters and motor-cycles that soon take on the feel of swarming mosquitoes rather than machines. Scooters, often loaded with 3 or 4 people, dart among each other and between cars with a hair-raising optimism that their sudden movements will be injury-free. Helmets, though common, are hardly universal. Unhelmeted, small kids, in particular, who are sandwiched (indeed, seemingly suffocated) between parents, appear oblivious to the harm that I believe is not just apt to happen, but a dead on certainty. Cars, like the ones we traveled in, come up on the bumpers of these two-wheeled vehicles so damn closely that so often you can see what kinds of screws hold their license plates on -- and this is at cruising speeds. Add to this mix the suicidal brand of pedestrians who actually deign to enter this war zone and you have the dictionary definition of chaos.

The notion of lanes is not even paid lip service. Are you kidding me? I'm telling you, it's a huge waste of paint. Sure, there is oncoming traffic. But, that gives no assurance whatsoever that the oncomers own their lane. They must share it with the cars and scooters that pass from the other lane, sometimes three abreast, in what I can only describe as a fiendish game of chicken. I am amazed as much as I have ever been that accidents are not just more frequent, but hellishly repetitive.

It is truly a video game on wheels, but I hesitate to learn in whose hands the controller rests.

The Gilis -- How You Say Island Bliss

I know it would be an exaggeration to say that here on Gili Air we have truly reached the other side of the planet, in all things literal and figurative. But, we are getting close. Gili Air is a tiny island, maybe 4 miles around. It sits in the South China Sea about a 4 hour ferry ride east of Bali alongside its island sisters Gili Meno and Gili Trawangan. These tiny islands serve as stepping stones off the coast of Lombok, an Indonesian province that will soon be a rising star for savvy jet setters. Stepping off the longboat that brings us to Gili Air, your personal decompression process begins to take hold. Not that what preceded this destination was stressful, but this place sets the standard for all that is laid back. It is one thing to say that there are no roads here or cars as was the case in Koh Phi Phi, but the difference between Phi Phi and Gili is the difference between New York and Mayberry RFD. There is only a dirt path that hugs the shore around the island, and the only thing that moves faster than the always strolling humans is the occasional pony-drawn cart and a random bike. There are a few bungalow-dotted "resorts," a string of beach front bars and eateries, and, after that.....nothing.

This is an island devoted largely to divers. There is really nothing else to keep you here except perhaps a driving ambition to lower your blood pressure. No credit cards here, no ATMs. Things here are pretty much a half step ahead of the barter system. Our hotel, Gili Air Bungalows, offers 4 steeply roofed thatched bungalows, each with a front deck and a bathroom in the rear that is open to the sky. Sink, shower, and toilet -- all alfresco. Pretty cool. The pool is salt water as is the tap and shower water. Bottled water is, naturally, essential. The beach bars offer covered, raised thatched platforms each with overstuffed pillows you can lean against while you throw down your Bintang beer and your shrimp or calamari schnitzel. There you can while away the afternoons between dives or after dinner hours, reading, sipping cocktails, playing hearts and trading stories. And the dress code? Let me just say that dressing for dinner means putting a tank top over that bathing suit. And, if you simply insist on footwear, let it be flip flops.

Oh yeah, there's stress here -- will it be tequila or beer, red snapper or calamari? It really doesn't get much more complicated than that.

Night Dive

When I asked Alice, our dive master, whether a night dive would quicken or slow the pace of breathing, she said either was possible. People are either so excited or apprehensive that they use up the air in their tanks more rapidly than is otherwise the case. Or, she said, for some, breathing slows for those who find this adventure to be a remarkably relaxing experience.

Actually, I found both to be true. I freely admit my apprehensions at the prospect of descending to the ocean floor in total darkness. Wondering whether you'll get separated from the rest of the group and feel the ultimate sensation of being lost, was in my mind not so much indulging in paranoia as it was recognition of a possibility that was uncomfortably greater than zero. We would have underwater dive lamps, of course, but their range was hardly limitless, and (definitely allowing my paranoia to take center stage) I felt the beam in mine was weaker than it should be.

And, so we descended as the sun was setting out over the South China Sea. It was Christmas eve. The drill was to stay together in a mute, marine conga line with admonitions not to bunch up too closely lest one whack a fellow diver in the head with an errant fin. There would be a dive master at the head, middle and rear of the line ostensibly to prevent strays. Well, that didn't last very long. Not that anyone was lost, but by the end of the hour dive, most of us observed that at least at one point in the dive we had been the last in line with nothing behind us but black and endless ocean.

As we settled in to this weirdly new environment, I relaxed and began to understand what Alice meant by the likelihood of one's breathing slowing. None of us knows what it's like to be in the womb, of course, but this has to be a damn close approximation. Movement slows, effort eases, and each breath extends longer and longer. The 86 degree water temperature soothes and relaxes. And, the pace is slow -- very slow.

As planned, late in the dive, we form a circle on the ocean floor sitting on the sandy bottom extinguishing our dive lamps. Blackness you cannot imagine. You know there are people all around you, but you are alone, believe me. Lily, Jesse, Alex, Colin and Shanti might as well have been a thousand miles away. And then, magic. On cue, we all start waving our arms as if in some legless dance routine, and in front of our eyes appear phosphorescence -- tiny, tiny marine life that appear to you as thousands of tiny fireflies or microbursts of a thousand fireworks. Awesome.

There was no evidence of Santa or reindeer that night, but there was no question that this was a pretty amazing way to celebrate the arrival of Christmas.

Singapore, the New Cool

Move over New York. You too, San Francisco. There's a new, cool dude you can learn something from. It's Singapore. It's modern, it's colorful, it's lush, and it is very, very cool. It is a city that reminds you of the old tale of the blind man trying to describe an elephant -- it depends on what part of the body he touches that reveals the creature's appearance. The trunk, the leg, and the tail -- they all tell very different stories, and Singapore is much the same. It can be a modern, jet set-worthy, splashy shopping experience. Gucci, Prada, Rolex, Dolce and Gabbana, Calvin Klein, Louis Vuitton, even Starbucks. You get the picture. It has wide boulevards lined by a gorgeous canopy of trees and dotted with marble benches for the weary shopper. But, it is also a city that pays tribute to the best architectural elements of British colonialism. Beautiful white-washed buildings all flowing with graceful arches and large, welcoming courtyards. This style is typified most elegantly by the Raffles Hotel, now in its 123rd year. But, Singapore is also a city devoted to its ethnic neighborhoods -- Malaysian, Indian, and Chinese. Here, the streets are narrow with small shops and restaurants seemingly piled one atop the other as is so typical for so many parts of Asia.

It is a crowded city. Make no mistake about that. After spending almost all of our three weeks in relative backwaters with no roads or cars, sharing sidewalks with what strikes me as one-third of the planet's population was unnerving and alien. The chaotic flow of pedestrian traffic, often elbow to elbow, paints the same picture for me as the hysterical movements of ants whose nest you have just unearthed. Nothing like post-Christmas shopping to get the juices flowing, I guess. And, the heat – formidable. Not that it is any hotter than Thailand or Indonesia, but it's amazing how it wears on you when you can't shuffle around in nothing more than your swimsuit.

Lastly, a word about the food. It reflects its people: Chinese, Malaysian, and Indian. Every nook and cranny offers a fabulous diversity of cuisine. Having gorged ourselves for weeks on Thai and Indonesian food, Lily and I stopped for a change of pace -- middle eastern fare offered up by one of the many open-air sidewalk cafes. My grilled lamb was delicious, but the shawarma Lily had was to die for. Maybe one of the tastiest treats of the entire trip. I went so far as to inquire in the kitchen how they made it only to learn that the chef whose recipe it was had died some months earlier leaving it in the hands of a supplier to deliver the goods to the café. With a shrug, the current chef smiled and suggested that it was no doubt some combination of the 4 Cs that did the trick: curry powder, cumin, cardamom, and coriander. I will experiment when I get home.

Singapore: whatever you want, it's here.

And on Reflection

On another 14 hour flight. This one's from Hong Kong to Chicago. At the moment, however, it's hard to think about anything but a very young, and very unhappy, passenger whose screams may break some windows before he's done. My hope is that the steady drone of the engines will soothe both his and my jangled nerves. The flight plan for United 896 appears to take us over Russian air space. I presume the Russkies are expecting us.

Our vacation is over. Months and months of planning and coordination and, in a flash, it's done. Isn't it always the case? But, the memories of this one will last a long, long time. For Lily and me, traveling with Jesse and Alex once again (and Laura now too) reminds me how wonderful it is to do that, although no reminders are needed. Jesse is fast becoming a very accomplished guy: a 3.95 g.p.a. in grad school, an internship upcoming with the State Department in Mexico City, a graduate degree in June, and nuptials in September. A crowded agenda. He is so grounded and well-prepared for whatever lies ahead. His days as troublemaker par excellence are rapidly vanishing in his rear view mirror. He is master of his fate, and I love that about him. When he mimics someone's voice, when telling one of his wonderful stories, he sounds like a stereotypical Russian, no matter what the nationality of the person he's depicting. I find it hilarious. He and I are ruthless hearts players, and it is not uncommon for newcomers to our games to indicate that maybe they aren't quite ready for this experience. But, we enjoy ourselves immensely.

And Alex? Here's a guy who's been traveling for a year. From Tierra del Fuego to Swaziland to Vientiane to Perth. And soon, Kathmandu and Mumbai. Mountain trekking, skydiving, shark cages, bungee jumping, safaris, and scuba. He has not been short changed in this adventure. What was once a kid with learning challenges and self-esteem concerns is now an emerging man of the world. When once reading was a painful exercise for him, he now devours books during his frequent solo journeys to the middle of nowhere. I know I am biased, but Alex may be the funniest person I know. Many people make me smile; Alex makes me laugh. Out loud. What could be better? Together Jesse and Alex take great pleasure in pointing out my foibles, both physical and behavioral. It is one of the constant drumbeats of our time together. Lily is spared this; she's their mom, after all. I, however, am fair game, and that's fine by me. They kid because they love, right?

For the days we spent together in Indonesia in our shared scuba experience, I found myself watching not just the amazing marine life, but Jesse and Alex too. They would probably be embarrassed to learn this, but experiencing these fabulous underwater jaunts with them and Lily, together as a family, was at least as amazing to me. It provided one of those quintessential "pinch me" moments.

So, this adventure is now history. In this family, though, it is always about the next trip. On to Provence, I say!

Steppin' Out

There comes a point when you say to yourself, "okay, the ball's in your court. It's time to get out there and meet people." After a year in Charleston, we have been swept up in a wave of extrovertism (if that's a word). While I have been out and about for the past year making an easy fit of my new retirement fatigues, the same could not be said of Lily. Whereas I have been doing a steady meet and greet every morning in my jaunts to the beach with Mojo, Lily has been encased, as it were, working in her cave, which we alternately refer to as the office or guestroom numero dos. I have been flapping my gums for months meeting a wide array of dog owners, getting to like some, making my own contribution toward our assimilation into the South Carolinian life style. But now, Lily is retired. And, in anticipation of the event (which officially occurred last Friday), we have been looking for avenues to pursue to glad hand and embrace the entire Wild Dunes Community.

Our first shot in the dark came with the local bridge club. I know, I know it sounds so terribly stolid -- so old school -- but, hey, it's a start. ily and I do enjoy the game although we find it so much more enjoyable when it is accompanied by major servings of wine and op-portunities to chat amiably with our opponents. As it turns out, the group we joined could not have been nicer: convivial, welcoming, knowledgeable. What the small print disclosed, however, was that the median age of the group was somewhere around 112, maybe a bit less. I mean these folks don't just remember the Great Depression; some were walk-ons for the movie version of the Grapes of Wrath, I'm quite certain. That's old in case you're missing my point. But, we have gone several times now even including their early bird dinners which begin about 5:30. My God, it's still light then, and it's winter for crying out loud. Stay tuned on this one.

Beyond this, we have enrolled (drum roll, please) in the Wild Dunes Yacht Club! Please, please try to refrain from laughter at this point. Really, wait just a second. First of all, you don't have to be a boat owner to join. This is a good thing since, first, we don't own a boat, and second, we are as comfortable in small boats as many people are in straight jackets. Second, it appears that the primary unifying force of the club is to get people together to drink and eat. Not necessarily a bad thing. And, maybe best of all, a number of the members don't clearly remember a world without the internet. No Civil War veterans here. Lily and I went to one meeting a couple of weeks ago and were delighted at the wine selection, and the care free camaraderie of the attendees. We look forward to the next event.

I'm even thinking of trying to find the perfect ascot for these events. Maybe one with little anchors in it.

The Bushido Challenge

Everybody loves a challenge. It focuses the mind. Gets the juices flowing, they say. "Don't tell me I can't beat that guy, " or "don't tell me I can't beat that record." Where would "machismo" be without a challenge, right? In the food world, the notion of challenge can take several, less than elegant, forms: competitive speed eating comes to mind. Or, perhaps, Man vs. Food which routinely endeavors to shock the world with ungodly volumes of consumption.

And, so it is here in Charleston where the beauty, elegance and grace of sushi creation are savagely re-directed to the more primeval elements of "the challenge." In this case, the venue is Bushido, a sushi restaurant in the West Ashley section of Charleston, where a steady stream of combatants come to test their will against the almighty spicy tuna roll. Some call it the Bushido Challenge, some call it the spicy tuna roll challenge, but the game is the same: to earn the title of "Legend of the Roll" one must consume in one sitting 10 spicy tuna rolls -- all hand-rolled -- in which each succeeding roll is increasingly spicy. The first few are deceptively easy, but the last few are laced with ever larger infusions of habanero peppers and thai chilies until the last couple fairly spontaneously combust if left unattended for more than a few moments. It is told that more than four hundred hearty, if delusional, souls have attempted this, and only a handful have succeeded.

I love spicy food and had looked forward to experiencing this diabolical, if ridiculous, challenge. Thirty years ago, when Lily and I were in Chiang Mai, Thailand I humbly met my match with a dish that caused my tears to flow as no other event in my life had up to that point (save perhaps the heartbreaking loss by the Yankees in game 7 of the 1960 World Series). I remember telling the restaurant proprietor that I was up to taking his best shot and I was taken down. Hard. I failed that day and now saw Bushido as a much delayed chance at redemption.

When we placed our order with our waitress, she sternly said to me, "You don't want a number 10. Believe me." Sadly, I folded, taking her at what had to be her very experienced word. Frankly, I think I may have been intimidated. I went with a number 6 which she said was the spiciest she had ever handled. (I had no intention of eating all ten and going for the Legend accolades. It wasn't just a matter of the cumulative spiciness that loomed, but the sheer volume of all that food.) I was on red alert as she placed the fiery red conical torpedo in front of me. Waiting for the alarm bells to explode as I chewed, I was somewhat surprised that while this roll was most definitely spicy, even fiery, it was not a killer. That silver bullet lay some what higher up the food chain, as it were.

What was so entertaining, though, was to look around and see others there who were unmistakably there for the challenge. They were the ones who could easily be mistaken for being seasick as they sat rubbing their heads -- in disbelief possibly -- with a vaguely green pallor, a vacant stare, and beads of sweat popping up all too obviously on their foreheads. They were up to their eyeballs in tuna, peppers and chilies and their bodies were in active revolt. One poor soul, who had just eaten numbers 9 and 10 had bolted outside with a carton of milk in his hands. Too little too late, I was thinking. Another guy, at the same table, looked as catatonic as one might be and still be considered a paying customer. The girlfriend of the guy with the milk told us there was no way her boyfriend was going to sleep in her bed that night. It was the couch for him. No sirree, no unnecessary risks for her. A third guy came with a large group all the way from Macon, Georgia for the sole purpose of doing the challenge. He told me there was no way he could return home without victory -- here celebrated by the issuance of a headband with the Bushido name on it, a $25 dollar gift certificate, and the promise of lifetime bows by the sushi chefs whenever you enter the restaurant. He was sitting there with numbers 9 and 10 on the plate in front of him daring him to complete the challenge and possibly a call to 911. His vacant stares told me he would be a while and so we left not knowing his fate.

As for me, when I decided to go for the number 7, my experience soared (or, perhaps sank) to a new plateau. After a few bites, I realized I was now literally on fire and wondered briefly if I should have the staff stick a fire extinguisher down my throat before I was totally engulfed in flames. Instead, I unceremoniously bolted out of the restaurant leaving Lily somewhat agape. I ran to the nearby grocery store and sprinted to the yogurt section where I immediately tore off the top and wolfed down its contents desperately hoping for some relief. When I got to the check out counter empty container in hand, the lady there gave me a knowing smile and said, "you're coming from Bushido, aren't you?"

I will leave to others the adventure of sampling the numbers 8, 9, and 10. It is said, I believe, that it is a sign of wisdom to know the limits of your strength. Or, that's the story I'm sticking with.

The Prodigal Son Returns

I stared at the computer screen transfixed. I was watching a flight tracking site as it ever so slowly recorded the progress of Alex's return flight to the U.S. from Qatar. It was just a blip on a world map, but that blip contained a son who had been gone for almost 15 months. That's a long time. The flight tracker gave me more information than I could possibly use: altitude, speed, heading, anticipated arrival time, etc. Everything but what they were serving for lunch. The blip inched its way into U.S. airspace and I experienced an odd sense of relief. As the altitude lowered in the plane's approach into Dulles, I actually got excited. But, it's not like we were there to greet him. No, that would come later once Alex had a couple of days to re-acquaint with friends who were just a tiny picture on Facebook or a faceless email account for so many months. I found it very amusing that literally an hour before his plane landed we got a postcard from Alex that he had sent from Nepal six weeks earlier, and, in his last line, he wondered whether it would arrive before he did. Just barely.

We had seen Alex twice in his travels, once in South Africa and again in Indonesia. Each was a sensational treat to have a reunion in such ridiculously exotic surroundings. But, having him home would be a treat second to none. After a whirlwind week of dinners galore with our friends in the D.C. area and then late nights with his friends, it was all pretty exhausting. We did return home to the Isle of Palms where Alex saw a far different house than the one he left in the closing days of 2008. And, he met Mojo for the first time who --doing his best Labrador routine -- was quite excited to see this tall, lanky stranger.

The effects of this trip will be with him for a long time, for sure. How could it not be? The other day, when we were driving through local streets, he spotted an animal and stared at it intently until he realized it was not a goat, but merely a dog. Maybe not what you're apt to see in India, Nepal or Java, but really quite ordinary here, right? Really, his whole persona needs a re-boot to get into the flow of this strange new land, the U.S. Some friends have asked us whether we thought Alex would have any re-adjustment issues having been away so long (and in such wildly different environments). I think the jury is out on that one. It may depend in some measure on how successful he is in pursuing his dream of working in sports media. It is a venture where he has focused his energies, and not just here but also abroad where he spent considerable time tracking down job possibilities and mapping a plan to guide him when he hit the ground.

Alex will be fine. Now, if he could only learn to pick up his stuff that has spread eerily like a lava flow around the house.

The Race

It was an impulse really. I did it without thinking. The good folks at the Wild Dunes resort here decided to sponsor a 5k run, on the beach. They called it the "Tortoise and the Hare Beach Run." We had just returned from Colorado where we skied for the first time in 13 years, and, frankly, my legs felt like lead. And, to be honest, in my more than 30 years of running, I had only participated in two previous races and they were more than 20 years ago. I think maybe deep down I thought that among the likely crowd for this one, I could do pretty well since I had been running almost daily for weeks. So, I signed up.

I showed up at the appointed time and sneaked glances at my competition. I was not encouraged. While there were a few souls appearing to be above the age of 40, most were in their early 20s. Jackrabbits, all of them. I was easily the oldest entrant. Certainly, no one else was sporting a white beard. Still, I thought I might do respectably. Lest anyone but the most oblivious think this was an event on a par with the New York Marathon, I could detect several distinguishing features. First, there were about 35 of us, not 35,000. Second, there were no crowds lining the course, although I can tell you there were many mosquitoes and sand fleas. Third, I don't think you're apt to see a human-sized tortoise and hare in full costume at the New York event. And, lastly, while we would not be touching down in all five NYC boroughs, we would be asked to run up the beach to a marker near the 18th hole and return to the start.

When the call of "Go!" came forth, I realized that one of the jackrabbits was already a hundred yards down the course before I had even turned on my ipod. Very humbling. But, I gathered myself to get into the fray and found myself, if not near the front of the pack, at least within hailing distance of it. Well, sort of. I realized my pace was a good bit faster than I would normally indulge in, but, after all, this was a race, not a jog. I got into my rhythm and tuned almost everything out except my music and the stares, some admiring, some quizzical, of the folks who had come down to the beach for an early morning stroll.

As I turned it on for the sprint to the finish line, I realized there was no one around me. Most of the jackrabbits had already finished and the rest of the field had slowed under the obviously torrid pace I had set for the them. At the finish line, there was one guy -- the one in the hare outfit -- who was there to give me a high five as I crossed the line. No cheering crowds, no bands playing. No champagne. Silence. I'm thinking to myself, why did I do this? I could have slept in and gone for a run later (indeed, without paying for the privilege).

I grabbed a couple of glasses of water and my race t-shirt and headed home. As I was leaving the area, I heard someone call out my name. I turned around. It was the hare. In his hand, he had an envelope which he handed to me. Apparently, the youthful winner had no sooner crossed the finish line than he had raced himself right off the beach and into a waiting car that would carry him and his family away from the resort and to, presumably, home. The race organizers decided that the award for the first place finisher -- a free massage at the spa -- should go to me! I didn't ask why. But, it was hard to stop laughing. And, sure enough, when I opened the gift certificate, it said "to the top male runner." I decided to aggressively delude myself into thinking how that might be the case.

Please tell me they didn't give it to me out of pity.

Adjusting (Or Not)

You've been there, right? You walk into someone's house who has a couple of kids -- and enough years have rolled by so this is not a recent experience for you -- and toys are strewn everywhere. So many, in fact, that as you ease your way into a family room you are more frequently stepping on things that squeak and honk than on a flat surface. Some things may even be sharp or large enough to cause a random meeting between your nose and one of those family room walls as you stumble your way to a chair. In a perverse way, this is what Lily and I are feeling these days as our community morphs from its winter ghost town identity to thriving metropolis. Spring has come to Charleston, and so have the tourists. They are everywhere, and they are there all the time. I went to the beach yesterday -- which for months has been more secluded than the Fortress of Solitude -- only to find actual people roaming the beach, making sand castles, burying each other, or just sunbathing. It is so odd that in an expanse that is so wide and deep and with such an infinite horizon that even the most claustrophobic feel at ease, I sensed a claustrophobic-like moment welling up in me. Who are these people and why are they upsetting my personal universe?

At night, when in previous months you would be much more likely to see deer roaming the streets than people, you now see hordes (well, what seems like hordes) of folks walking about like it's noon. Voices come from everywhere. And the trash! Beer cans, wet towels, pails, and partially buried toy tractors and trucks are all too visible on the beach. When driving, what had once been an environment where the local stop signs were as needed as they would be on the lunar surface, they now must be rigidly obeyed. During the day, be-hind the wheel, you feel like you're in an amusement park arcade as you anticipate the constant darting out into the streets by small urchins untethered from their parents. Not that the parents don't enjoy their jaywalking too. And the traffic! Now, you actually have to plan ahead to wander out to the Piggly Wiggly lest you get caught up in a line of cars so long and serpentine you feel you're in an ant colony's conga line.

I was sharing these observations the other day with the nice lady who sells us Mojo's dog food, and she nodded knowingly, as only a long time resident could. She told me that when she and her hus-band moved here from Ohio 12 years ago they, too, soon enough came to love the off-season and were quick to take up the spiritual banner against this dreaded species they call tourists. She also told me to lighten up.

So, now I have to deal with the fact that I am on the fast track to curmudgeonhood.

A Prayer for Captain Tony

They put Captain Tony down today. This bear of a dog, this absolutely wonderful best friend to Jim, Lily's brother, is gone. So very, very sad. Our hearts go out to Jim, Ivy, and Marley, but, in the end, this was Jim's dog and I believe his hurt will be felt the most. To people who do not own pets, or who do not fancy themselves as dog lovers, Captain's passing will not seem particularly newsworthy; but it is.

We first met Captain Tony, a burly, lightly hued golden retriever, when he did time at the animal shelter in Alexandria, Virginia. From the get go, he displayed his lifelong habit of nudging his head under your hand for some attention, some special handling. If, moments later, you would pull your hand away, his head would dive right back in there. He simply craved a little attention and affection. And, it was humans he was drawn to, not the companionship of other dogs. He came into our lives when Jim and Ivy had yet to find a place to live that would accept pets, but Jim knew he had to claim this wonderful beast because dogs like Captain Tony don't hang around animal shelters very long. Until they could find a pet-friendly home, Lily and I agreed to give Captain a home although he would have to share it with our eternally juvenile chocolate lab, Hoover.

Captain Tony was deaf, or mostly so. This did not make him seem disabled or damaged to me; rather, that quirk seemed to make him even more special. We fairly quickly learned that if you wanted to communicate with this guy, you had to face him head on. You needed eye contact. And, once that was established, we did fine. He did scare the bejesus out of us the day he suffered his first seizure in our home, and the terror we felt still resonates with us. His contorted body and wild flailings froze us in place. We didn't know if he was dying or if he would throw himself through a window. And, afterwards, when he was so disoriented that for minutes he did not know where he was or who we were, were moments that were as heartbreaking for us as they were troubling to him. But, through medication, this issue, too, was safely negotiated.

When Jim claimed him from our house, an era of almost magical camaraderie was born between these two. The fact that they were of two different species was so besides the point. They bonded as few animals and people do. Their hikes, their trips to lakes and streams and to the beach were so special because for each of them, that was what they most loved to do. And, to share that with another being who feels exactly as the other makes for an extraordinary relationship.

As the years wore on, and Captain Tony slowed his pace, he took on a dignity that, yet again, was special. He had a huge head and when he sat on the beach and barked at some unseen goblin, he had the demeanor of a lion. A very agreeable lion. Of late, he developed bone cancer and the dreaded countdown began. A few days ago, when I discussed Captain's fate with Jim, he told me he had done some research online looking for answers as to when it is, exactly, that marks the time that one should put down an animal. What he came away with was the notion that when a dog can no longer do what he loves to do, then maybe it's time. It resonated with Jim, but that didn't make the decision any easier.

At mid-day today, I knew the moment was at hand and both Lily and I felt a great surge of sadness. Having lost Hoover a few years ago, also to bone cancer, we knew the extreme despair of knowing the time has come, but also realizing that your great friend, who trusts you completely, does not share that realization. And there is no way to tell him. It is one of the heartaches of being in receipt of unconditional love that makes this so difficult.

I told Jim I would wait a couple of days to speak to him. It's just too fresh today. But, our thoughts and love are with that family.

Hello. Good-bye. Again

You know the time worn phrases: no grass grows under his feet; a rolling stone gathers no moss; he's got ants in his pants; shpielkes (for those of you with Yiddish tendencies). The ultimate truth remains the same: they come and they go. And, so it is with Alex who left at dawn this morning for points West. San Diego, specifically. Here in a flash and gone the next moment. The rhythms of life, eh? In this case, Alex was gone for 15 months, traversing four continents and communicating mostly by email and skype except in those rare moments when we could actually catch up to him in person in those special passages of time overseas. We are no different than any other parent, really. We watch our children grow and take their own baby steps to achieve their dreams, and we watch from the sidelines like so many cheerleaders at an athletic event. But, we are mostly helpless. Children grow and leave, maybe to the next town, over the mountain or maybe to the next ocean. It's all the same. In this case, Alex is off to pursue his dream of becoming a media mogul and can only watch its twisted path that leads who knows where. Lily and I certainly had no expectations of spending much time with Alex after his return from his 15 month global odyssey; but, that doesn't mean we weren't choked up at his departure this morning. We helped him load his car, helped plan his itinerary West, made some sandwiches for him, gave him some traveling money, and then, poof(!) he was gone…again. At least now he would be within reach by phone. At least now he wouldn't be off on some incredible third world jaunt unreachable by normal means. Small comfort.

Isn't it just an extension of the time when you watch them take their first baby step and let go of their hand in that magical moment to see if they can do it on their own? I wonder if that visual image ever changes no matter how much time has elapsed and how accomplished they have become. This is new to me; I can offer myself no expert advice. We will watch, though. But not from a place where we can help dictate a result. He's on his own now, this kid.

We'll keep the light on for him.

It's Free (Sort Of)

I promised myself I would never do this. Never, ever, ever. For as long as I can remember, I always tossed them out when they came intruding into my mailbox. You know -- those ever so superficially alluring promos from mostly real estate interests of one type or another promising free this or free that if all you would do is come on down and listen to a little spiel about their product. We know, and they know (and they know that we know) that this is a little scam to pry loose thousands of dollars from us all in the name of an "enhanced vacation experience." I always said to myself, what dummy would actually fall for this thinly veiled mockery?

Well, apparently, I am more of a dummy than I gave myself credit for, or, at least I've become one since retiring. So, what happened here? I saw the envelope in the mail: a promise of a free cruise. Even knowing what this was about, I was feeling a bit mischievous and curious, and decided to call the folks just to see what it was like to speak to the devil. The nice lady at the other end of the line asked me only to come to their office in Charleston with Lily (and proper identification, please) where we could pick up our free cruise voucher after a "brief" encounter with company "representatives" who would merely introduce us to a wonderful new product before the voucher could be issued. I laughed and agreed. When I told Lily about this, I told her it would be a hoot to do this and she could count on me to nap through what I figured would be a cutesy video presentation. I encouraged her to bring something to read.

I had no idea what I was talking about. Zero. After being introduced to our personal representative, Shannon, whose job no doubt was to soften the first lines of our resistance, we were ushered in to a large room. Here, the subzero climate they maintained was not the primary distraction only because Mike was. In rolled this large sized man with a voice that knew no volume control. I could be wrong about this, but I think Mike's last name was Megaphone. And, Lily and I were sitting in the front row within spitting distance of the mammoth air conditioning vent that was actively trying to single-handedly create the new ice age. I felt as if our hair was being bent backwards by the force of the sonic waves coming from Mike's mouth. With Mike finding it to be presumably an effective selling technique by making his presentation interactive, it sealed the deal that there would be no napping or casual reading while he held us hostage.

As Mike and the air conditioning terrorized us, we were showered -- no, make that inundated -- with facts and figures that made it all sound as if this real estate "time share-like" proposal was indisputably a deal that only an idiot could decline. We'd save thousands, and over the 40 year plan that was on the table we would travel the world for pennies. How could you lose? Although I was wearing a t-shirt, I felt as if I were wearing a shirt and tie that were three sizes too small. I felt that somehow they had managed to artificially increase the air pressure in there far beyond normal bounds. Indeed, the fabulous relentlessness of Mike's performance, made me feel like I was in the middle of the original Terminator with Arnold Schwarzenegger ruthlessly pursuing me with absolutely no chance for denial or reprieve. Or mercy. I felt some compassion for those facing what they euphemistically call "aggressive questioning" by law enforcement or the military. My head was swimming. I felt hunted.

Almost two hours later, Lily and I managed to fend off Mike and Shannon's final stabs at our vulnerability and, almost begrudgingly, we were issued our voucher for a free cruise out of Charleston to points South. We were so stressed out, we couldn't wait to get back home, grab two beach chairs, Mojo, and the largest rum drink I've had since my junior year in college. We headed to the beach to watch the last rays of the sun... and decompress.

The funny thing here -- lost in all the combat sequences we had just survived -- was that Lily and I have never thought of ourselves as cruise candidates. Just not our style. Our sense of it is that it's a place for spandex, coiffed hair and garishly mismatched deck wear. And, of course, a non-stop eating experience where food is available in every nook and cranny of this floating refrigerator.

But we're going alright. This is our only way to finally defeat Ahhnold.

Mojo's Knees, Redux

When we first got the news that Mojo -- at the delicate age of maybe a year and a half -- needed surgery for a bum knee, we knew we were in for a tough slog. We were told it would take on the order of 3 months until his body could heal and he could fly free of his leash once again. Like in all things canine, it's tough to explain to the guy that this too shall pass; that his goofy Elizabethan collar would be temporary; that our joyful forays of chasing one another around the house must be put on hold; and that his weeks long rehab might be fun, sort of. We followed the script and kept him under a proverbial lock and key -- indeed, virtual house arrest -- for the past 2 months. I kept telling the folks, who had become accustomed to seeing Mojo and me in the early morning hours on the beach, that his re-appearance was almost imminent and that I would bring a bottle of champagne to the beach in mid-July to celebrate his rediscovered freedom.

All that was until the other day when I brought Mojo back for some scheduled post-surgery x-rays. The surgeon matter-of-factly advised me that while Mojo's recovery from the surgery was going swimmingly well, Mojo's other rear knee was in need of repair as well. He showed me the x-ray and tried to point out in detail the growing fluid on the bad knee and the loss of muscle mass there. To the surgeon, it was not an "if" question, but a "when" question. He opined that the final tearing of the tendon could be in 6 weeks or 6 months, but it was coming as surely as next winter. In a flash, "deflating" had a new poster child. My mind had already been on a schedule that would envision a return to the beach for the rest of Mojo's life in a matter of weeks. We could get through this unfortunate delay knowing the finish line was looming. Hearing that any such prison break would be, at best, temporary, forced my brain to entertain a mid-course correction of my expectations. It could be done because it has to be done, but I think it's going to take a while to sell me on it.

And, this does not begin to confront the issue of cost, which, as they say, ain't chicken feed. As I became fond of telling folks, it's not as if Blue Cross covers these procedures. I suspect they wouldn't look too kindly on a bill submission for MCL surgery for a four-legged dependent.

I am taking some comfort -- perhaps as a delusion -- that the angst here is all mine and not Mojo's. I try to think that dogs don't appreciate the passage of time -- more specifically, the painfully slow passing of it -- as humans do. They truly live in an "it is what it is" world. Right? I'm clinging some to the notion that notwithstanding the physical discomfort and a replay of the slow rehab process, Mojo is not thinking, as I am, "when the hell can we get back to the beach?" I want to be right about this.

Maybe I'll age that bottle of champagne a bit more.

"Will you still need me, will you still feed me......."

Back in the mid-60s when Paul McCartney wrote "When I'm 64," I barely gave it a thought. It was a nice enough song, but one that definitely took a back seat to a host of other Beatles tunes and, for that matter, almost every other piece of music from that fabulous era. If I had given the thoughts behind this song even a nanosecond of my attention, I would have shrugged and concluded, "that's for other folks." And, of course, that would have been right......in 1966. But, we're not in 1966 anymore, are we? It's 44 years later and now its lyrics and sentiments resonate a bit more personally than they did back then. Why? Because today I turn 64; that's why.

Mostly, as we age, we become avid devotees of the "denial" approach to problem resolution as we still, despite all obvious indications, try to siphon off our latent fears that things are most certainly going downhill. What we hear is such tripe as, "60 is the new 40" and so on. Well, I hate to tell you, but 60 is still 60, and 64 is still 64, and until the human species can reliably extend life well into the hundreds, we are marching, unrelentingly, to our expiration dates.

Do I take solace that I can still run 6 miles or swim 60 laps? Of course. Do I try to tell myself that my parents were not remotely in the same shape I am for this age, and that bodes well for me? For sure. Am I convinced by all that? Sometimes... as when I indulge in one of my flights of denial and delude myself into thinking it so. Maybe it's a pattern for baby boomers who have never taken well to notions that they are not special or cutting edge. We are immortal, no?

100

I do have to say that the image conjured up by Mr. McCartney of the person who is 64 is of someone who, in my own mind, is hopelessly infirm and tottering on helplessness. I know I don't feel that way and look forward to many more adventures before I pack it in. But, I would be lying if I said that turning 64 isn't a dour reminder of something I don't want to confront. Am I drooling yet? No. Am I googling nursing homes? Hell no. But, there's something so arbitrary about a number. Is 64 so wildly different than 63? Of course not. Damn you, Paul, for making me think it is.

Nap time anyone?

Jailbreak

We reached the end of the wooden walkway that leads to the edge of the beach. I reached down and spoke softly to the patiently waiting Mojo. "Be careful out there" I whispered to him and then released the latch on his leash and sat back to watch his ecstasy. It was his first day unleashed since early April when he had knee surgery that would require more than three months of rehabilitation. From his ridiculous "Elizabethan" collar, to his underwater treadmill sessions, to his slow return to long walks, to his trots with me around Wild Dunes, his surgeon finally pronounced him ready to return to the scene of the crime, as it were. He was joined on that walkway by his long time compatriots, Bosco and Mabel, the great danes who live next door. Mabel, too, was excited to see her buddy again. In a flash, he was sprinting to the ocean, his home away from home.

If one can paint a picture of happiness, then this was a Rembrandt. Mojo flew to the water and began his eternal pursuit of minnows in the shallows. He fairly leaped vertically as he tried to pivot and intercept the elusive fish. His motions were akin to a frenetic, spastic dance to a music that has no rhythm, but which has a satanic beat. For a creature that has only two goals in his life -- to catch a squirrel and to catch a minnow -- this was serious, if joyous, business. I brought with me three tennis balls to keep him entertained, but they were wholly unnecessary. The minnows, or, more accurately, the promise of minnows was all he needed. Even his other compatriots, Lucy the boxer, Betsy the goldendoodle, Sandy, the miniature something, and other assorted labs were most surely a distraction, but they were only a diversion from the main event. Center stage was reserved for the ocean.

The fly in this ointment is the knowledge that Mojo will be facing more knee surgery in his near future, this time on his right leg. The surgeon told me it was not an "if" question, but a "when" question as to when the other shoe would drop, so to speak. Lily and I held our collective breath as we watched Mojo sprint to the ocean wondering if he'd pull up lame and face a maddeningly hasty return to being under house arrest. In a way, we were already preparing ourselves for this. But, this was of no interest to Mojo who cared only that he could dive through some waves, lie in the shallows, and chase those infernal minnows. Today all went well.

This is how you spell happiness.

Adieu, Mon Ami

I hope I'm not alone in this. Tell me you don't have a favorite t-shirt somewhere, or maybe a fleece, or an old pair of jeans, that has out-lived its expiration date by, let's say, 15 years. You know what I'm talking about. Clothing that's so old it not only looks weathered, but it knows your history; it knows your secrets. It is almost holy in its rankings among your belongings. You put these garments in the laundry and you dearly hope they survive the spin cycle. Why you keep them is obvious. They feel great. They conform to your body in a way that reflects that they are practically human. They know you, right? So what if they are a bit torn, a bit weathered, a tad faded. They are your friends. They understand.

So, when it comes to parting with them you feel a sense of loss that is wholly out of touch with reality; totally out of line with "normal" expectations. They have become a part of you, and tossing them away is akin to tossing away a loved one, sort of. They deserve a fitting burial, no?

This tragic moment happened to me this weekend when I ever-so-re-luctantly parted with a t-shirt I loved. It was one I picked up in New Zealand 14 years ago when we were traveling there with Jesse and Alex. It was a muted peach in color -- or at least it became muted af-ter its 4,000th washing in 2003. Over time it became beatifically soft as only a bit of clothing that lasts so long can become. On its back it touted A.J. Hackett Bungee Jumping, an outfit that was responsible for Jesse's leap into thin air at the tender age of 13 off the Kuwara Bridge outside of Queenstown, New Zealand. A leap that launched an adventurous and -- some would say -- fearless attitude toward life that has suited him well over the past decade. Some would say too well, but that's another story.

And so, when I realized that its threadbare leavings were not up to yet another spin cycle, I made the terrible judgment that its expiration date -- long overdue -- had actually arrived. Life support was no longer an option. The shirt was now semi-transparent and was deserving of a fitting adieu. I touched it with a sensitivity I likely had never before managed; the kind you would experience maybe with a loved one with whom it was time to say good-bye.

I will get over this, of course. But, don't tell me there aren't memories embedded in that t-shirt's weave. Don't tell me there isn't something more important here than discarding your every day piece of trash. I won't hear of it.

Treasure your old garments. They know you as few do.

Life Among the Giants

Mojo has a couple of friends, Mabel and Bosco, whose mere appearance casts shadows across whatever landscape you happen to find yourself in. Mojo is not exactly small in the world of canines; he's about 75 pounds, give or take. You know he's there. But Bosco is to Mojo what Mojo is to a cereal box. Bosco, and his mom Mabel, are great danes and they live next door under the same roof as their guardians, Brian and Jan. I see Mabel and Bosco -- oftentimes referred to around these parts as "the ponies" -- at the beach every morning where the vastness of the shoreline can make even these behemoths seem average-sized. But, indoors, they can make your 2,000 square foot house seem like nothing more than a large efficiency in a flash. They fill the space, as they say.

This weekend, Lily and I became dog sitters for the ponies as both Brian and Jan had to be in Chicago for a funeral for Jan's mom. When Brian asked me if we would take in the big galoots, I didn't hesitate. I knew they got along famously with Mojo, and I knew this would help out Brian and Jan. The plan was for Bosco and Mabel to stay at their home with me coming over to feed them, walk them, and take them to the beach in the mornings. For a day that worked. While Lily joined me in our early morning beach outing, and was a huge help, I still felt like it would have been helpful to have a third eye and, perhaps, a third arm. Bosco has a tendency to want to explore the rear regions of the deep beach, while Mabel actively seeks out both other dogs and the stray passer-by against whom she does her famous lean which can bowl you over if you don't pay attention. All the while, Mojo is doing his frenetic "dance in the shallows" looking for minnows, or alternately, leaving tennis balls all over the place which he has passionately chased, but not so passionately returned. And, one of them is surely pooping somewhere during all this, and not always where it's most convenient. Shepherding these three brutes to more or less head in the same direction is like the proverbial herding of cats. Very big cats. When you finally get them on leashes to get them home, the odds of your getting twisted into a pretzel are of a sort that even Vegas smiles on. So -- this is more than a one-person job, at least for me it is. But, day one, went swimmingly. A good time was had by all.

Day two, however, large and very noisy thunderstorms altered the landscape in more ways than one. Mabel fears thunderstorms the way you and I fear not being able to breathe, so when storms arrive (or even when they're still in the distance), the poor girl goes into manic mode, drooling, tail curled downward, all the while seeking a safe haven. This is what happened this morning. In an effort to ease her stress, I cajoled her and Bosco -- who is fine with all this climatic drama -- to come over to our house where at least Mabel would have the comfort of human company.

As I write this, this is still a work in progress. What I can say is that Bosco and Mabel follow me around the house in a way that makes me feel like I'm being trailed by two small continents, one on either side. Mojo darts in and around the continents with a toy in his mouth seeking a playmate, two-legged or four -- it doesn't matter. I feel the need for space.

Sunshine could really help here.

We're Gonna Need A Bigger Boat

You remember that line, right? Roy Scheider utters it in a moment of awe and horror as he takes in the spectacle of the great white thinking lunch thoughts next to Roy's hopelessly undersized boat. Funny how that line flew into my consciousness as Mojo did his level best to re-enact Captain Sam Quint's role in "Jaws" this morning. What Mojo clearly didn't appreciate was that, in fact, he was actually reprising the title role from the 1939 classic "Idiot's Delight."

This morning's jaunt began innocently enough: bright early morning sun, a beautiful low tide, lots of dogs. But, when someone shouted "shark," that was reason enough to know this was not going to be your ordinary morning. As we turned to the ocean shallows, the large silvery dorsal fin was unmistakable, and while he was no mammoth great white, he was no minnow either. Both two-legged and four-legged life forms immediately got out of, or steered clear of, the water......except Mojo. To the extent that Mojo can be said to think actual thoughts, I felt he was saying, "Damn, that's one big minnow out there!" Not needing any further encouragement, and having batted zero for a thousand in this summer's endless attempts to finally land a minnow, Mojo dove into the shallows and attacked the shark. Let me repeat that: he attacked the shark. With his front paws sitting astride the dorsal fin, I feared the Mojomeister was on the verge of having a sushi breakfast were it not for the deft escape maneuver of the shark who proved to be the far wiser of the two animals in this one act play. You could just hear the shark thinking, "What the hell is that lunatic black thing on my back?" as he slithered off to deeper waters.

Normalcy ensued for maybe another 20 minutes or so until the shoreline was visited by yet another shark, this one, to my eyes, even bigger than the last one. (I think the first one went back for reinforcements.) Mojo, having learned nothing from his first encounter, dove into the ocean yet again in pursuit thinking, no doubt, how this really was his lucky day. Never, ever, had the Isle of Palms been visited by such fabulous minnows. In proving yet again how stupid people can be when faced by moments of trauma, I ran into the ocean after him waving my plastic ball launcher as if this were weapon enough should things get dicey. Fortunately, this shark came from the same smart family as the first visitor and found a way to get away from the shark-surfing Mojo and retreat to live another day.

My friend, Brian, tried to convince me that Mojo was not acting stupidly, but was actually indulging in an act of heroism; that Mojo was, in fact, putting himself in harm's way to save his buddies from an unsavory fate. This is what I will let others think. I would say that Mojo and I know better, but clearly, Mojo does not. When we returned home and I watched Mojo eating his usual breakfast of dry, boring kibble, I wondered whether thoughts of sushi or shark tartare danced in his head.

Next time, big fella, next time.

Seared Sea Scallops in a Tangerine Reduction Over a Mango and Avocado Salsa

When you're at a loss for what to do for dinner tonight, try this out. I'm telling you, your children and your children's children will be talking about this for a long time. A taste explosion!

ingredients
- 3 large sea scallops per person
- 1 ripe avocado
- 1 ripe mango
- 1 package string beans
- 1 can garbanzo beans
- 1 good sized scallion
- 1 good handful of cilantro (chopped)
- 1 medium handful of sundried tomatoes
- 1 medium handful of pine nuts
- olive oil
- toasted sesame oil
- 1/2 cup fresh tangerine juice (or, in a pinch, orange juice)
- 1/8 to 1/4 cup soy sauce
- 1/8 to 1/4 cup lemon pepper oil (or the flavored oil of your liking -- maybe basil oil, for example)
- 1 lime
- ground black pepper to taste

the scallops
1. place scallops into a hot pan that has been coated nicely with olive oil. use medium heat.
2. sear scallop bottoms until nicely caramelized. flip and do the same to the reverse side.

the mango salsa
1. chop mango into smallish pieces. same for avocado. add in chopped scallion and chopped cilantro. add in the juice of the lime and the toasted sesame oil. let stand.

the tangerine reduction
1. into a saucepan, put tangerine juice, soy sauce and lemon pepper oil. place under medium heat and allow the mixture to reduce.
2. when the sauce has thickened, let simmer and spoon on to scallops

stringbean chopped salad
1. blanch stringbeans for no more than two minutes in boiling water. drain and put in a bowl of cold/ice water. drain that bowl and add the stringbeans and drained garbanzos to the bowl. add in sundried tomatoes.
2. in a pan, toast pine nuts either with a little olive oil or without -- your choice. add in pine nuts to beans.
3. sprinkle the mix liberally with olive oil and black pepper and stir.

Serve scallops atop the mango salsa with the bean salad on the side. spoon your tangerine reduction over the scallops.

Wham! One great dinner!

The Ceremony

On September 19, Jesse and Laura got married. Here is the ceremony that I prepared for them......

I'd like to welcome all of you to this wonderful celebration we're having today. I have to tell you, I find it both amazing and incredibly heartwarming not just to see so many familiar faces, but to realize the distances -- in many cases, great distances -- that so many of you have traveled just to be here. We have folks here from Mississippi, of course, but also Louisiana, Colorado, California, Oregon, Florida, Massachusetts, New York, Ohio, Illinois, Maryland, Virginia, Washington D.C., Delaware, North Carolina, and, yes, even a few from South Carolina. Have I left anyone out? I want to thank all of you for taking the time, for making the effort, to be here and sharing in what is obviously a very special day for us.

Before we proceed, may I ask please who is presenting the bride? Thank you John; thank you Gail.

Laura and Jesse, imagine meeting you here today. Who would have thought even just a few short years ago that one day the three of us would be standing right here right now like this? But, here we are. And, what an extraordinary day it is. I suspect everyone here, if asked, could describe for you in vivid detail the most special days in their lives, but, speaking for myself, I can tell you that there are precious few of them where we can honestly say that we find our-selves surrounded by all of the most important people in our lives: Your family, your friends -- all the people through whom no doubt you can trace every significant step (and misstep) you have taken along the way. There are some people here today who know you as no one else does. They know your strengths, your weaknesses, your idiosyncrasies, your history, your secrets. And, they love you. So, as I say, days like this don't come along very often. Enjoy these moments and remember them.

I know your relationship started seven or so years ago as a dating one. But, I seem to recall that at some point fairly early on, you deepened that relationship by becoming good friends as well. You learned to trust each other, to rely on each other, and to look out for one another. Essentially, you began the process of becoming partners in each other's lives. Believe me, I know there were no shortages of parties and good times in those years, but all of us here also know that since those days the two of you have gotten down to the business of sharing your lives together when it's not all parties and good times. You now know what it is to pay the bills, to put food on the table, to share in day-to-day responsibilities, and to ride out stressful times. You also know what it is to make plans with a keen eye on each other's likes and dislikes, not just your own fancies. And, yet, through all of this, you have remained sure of each other's feelings and, best of all… you have remained happy. The trust the two of you have built up in one another is not something you get automatically by simply signing a marriage license; you have to earn it. And, each of you has done just that.

Jesse -- I know you will recall the steady drumbeat of advice you got from us when you were growing up, especially from your mom: don't you dare get married before you turn 30, we said. We told you that you really don't know who you are until then; we told you that you would evolve and grow and that your tastes and values at age 30 will bear little resemblance to those you had at age 20. So -- if you don't know who you are, how can you expect to go about the business of successfully selecting a partner for life? You remember that, right?

Well, Jess, it's not that we were wrong, not really. We thought that was sensible advice. What we hadn't counted on… was Laura. Laura, as you know, you have long since become a part of our family. I sometimes feel as if we have literally traveled the globe with you, from Europe to Costa Rica to Indonesia. I don't remember when it happened exactly, but at some point Lily and I stopped being "ma'am" and "sir" and we became just plain old "Lily" and "Jeff." And, I have to tell you how delighted we are in the evolution of our relationship with you.

But, apart from our travels with you, Laura, you and Jesse have truly traveled the world as very few ever get to do --- from Africa, to Europe, to Central and South America, and to Southeast Asia. Those have been amazing times for you both, but I also suspect they were testing times for you as well. You don't need me to tell you that oftentimes, when you're traveling under less than the best conditions -- something the two of you know a little something about -- qualities such as patience and tolerance are not the ones that always come to the fore so easily. To me, then, what made your travels so special was not just that they enabled you to learn more about each other, but they enabled you to strengthen a relationship that was already strong. Best of all, they enabled you both to envision a future together as well. That's why I'm thinking that among the many, many irreplaceable memories each of you have of those journeys are not just the destinations you reached, but memories of how you traveled together as well. Somewhere down those roads, Laura, you not only wowed Lily and me, but, far more importantly, you wowed the fellow standing next to you today.

So, Jesse, here we are today seeing you getting married at age 27 and not 30, which means, Laura, that I can say to you that, in your wonderfully disarming fashion, you pretty much singlehandedly shattered one of the basic parenting lessons we had for both Jesse and Alex. And, I am here to tell you how happy we are that you did…this one time. And, Jesse, how happy we are that you so totally ignored our advice...this one time.

I think what I'm going to say to you here may sound a little trite, Laura, but I promise you that is not my intention. Your bright, sun-shiny disposition just makes things better. Your graciousness and your generosity are of a sort that simply cannot be manufactured. You are truly genuine. Gail and John -- I have to tell you, you've done good here. You have raised an amazing daughter. Indeed, if I may say so, you have raised three amazing daughters. And, Laura, just as we have come to embrace you, so has your family embraced Jesse both as a son and a brother. From Jackson to Pickwick, you and your family have always made Jesse feel relaxed, comfortable, and loved. And, for that, Lily and I are truly forever grateful.

Jesse -- the personal growth you have shown over the past several years has been simply stunning to me. I can say this, of course, be-cause, as your father, I am hopelessly and irretrievably biased. I raise this issue here only because it sheds light, in part, on why we believe your future with Laura is so promising. You know, Jess, there was a time in your life when your inclination was "to go it alone" and when you would engage in decision-making essentially by falling back on your own instincts, really to the exclusion of everything and every-one else. I can say honestly that is simply no longer the case. Not from what I've seen. What you have gained is a measure of humility and, in my book, it is humility that is a basic building block in any enduring relationship. You have learned to learn from others and to trust their judgments alongside your own. Nowhere is this more in evidence, Jess, than in your relationship with Laura. Just judging from our own conversations in recent months when we've talked about your life plans, your goals, your aspirations, I am struck by how mindful you are of Laura's happiness, not just your own. And, I have to tell you, this is a wonderful omen.

You will recall that some months ago I asked each of you if you would share with me what you believe you have learned from one another. Jesse, you told me that because of Laura's influence in your life, you are now more patient, more tolerant, more mature. You say you see yourself now as a far better person since Laura entered your life, and those of us who know you best see how much easier it is for you now to get outside that once stoic exterior and express your feelings more openly. Essentially, Jesse, Laura has begun the process of opening you up, and how wonderful is that?

Laura, you told me that because of Jesse you are now far more adventurous and that you see yourself as a far more independent and confident person than you have ever been in your life. You told me also, Laura, that because of Jesse you now strive for better things in your life. These are amazing qualities to learn from one another. What you don't know -- indeed, what you cannot know yet -- is that as each of you continue to grow and as you continue to share your strengths with one another, each of you will grow in ways you cannot possibly imagine. And, I dare say, they will all be for the good.

I'm a little bit older than the two of you, and I only have the floor for another minute, so, if I may, I'd like to offer a few of my own suggestions to you: be kind to each other, be generous with each other, laugh with each other, listen to each other, and remember that while it is so important for each of you to maintain your own separate identities in this relationship, remember also that whereas you were once two, you are now one. Think that way. I'm smiling as I say these things to you because I know you know these things; I know you understand them, and I know you try to practice them. I'm also smiling because as a father, and a father-in-law, nothing could possibly make me any happier.

I know the two of you have vows you would like to exchange, so, if you would, please turn toward each other and repeat after me.

Jesse: I, Jesse, take thee Laura to be my wife, to have and to hold, from this day forward, for better – for worse, for richer – for poorer, in sickness and in health, to love and to cherish, till death do us part.

Laura: I, Laura, take thee Jesse to be my husband, to have and to hold, from this day forward, for better – for worse, for richer – for poorer, in sickness and in health, to love and to cherish, till death do us part.

May I have the rings, please?

Jesse, please repeat after me: Laura, accept this ring, and with it my promise of faith, patience, and love, for the rest of my life.

And Laura: Jesse, accept this ring, and with it my promise of faith, patience, and love, for the rest of my life.

Jesse and Laura -- In the spirit of God, and with the hopes and wishes of your family and friends, may the happiness you feel at this moment stay with you the rest of your lives. By the authority vested in me by the State of South Carolina, I now pronounce you husband and wife.

Jesse -- You may kiss the bride

Ladies and Gentlemen, may I present to you for the first time, Jesse and Laura Golland!

Epilogue

When I was getting dressed for the ceremony, I reached into my bureau looking for a nice watch to wear for the occasion. What I came across was a watch belonging to my father, a watch that had not been worn for the 24 years since his death. I put it on. Lying next to it was my mother's wedding ring, untouched since her passing 18 years ago. I picked it up and put it in my pocket. I felt like I was in a circle now completed. I felt whole.

In the ceremony, I said to Jesse and Laura that this would be one of the most special days in their lives. What I had not realized, but soon did, is that this proved to be one of the most special days in my life as well. Surrounded by almost all of the most important people in my life and Lily's -- family and friends -- and feeling the good will, support and love coming from all, I knew this would signal a moment that would be with me forever. Thank you, Jesse. Thank you, Laura. I love you both so much.

Go and Then Stop. Repeat, and Repeat, and Repeat…

Let me make a friendly suggestion. When next you contemplate a dashing, daring adventure far from home, give a thought or two to how logistically crazy it will be to get there. I say this as we board our fourth flight of the day. Count 'em: one, two, three, four. Don't ask me what day it is or what time zone we're in. I haven't a clue. I do know we're in Turkey. At this moment, we are awaiting the departure of Flight 2560 on Turkish Airlines from Istanbul to Dalaman, on the country's southern coast. Charleston feels very far away.

This was a trip planned long ago when we knew we'd barely close out Jesse and Laura's wedding before having to execute a hairpin turn within 36 hours to ready ourselves for this wonderful adventure to Turkey and Greece. We knew it would be a long journey, but knowing and doing are two different things. Why is that?

Up at 7 to see Alex off for his return to San Diego, we later make it ourselves to the Charleston airport. One hour wait here. One flight of one and a half hours. Arrive in Philadelphia. A three hour wait here. One eight hour flight to Frankfort, Germany. In Frankfort for four hours. One three hour flight to Istanbul. Wait in Istanbul for two hours. Finally, a two and a half hour flight to Dalaman. Let's run the numbers, shall we? Ten hours waiting in airports, fourteen hours in the air. That's a day, right?

Somewhere before Frankfort, I lost my train of thought. I think somewhere between Frankfort and Istanbul I lost my ability to reason. In Istanbul, I lost the ability to speak coherently. Will I re-member my name when we land in Dalaman? I am clutching our two passports with whitened knuckles lest I leave them in some god-forsaken restroom.

I'm not complaining, mind you. I can't wait to reach our destination and get the trip rolling. I'll rally, whatever my name is.

But, right now, fatigue rules.

Aboard the Alaturka

The Mediterranean is pretty spectacular wherever you find yourself on it, and the southern coastline of Turkey is no exception. The water has none of the turquoise you associate with the tropics, but it does sport an eye-popping sapphire, almost electric, blue. We are aboard the Alaturka, a Turkish "gullet" perhaps better described as a wooden sailing vessel. We are among eleven other passengers: five Aussies (including a couple of newlyweds), two Lithuanians into homeopathic medicine and beekeeping, a female Canadian journalist working for Reuters, three other Americans, one of whom is literally pedaling himself through eastern Europe and Turkey on his trusty but well worn bike, and one non-English speaking Turkish dude, Umete. Except for Umete, we are all united by a common language, a love for travel, and a fondness for storytelling.

What is not to like about this? Nothing, I tell you. We all have "staterooms" below, but they are small enough to test even Clark Kent's legendary skills at costume changes in small places. And, the bathrooms each of us gets are so microscopically tiny they should issue elbow pads as standard equipment. As a result, all of the action is on deck, including sleeping. I mean, why sleep in a claustrophobe's hell when you can bed down on commodious pads with your blanket and pillow and fall asleep under the stars? As for day-time activity, I know this sounds stressful, but we eat, drink, swim, nap, read, mingle, and repeat. This cruise is not for the antsy.

I thought the sunset last night was as good as it gets, but I was wrong. This morning's sunrise was a psychedelic pastiche of neon pinks and blues against a foreground of the steep Turkish hills that slide into the sea, each a different hue of black.

Spectacular.

Close Quarters

An interesting study in human relations, this gullet excursion. The challenge: close, sometimes very close, physical proximity for 4 days to 11 other travelers none of whom you have ever laid eyes on before. As in any forced encounter, some interactions fare better than others, but you know deep down you'd like all of them to work as well as possible since you're virtually nose to nose with these folks for more than just afternoon tea. What this means, among other things, is putting up with Umete's snoring a couple of feet away on the deck's night time sleeping area, or Herb and Judy's effortless (and, sadly, continuous) attempts at dominating breakfast, lunch and dinner conversations.

For us, the experience worked well, first and foremost, because -- with the exception of Umete -- all of us spoke English. Immeasurable barriers were overcome as a result of this good fortune. I mean, it's not like we needed to immerse ourselves in Swedish or German to get by. Rather, bonded by everyone's love for travel stories, an avalanche of information and opinions were the order of the day. Want to know what the life of a journalist is like? Done. Want to know the nuances of beekeeping? Done. Or, maybe you just want to know what it's like to pedal your way through eastern Europe. Done. Even Herb and Judy's voracious appetite for the spotlight could not disrupt this totally pleasurable atmosphere.

This may be a bit of an exaggeration, but we ate every nine minutes -- or, so it seemed. A wild pastiche of tomatoes, potatoes, nutella, bread, cheeses, pink deli meats, grilled chicken or beef, pasta, and the ubiquitous olives. Not gourmet, for sure. But, plentiful, tasty, and satisfying. The scenery is spectacular: mountains falling into the deep blue Mediterranean, a smattering of ruins, ancient castles lording over the sea from protected heights, and gorgeous sailing vessels dotting the waters. Swimming off our boat revealed to us not only how warm the water was, but how incredibly salty it was as well. We had floats and noodles to bask on, but, seriously, it would take more than a little effort to sink.

One last note: sleeping on deck was awesome. Lulled to sleep by a gentle rolling of the boat, you could try to keep your eyes open just long enough to take in the full moon and its beams traversing the sea like a yellow carpet leading directly to your eyes.

Not a bad way to end the day.

Rhodes

We are staying in a hotel whose building dates back 800 years. It begins to tell you the story of this epically historic site which has seen the likes of the Lycians, Romans, Ottoman Turks, English crusaders, and, in more recent times, the Germans, Italians, and Greeks. It lies at the metaphysical and literal crossroads of history and geography as, over the centuries, marauding powers, traders, and crusaders criss-crossed the eastern Mediterranean in pursuit of religious purity, riches, power, or some other greater glory.

One can begin to envision what all this might have looked like way back when, but for the impossibly numerous shops carved into these ancient buildings: jewelry, fine clothing, artwork, leather goods, souvenir emporiums, and t-shirt shops. And, this is to say nothing of the seemingly endless array of rooftop and sidewalk cafes that vie for the tourist dollar at every opportunity. You've got your souvlaki, grilled octopus, yogurt, stuffed grape leaves, prawns, all with tomatoes, onion, and parsley and the ever-present and tasty olive. Factor in the waves of folks arriving by cruise ships which dock from time to time, and you have all the ingredients for a shopping and eating frenzy that may have no peers. At some level, this commercial onslaught is insulting given the very serious history of this place. At a lighter level, however, the sensory overload presented by these shops and eateries seems engaging, entertaining, and even comical if you're in a more relaxed and whimsical mood. Which we were.

We have a safe haven from all this at our hotel, the Sotiris Nikolas, nestled near the western walls of the Old City beyond the rabble.

We reach it by a narrow alley whose cobblestones, like those every-where here, are still impossibly rounded despite centuries of traffic. The Nikolas exudes charm no less than Cary Grant once did with rooms having arched doorways that lead to a protected wooden patio overlooking a rear garden that has enough green to balance out the stone walls that rise above it. The proprietor, Marianne, is of Danish descent, and she is exactly what you want in a hotelier: charming, helpful, funny, obliging at every turn. Breakfasts are up on the roof, and there amid the bountiful offerings of eggs, fruit, pastries, bread, coffee, cheeses (and, yes, olives) lies the city and harbor beyond.

Perfect.

The Gateway to Heaven?

Ask yourself to name the three most beautiful places you've seen on the planet, and ask yourself why you made these choices. Was it a beautiful beach, a majestic mountain range, the most charming of cobble stoned villages, or, maybe, a lush tropical paradise? Then, narrow your choices down to one. How can there be just one best, one most beautiful place?

I thought that myself until we came to Santorini. The pictures I had seen over the years seemed stunning, but I also knew this place to be a popular tourist mecca -- something that tends to erode great beauty very quickly. Does Santorini have tourists? You bet. Does it have a thousand jewelry, t-shirt, and souvenir shops? Of course. But, all of them combined cannot begin to put a dent in the overwhelming grandeur and sheer mind-bending, breathtaking beauty of this place. Most of the island is a huge rock, but at its western façade, it serves as a fitting foundation for the small, white-washed towns that hug the cliffs along a fantastically sparkling Aegean Sea with views to the horizon so vast and so sweeping you swear you can see the curvature of the earth. The Caldera, as they call it, or the volcanic remains of what was once part of this island, jut out of the sea just enough to give a proper sense of size and distance to this matchless vista and give context to sunsets that are so breathtaking they can make you cry.

The towns of the west coast are a vertical jumble of white-washed buildings and blue-domed churches. They seemingly overlap one another so that from a distance they appear to be one rolling structure. Trying to identify a particular hotel or restaurant from a distance, as you move higher or lower along the aerie-like paths that hug the cliffs, is a game in itself, not entirely unlike "Where's Waldo." From the water, the towns and cliffs give all the appearance of snow-capped mountains, the cliffs a deep reddish brown capped by the sea of white buildings on top.

Somewhat like the Amalfi coast in Italy, Santorini's famed western slope towns are not for the poorly conditioned. Everything is either straight up or straight down. Even getting from our hotel bedroom to our bathroom involved a hike of several steps up and then a steep staircase down. (In the middle of the night, this is not a task taken lightly.) What this presents is an endless opportunity to see everything from different angles -- from above and below -- as you navigate vertically. In one moment you are looking up at a church dome; in the next, you're taking a picture of the same dome from above.

The alleyways of these towns, notably Fira, and the crown jewel, the achingly beautiful Oia (pronounced Eeya), are almost narrow enough to span with your arms. There are no cars here; there is simply no room. Automobile traffic is relegated to streets inland and to the flatter parts of the island. But, the manner that these alleyways connect, sideways and vertically, give you the feel sometimes that you've landed in a life-sized M.C. Escher drawing where all paths seem circular and without resolution.

As in Rhodes, there seem to be cafes and restaurants every nine feet. I have no idea how all of them survive, but I'm told they do. You pay for the view, of course, but mostly that is a price we're willing to pay. Order your "tomato balls" -- deep-fried tomatoes in a chewy crust -- or deep-fried stuffed olives, or cheese plates, or, for heartier fare all of the beef, lamb, octopus and calamari dishes you can imagine.

Ply yourself with local Greek wine, put your feet up on the railings, and breathe deeply.

As they say, beauty is in the eyes of the beholder. For me, the eye-popping effect of these starkly white-washed cliff hugging towns against the matchless backdrop of the Caldera and the Aegean, all from a height that seems miles high, is as good as it gets. Is it perfect? No. Is it close? Oh yes. At this moment, I am sitting on a chaise by our pool staring out at a scaldingly sun-washed sea that, as I say, seems to be miles below. There's a cool breeze blowing, and even the monstrous cruise ships that lurk in the harbor seem no bigger than toys. They are no threat to us right now. We will enjoy cocktails later as we watch the world-famous sunsets here where the sea takes on hues of pinks and reds and the white facades of these towns turn peach in color. Dinner lies beyond. Somewhere.

You Can't Get There From Here. Really.

(October 7) Ok. It's been just about a perfect trip, right? Lots of sun, gorgeous settings, great food and wine, and great company. We are smiling, relaxed, and nostalgic about leaving.

Leaving? Who said anything about leaving? At midnight on the eve of our departure from Paros, we hear a knock on our door. My thinking is this is never a good sign, and this time is no exception. It is our local travel agent who comes to tell us that the air traffic controllers of Greece have gone on strike, and our flight to Athens (and then home) has been cancelled. We will now need to take a ferry to Athens, and wave bye-bye to our flight out of Athens should it actually leave. Which it did. Without us.

What now? Plan B. Get to Athens, get a hotel near the airport and then start the always endless slog of dealing with the airlines to re-book our departure. One of the dark, little secrets of the airlines is that when you miss a flight and you're using more than one air carrier, they always point the finger at the other guy. Your problem is never their problem. And, so it was with us. Lufthansa told us we would have to deal with United, and United told us we were out of luck. They could maybe get us out five days later and we would have to buy new tickets at a cost of about $5,000 per couple. That's right. $5,000. This is not a typo. Sensing this was not an option, we toyed with the idea of staying in Athens, see the sights. Or, maybe go back to one of the islands and wait it out until United deigned to give us mileage tickets at a fairly nominal cost. In the meantime: souvlaki, ouzo, repeat.

What happened instead was we tried another United phone number and were met with a far more compassionate lady who tried her level best to re-acquaint us with the U.S. of A. without draining our bank accounts. She tried to get us on any flight back to the U.S. This meant possible trips to New York, Charlotte, Chicago, Miami, Atlanta, Houston, Detroit, and even Canada. Nothing. Zilch. Nada. (Vegas. She should have tried Vegas. Anything is possible there.) We were stranded. I had visions about now having enough time to learn Greek, or, at a minimum, increase my tolerance to ouzo. I wondered: would Mojo remember us? In fact, would he be cared for since our house sitter had other obligations going into the weekend? Huge stress on this one. (Through a series of emails and texts we were able to get word to our neighbors to take the little guy in. Problem solved.) After rolling up $300 in telephone charges, Compassionate Lady at United forged ahead to find us some minimally sensible solutions, and, amazingly, she found one. We could leave the next day, but would have to stay in London for a couple of days.

Fish and chips anyone?

Reminiscing

Why is it we really get into reminiscing just when we don't have the mental capacity to do that successfully? I know, I know -- when you're young, and have wonderful mental acuity, you don't look backward; there's too much that lays ahead to ponder what was. And, when you're young, the next step is always so cool and to be envied that you don't want to waste a moment on some lame memory that happened when you were, let's say, a toddler. If you're 8, you want to be 10. Ahh, double digits! When you're 10, you crave 13. To be a teenager at last! When you're 14, you can't sit still until you're 16 so you can drive. Freedom! And, when you're 19, you ache for 21 so the whole deal can be legal and you can be treated as a full-scale, honest-to-God adult, just like your parents and teachers. Everything is forward looking.

But, when you get into your 50s or 60s, I guess your head is so crammed with memories, you just have to have an outlet for them before our heads explode from over-capacity. And so we reminisce. Or, at least we attempt to. This past weekend, our good friends Randy and Cathy came for a visit. Our relationship goes back decades, and for Lily, back to college days. We were married within a year of each other, shared summer beach houses for years, raised each other's kids, skied together, traveled together, partied together. You get the picture: we share a lot of history.

So, there we were, sitting around the dinner table the other night calling up days of yore, drinking way too much wine. We were trying to recall a charades game we all enjoyed, played some time in the last millennium. Ancient history to all but those steeped in Greek history. It was a contest between the girls and the guys, or, as we entitled them, the Powder Puffs and the Bulls. No stereotyping back in those days, oh no. What we couldn't get straight -- in 2010 -- was exactly who was there. Was Syl there? Randy thought so. Was Maggie there? She had to be, right (even if her name back then was Marge)? Did the Powder Puffs prevail? None of these matters could be resolved. In a desperate effort at resolving the vagaries of history, Lily reached through the cobwebs of her distant past and went to what had to be an unassailable source: some old poetry she had written commemorating the famed pantomime event. I mean, what better documentation of history than old poetry. So what if it wasn't Homer, Sappho, or Aeschylus. Sadly, all we got from that effort was that there was apparently some guy named Allen at that charades event, and none of us could even remotely think who that might be. I called Maggie, one of the most intelligent people we know on planet earth, and all she had to say was "what charades party?" Not helpful, but why should she be any different? We thought she was a participant that long ago night, but our memories are -- how you say -- not to be trusted.

And, so the evening wore on. We tried to reconstruct which beach houses we rented in chronological order. Consensus was as ascertainable as an elusive ghost on some far away mountain. Our minds were mush, and while some of that could no doubt be attributed to the wine, equal parts of the blame rested with our over-used and way too cluttered heads. I guess this is why history is written and why extemporaneous accounts are so valued. As the event, whatever it is, vanishes in the rear view mirror, so does our ability to re-create what happened. Is it fun to try to reconstruct personal history? Absolutely. Is it productive? Not a chance in hell.

And, why should we expect it to be any other way? We can't remember what we had for lunch just yesterday. Nor can we recall who that actor was in that movie (whose title is also a bit too elusive at this particular moment). You know the one. It's on the tip of my tongue! It took place in Vienna. Or was it Rome? And, the star went on to play a major role in that spy movie. You know, the really popular one that led to a TV series that starred the guy who used to be bit player in that old James Garner flick. And, on and on it goes.

It's all there. In our minds. Somewhere. Probably not far from where we left the car keys or glasses, wherever that might be.

A Winter's Morning

It was 26 this morning; no doubt colder with the wind chill. Another day in the "mild winter" world of Charleston. As usual, Mojo came over for a "visit" to my side of the bed about 7:45 -- you can count on it -- and it doesn't take a psychic to know what was on his mind. With his head resting on the bed and those soft brown eyes forlornly looking up at me, he was wondering if this, at last, might be a beach day. Lately, it's been so damn cold in the morning that going to the beach with him just wasn't an option I was so terribly interested in. I mean, who wants to subject themselves to wind chills of 13 degrees on a windswept terrain that is disturbingly lunar in its personality, devoid of life but for the occasional passing pelican? But, this morning I reacted differently. Mojo is headed for knee surgery in two weeks, his second in 9 months. For three months following that, there will be no beach time for him at all. Just house arrest and rehab. How could I say no?

I bundled myself up in more layers than the best lasagna; a veritable Pillsbury dough boy was I. Or, maybe the Michelin Man. I thought it would take a crane to get my coat over the last of my fleeces, but I managed to waddle to the door like a sumo wrestler and took a wagging Mojo with me. He was naked, naturally. And, very excited.

Pulling me as if we were about to be overtaken by a maniac bear, Mojo and I reached the beach in near record time. As is our ritual, he sat patiently while I got his leash unhooked and then waited for me to give him two pats on his side whereupon he launches like a rocket. Eat my dust. As I walked on to the sand, I immediately noticed that the sand was frozen! As crunchy underfoot as a graham cracker crust. The sun was bright, if not warm, and the wind blew the few errant particles of sand like whirling dervishes across the desert. Seeing that I was the only game in town, Mojo returned half-way from the water's edge to urge me to get on with the business at hand: the flinging of tennis balls far out into the ocean.

Some would consider this tantamount to animal cruelty notwith-standing the (somewhat) warmer temperatures of the ocean water than the ambient air. But, this was not about human activity; it's all canine. As my brother-in-law-Jim would tell me later, think of Mojo's coat as a built-in down-filled parka. Warmth is not so much an issue. Except to the canine's shivering owner. And so our little dance proceeded. I would launch a ball as far out as I could into the icy waters and Mojo would leap over and through waves to track it down. He returns, drops the ball near my feet, shakes off the ex-cess ocean, and expectantly waits the next throw. Throw after throw, throw after throw. Spring, summer, winter -- this exercise knows no season. I stand at the water's edge my toes secure in the L.L. Bean waterproof boots that I simply never thought would see the light of day once we moved down here. But, here we are and Mojo's cease-lessly wagging tail tells me I've done good here.

As is his fancy, Mojo will approach anything with a pulse, no matter how far he has to roam, if only to drop the ball at their feet in the hopes -- indeed, with the full expectation -- that his new playmate will pick up the nasty, slobbered-upon orb and toss it into the ocean, where it belongs. This morning was no exception. In the distance, a solitary figure approached so hooded and wrapped it was impossible to determine age, sex or anything else other than there were two arms and two legs belonging to this person. As advertised, Mojo ran to him/her looking much like the deranged epicenter of crazed play that he is, and dropped the ball at the person's feet. Getting the idea, the person tossed the ball into the ocean and repeated and repeated as the two of them worked their way up the beach. As the figure approached, it became clear it was an older guy. I apologized and said what I often do which is that the lucky devil is now Mojo's new best friend. He smiled and said, "That dog is just full of life, isn't he?"

Tough to argue with that.

The Coach

He walked among his players before the game. Words of encourage-ment. Last minute reminders. Against a backdrop of gangly 15 year olds, he stood out in his nifty new black suit and yellow tie. But, the professional look this attire offered provided no disguise for the ner-vous energy Coach G was exuding. He was clearly anxious; distract-ed. After a rousing victory in its debut performance, the San Pasqual Eagles freshman team had lost three straight. Despite endless rep-etition to hone offensive and defensive schemes, Alex's players still seemed to favor mayhem, chaos, and other forms of disorganization to the neater disciplines that might characterize older teams. But, over the winter break, Alex worked daily with the boys to create some muscle memory in his schemes in the hopes of creating a sem-blance of order out of the chaos.

From the opening tip, there was little chance this coach would sit for more than a few rare seconds at a time. Too much adrenaline, too much emotional commitment to the task at hand. Pacing, scream-ing, gesturing; arms folded, arms pumping, arms outstretched, arms on hips. Alternately begging, beseeching, cheerleading, threatening his players -- it had to be exhausting. As the game progressed, I saw something that surprised me. The kids looked poised, not frantic. You could see their purposeful efforts at running the plays as coached. It didn't always succeed, of course, but the coherent pattern to their play was unmistakable. Picks were set; kids were cutting to the basket looking for easy shots; there was movement away from the ball. The press was executed in a way that would lead to the easy baskets the coach had predicted. There was no coincidence in this. The coach allowed himself the occasional smile. During time outs, the coach was encircled by his team, and he spoke encouragingly. He casually draped his arm around the kids whose normal fate is to sit glumly at the end of the bench with little hope of playing time. Inclusion, I thought. Nice touch.

As his team's lead increased in the second half from 10 to 15 to 20 points, the coach relaxed. His urgings diminished. He got acquainted with his chair. He cleared the bench. Victory was at hand. The final? The Eagles 48, the San Diego High School Cavers 26. A rout.

When Alex joined us in the sparsely populated bleachers after the game, he was smiling beatifically. He was calm and in the mood for assessing where he and his team was. He spoke of what he sees as the triple demands of his job: managing egos, keeping kids motivated, and getting them to play together. He spoke at length and with feeling since these were things he had clearly given much thought to. And, how sweet to see all these challenges overcome all at one time and with his parents in the stands watching closely.

Where did this wisdom come from in this 24 year old? How did he get from "there" to "here"? Why is it that parents are so often taken by surprise by the progress of their kids? Maybe, I thought, when they don't live next door anymore, the progressions are all the more dramatic and more pronounced because you don't see the day to day growth they experience. It is incredibly uplifting to watch.

The evening for us was alternately thrilling, amusing and always endearing. We were not the only ones who were pleased. The Eagles' varsity coach came over to Alex after the game, congratulating him. "This was all you," he said.

High praise, indeed.

Fleeting Images

I saw someone yesterday I hadn't seen in a long time. It was me. A few fleeting images from an old video confirming that it's true I was once a teenager. I was at a wedding reception for my cousin, Bob, and, while I can't be certain of the date, I surmised I was about 15 or 16. My hair was dark; I was clean shaven; and I was wearing what was for that time in my life my trademark goofy black eyeglasses that looked more suited to Mr. Magoo than a wannabe man about town. I was not alone there. My sister, Susan, was seated at the other side of the large round table looking suave and sophisticated for someone about to leave her teen years behind. And, my parents were there. They weren't on screen for more than a minute, but even in just that short span it was electric to me. It sounds so silly and old school, but seeing them "live" and not just as a still image staring back at me from within a picture frame was transfixing. My folks have been gone for decades and so seeing their moving images, even the slightest of quirks or facial expressions or arm movements took on for me a far greater significance than they were owed. My father was the debonair guy I remembered, looking dapper in his dark suit, leaning over and sharing some secret with my mom. She played to the camera with a smile worthy of an old-time movie queen. They would not have been out of place in Monte Carlo.

To a lesser degree, I reacted the same way to seeing myself, simultaneously a total stranger and yet one and the same as the older and grayer guy glued to the TV screen taking it all in more than a generation later. Who was this guy? Could I have really been that shamelessly goofy? Was I really so awkward, so gawky? When I was

15 could I possibly have projected ahead and seen what I might be like some day? Could I do the reverse, and close my eyes in an effort to put myself back into the psyche of that strange looking teenager? I know that the young Jeff was incapable of such forward leaning thought, and I know as well that the far older Jeff has left his predecessor too far behind in too many ways to attempt a similar time-tilting somersault.

Those images, as fleeting as they were, stayed with me when I went to sleep last night. They played over and over in my head. I realized that my reaction is a reflection of the time I have been here on planet earth. In today's world, video is so ubiquitous, so accessible, so taken for granted, that young kids will always have their younger selves as company as they grow old. That mystery and excitement I felt in those all too fleeting moments will be lost to them. I don't know that I am jealous of them or that I feel some pity for their loss of amazement and joy that surely accompanies the finding of something lost and then found.

Stamped Out

I ever so vaguely recall in my youth a tepid effort by my mother to collect these silly little stamps at the local grocery -- the renowned S&H Green Stamps -- all in the not fully articulated aspiration of getting something for nothing. I mean, in my small and unworldly head at the time, that's the way it struck me. You buy food, you get stamps, you claim stuff you really don't need and, most importantly, you feel you've bested the system. We had these little books designed to hold these stamps and, despite my own doubts, we would watch their numbers grow with elevated salivation imagining all manner of trophy acquisitions that one could just not live without.

We now flash forward more than a half century and find history biting me in the ass. Why? Because our local Piggly Wiggly announced a campaign to issue "stickers" to one and all in the hopes that one great day we could all enrich ourselves with a potpourri of Cuisinart appliances and cookware. I'm not sure where I went wrong, but I ever so quickly pushed aside my decades-long impression of these kinds of promotions and embraced this one with a vengeance. Here was the deal: for every $10 worth of grocery purchases, you would be issued a sticker that had a picture of the lovable pig himself on it although that was hard to tell since each sticker was no larger than a mosquito bite. When the promotion expired in January, you would check your accumulation and come reap your reward whether that might be a new frying pan, coffee maker, juicer, assorted pots, etc. You decide.

What ensued was madness. First, the stamps were so miniscule, you had to almost place them in a special padlocked container just to get them safely home. Put them in your shopping bag? Forget about it. Put them in your pocket? Gone. I am convinced the good folks at the Pig designed these things to be so small knowing that 40% of them would never make it out of their parking lot. (Speaking of which, when the checkout ladies started spreading the word that a lot of customers were losing their stickers while returning to their cars, you could unerringly find an enterprising shopper or two kicking stuff around on the asphalt outside trying to dig up this lost gold.) Second, should you be lucky enough to get the stickers home, you faced the infuriating task of separating them and attempting to enter them in the microchip-sized slots in the flimsy "booklet" provided by the Pig. Stickers would stick to themselves, and it became de rigueur to mumble a fine litany of cuss words when attempting to roughly fit each stamp into its intended miniature slot. Third, irrational reasoning took hold at shopping outings when your shopping list would clearly become second banana -- if I may use that term here -- to sticker acquisition strategies. For example, maybe, just maybe, you feel a rising urge to buy another bottle of olive oil -- just so you don't run out -- even when there might be some weeks left in the supply you already had. And, thoughts like, "you can never have enough hummus" creep into your head when passing that stuff. Ditto for the Wheat Thins. And, God forbid you should find yourself at check out and find you're 49 cents short of getting another sticker. Panic sets in while you desperately reach across waiting shoppers in the checkout line behind you so you can stretch to reach the display of breath mints and chewing gum that would enable you to cross the magic line to that next, fabulous sticker. Fourth, whenever the shopper in front of you would decline the stickers he or she had just earned, you find yourself winking at the checkout girl asking if you could take the unclaimed stickers. And, lastly, you start working the neighbors asking them to give you their stickers if they were not otherwise collecting. These are the depths, I tell you.

After all this, the Day of Irony arrives and you have to figure out what you want to claim with your horde of hard earned stickers. Will it be the non-stick pan, the hand blender, the pour saucepan?? It is in that moment that it sinks in. The joy -- if one can call it that -- was all in the chase, not in the acquisition. Did we really need another frying pan? Would we ever use a hand blender? Didn't I already bemoan the number of pots we owned? But, choices needed to be made, and so choices were made. In a vaguely joyless move, I opt for a 2 quart pour saucepan and the juicer. The game is over. I can breathe again.

Lemonade anyone?

Open Seas

Like so many people, I love the ocean. This late afternoon we are being treated to a sensation we don't often feel even though we do live just steps from the beach. Seeking an escape from the shadows of the rear deck, we've taken up a perch on the ship's port side -- where the sun shines warmly and the breeze we felt before has subsided. My feet are up on the railing, my chair tilted back, a tequila and oj inches away. Lily is reading, facing the sun. There is near silence here too, something that has eluded us in the past 4 days. There is nothing, absolutely nothing, beyond these railings. Just ocean and sky. To our right a bit, the lowering sun has turned the sea ablaze, blindingly so. To our left, the ocean is slate blue and so very, very flat. It is as peaceful a moment as one can reasonably expect to enjoy. Other than the muted voices of folks at near-by tables, the only sound is the ocean's. More particularly, the sound the ocean makes as this large ship cuts through it on its way northwest. The sounds of foam and spray. There is a gorgeous randomness to the wave action out there. Some of it rolls away from us, some toward us. There are intricate patterns in the waves I have never noticed before, almost like a very fine latticework. Is it really possible these waves we are enjoying originated thousands of miles away? Brazil, maybe. West Africa? Who knows? But, I don't want these moments to go unnoticed. They are just too serene and too beautiful.

Our ship rocks ever so slightly, just enough to remind us we are not on land. No birds, no planes, no other ships. Just us.

I am happy.

Cruisin' (With a Better Attitude)

Ok. We're beginning to get the hang of this cruising thing. No epiphanies here, just some simple lessons:

1) We have learned how not to stub our toes (or, alternatively, whack our heads against the closet door) when entering and exiting the one-step up bathroom in the middle of the night.

2) We now understand that as black as it gets in our windowless room, it does not automatically mean that it is 3 a.m. It could just as easily be high noon. So, whenever I wake up I check my watch just to be sure we're not missing lunch. Our room is not really a badly appointed box; but, it is still a box. And, the insides of boxes are very, very dark.

3) We are learning the food can be quite good here. Last night: melon and prosciutto, lobster and shrimp, and a chocolate ganache. For lunch: shrimp and calamari fritters. Plus, the sushi bar is perfect for those all-important pre-dinner snacks. Gaack! I'm becoming one of those cruise types who eat 24 hours a day. Thank goodness we walk a good bit whether it's around in dizzying circles on the ship's rooftop track or on land, as we did today on our hike to Paradise Island.

4) We are finally learning to navigate around the 11 or 12 decks of this boat. The first day was a living, life-sized maze. I mean, really, how do you get from the Fantasia Lounge to the Ecstasy Dining Room?

5) Start drinking at 2 p.m.

6) And, last night, on Valentine's Day, Lily and I danced at our dinner table (as, I am quick to add, many others did as well) as our hosts broke out in an impossibly atonal version of "Amore."

Would we do this again? Absolutely not. Even, if it was, in fact, free? Let me put it this way, if I asked you whether you'd enjoy wearing shoes for 4 days that were a size too small -- for free! -- I suspect our answers would be remarkably similar. All I know is that three mornings from now, we will open our eyes and know with absolute certainty that the sun has risen.

Cruisin'

Close your eyes and imagine a place that is a perfect blend of Las Vegas and Disneyland. Apparently, garish met cutesy; they fell in love, and produced one fiendishly surreal progeny they called "cruise ship."

We are aboard the Carnival Cruise Line's "Sensation." And, I can sort of see the logic in that name since it is your senses -- all of them -- that are stimulated here (or, perhaps I should say assaulted). First, the décor is designed, I am quite certain, to give life to whatever feelings of seasickness you've been earnestly trying to suppress. The walls abound with large, wavy lines crisscrossed at random intervals with jagged zigzag lines. The carpeted floors are awash in bright, clashing colors and shapes that are as alien to the wall "art" as I am to the 400 pound fellow cruiser sitting way too close to me. Glitter and small panels of reflective mirrors dot the scenery, producing an overall effect that allows you the trippiness of an acid encounter without the assistance of drugs. Second, your ears are treated to everything except silence. Choose your poison: hypercheerful p.a. announcements, muzak, raucous bands, and the, shall we say, overly ebullient hot tub denizen who can speak only at ear-splitting decibel levels. Third, as we had been advised, the food is not just plentiful, it is thrown at you much like a virtual avalanche. We have barely scratched the surface of this, but already it is hard to be more than arm's length from plates overflowing with pasta, mashed potatoes, burger and fries. And, don't get me started with the crazily bodacious dessert display. I have concluded that 30% of the crew are trained cardiologists. Judging from the girth of a not insubstantial number of passengers, there are a number of folks here who know just a little about how to navigate a buffet table. Pay heed and just stay out of the way.

When Lily and I first "won" this "free" cruise after attending a manic sales pitch for resort time shares, we really should have narrowed our eyes a bit to read between the lines. Nothing is free and this cruise is out to prove this point with gusto. After we had learned of our so-called free ride on the Sensation, we were advised that we would be staying in bunk beds in an interior room. When I asked if we could move to a room with a king-sized bed, they cheerfully obliged -- in return for $550. What they didn't tell us is that for this extra sum they would simply re-arrange the twin beds by throwing them together and then fitting them with king sheets. Essentially, we paid $550 for a set of sheets. Drinks, excursions, spa treatments, dinner at Sinatra's table -- all extra. I am reasonably certain there is no charge for the air we breathe, but I'll have to check our statement on this later.

Our stateroom is -- how you say -- compact, much like a sardine can is compact. I'm okay with a single file rule when going to the closet or bathroom. But, as Lily will most avidly attest, it's a bit discomfiting to realize that your room is not only windowless, but pretty much at the bottom of the ship. The only living quarters beneath ours is, I believe, Davey Jones' Locker.

Off to dinner!

In Over My Head

When the nice folks at the Wild Dunes Yacht Club asked me if I would be interested in becoming their new treasurer, I was quite pleased that they would think enough of me to hold out such an honor. After all, Lily and I had not been members for very long, and surely there were other deserving candidates out there. The club, which places a heavy -- some might say disproportionate -- emphasis on good time party events, seemed like a natural fit for us, and, if I could help steer the financial fortunes of the organization to help it party on, so much the better. I came to this calling buoyed by the knowledge that I had been the unofficial "banker" for years in our group houses in Rehoboth, figuring who owes what to whom, and so it seemed like a marriage made in heaven.

The current treasurer, Doug, an eminently affable and princely fellow had promised to take me through the contours of what his job entailed, and, after a few months of dithering, I finally arranged to meet with Doug at his home here to receive my tutorial. He lives barely three blocks away. We sat around the kitchen table where Doug displayed for me a binder that was half the size of Belgium and that contained fourteen metric tons of financial history, receipts, necessary forms and tables, and balance sheets that mark the backbone of any semi-serious organization. It was at that moment that I realized I had underestimated -- woefully -- the nature of what I was being asked to do. This was no beach house account where mere scribblings on a piece of scrap paper and approximations were the order of the day. This was the real deal. General Motors could not boast a much more thoroughly articulated set of books than what lay in front of me.

As Doug patiently led me through the various sections of this fabulous -- and endless -- tome, my anxieties rose in much the same way
they might if I were in a line of skydivers and my time to jump into
space was rapidly approaching. With each page of double entries,
and with every introduction to a new form that the IRS would need
to have, my throat tightened. Was this what I signed up for? Really?
This was a job for crying out loud! Serious business! But -- wait a
second -- I thought I was retired.

I must have reached critical mass. At some point -- I'm not sure
exactly when -- I realized I was in WAY over my head notwithstanding Doug's calm assurances that this was merely his way of doing
the books and perhaps there could be other, less ritualistic, ways of
performing the same overall tasks. Too late. My head was swimming
amid an avalanche of receipts and inventory listings of wine bottles,
club soda, and paper plates. I knew -- I just knew -- that whatever
embarrassment I might suffer from backing out on my offer to become treasurer, a hasty retreat had to be trumpeted loudly.

And so, I decided I needed to tell Doug my decades old story of my
first exposure to accounting. It went like this:

In my freshman year at Washington University, I was (inadvisably
and temporarily) enrolled in the Business School. A required course
in accounting was on the table for first semester freshmen. I struggled with this course as I had never struggled with a class previously.
The material was so dry, so devoid of fun, excitement and adventure
that I quickly developed a huge mental block any time I dared to
dive into the material. I simply could not do it. It irritated my DNA.
Thus, it came as no surprise that I flunked the mid-term which, as
a newbie freshman, was the academic version of a death sentence. I
went to see my professor, a kindly sort who was headed to retirement
at the end of the school year. I pleaded with him to let me drop the

course, but he refused since it was against university policy to allow a student to drop a course unless he or she had a C average. I winked and said, essentially, what's the harm? Who's to know? Just let me get out and escape to the finer pastures of the liberal arts curriculum where I so obviously belonged. My professor refused... but he did hold out an olive branch. He said, "Golland, I'll make you a deal. Study hard for the final, do all your homework, attend all the classes, make an honest effort. If you show me any signs of intelligence, I will give you a C for the course and you can go off to a greater future in the liberal arts world." How could I refuse? I studied hard -- as hard as I could for material that was as stimulating to me as a bowl of tepid oatmeal. I went to class, I took notes, I did the homework, I studied as well as I could for the final exam. And, by gosh, I thought I did pretty well.

A few days later I decided to go to my professor's office to learn my fate. I knocked; he had me open the door. When he saw it was me, he said -- and for as long as I live I will never, ever forget his exact words -- "Golland, you showed me no signs of intelligence." I died, right there on the spot. My future evaporated in front of my eyes. My GPA was doomed to mediocrity, at best. Then, as if the Greek gods themselves intervened at that that very moment, my professor said that out of his desire (more accurately, pity) not to derail my college experience so prematurely he decided to give me a C for the course despite everything. It was a retirement gift to me from the soon to depart professor. The blood slowly came back to my ashen face. I dodged a bullet -- big time. But, lest there be any lingering doubts, business, and more particularly, accounting, would not be in my future. Ever.

Doug smiled. He knew at that moment that the gig was up. He knew he would have to find another candidate to be treasurer. For my part, I had dodged another bullet, this one almost a half century later.

I left Doug's house and smiled, so glad I had overcome my fear of the embarrassment I would feel for having let folks at the Yacht Club believe I would take the financial reins. I walked home barely feeling my weight. I was free. I would live to fight another day.

Running to Daylight

Imagine you are standing outside but you are boxed in, as you might be in a corral. As these things go, a small corral. Sharing the corral with you are 4,000 people who are so close to you you can not only read the labels on the insides of their shirts, but you can identify the space between their neck hairs. Any other place or time, you would likely become the target of a protective order. And, then, you are asked to run. The legs start, the adrenalin starts pumping, but there is absolutely nowhere to go.

This was pretty much the scene last Saturday morning at the beginning of the Cooper River 10K Bridge Run, an annual event of some celebrity here in Charleston. The overt task: run 6.2 miles through the streets of Mt. Pleasant, up the graceful span of the Ravenel Bridge, and then down the mean streets of Charleston to the edge of the historic district. The less advertised task: to keep from getting trampled from behind by a tidal wave of hyper motivated runners, and to pretend you are doing a nifty bit of broken field running as you dodge slower moving humans as if they are enemy linebackers. There were about 40,000 of us that day, mostly runners, but also a fair number of walkers. Some are with strollers, mini-baby racers getting their first taste of competition. Others are in costumes, as outlandish as you can get while still permitting the legs to run, as they must. One guy had his dog with him.

There are 12 "waves" or corrals, as I prefer to call them, that are set in motion, each at 3 minute intervals, as they ever so smartly unleash groups of only 4,000 at a time until the approximate crowd of 40,000 are set free upon the local streets. My wave is about mid-way to the rear, somewhat ahead of the tortoises and zombies who bring up the rear of the field. Notwithstanding the sea of humanity I stare at ahead of me (and, no doubt, the nearly countless thousands staring at me from behind), the energy and excitement is univer-sally shared as the countdown for each group is loudly announced. Temps are in the low 50s and the sun is just clearing the tops of the surrounding buildings. Perfect.

As many others do, I put on my earpieces and get the juices flowing even stronger as the running tunes I had selected fill my head with totally extravagant and unwarranted confidence. Funny thing about listening to music as you run. Naturally, you are very aware of the masses around you, but in a strange way the music turns you inward. You are alone with your thoughts. Only the occasional jostle from another runner, or the sudden swerve you need to navigate to avoid a collision brings you back outside. It's such an odd sensation to have such a solitary, personal experience amid the teeming hordes at your elbows and shins.

And, then, the bridge looms in front of you. It is as intimidating as it is gorgeous. As I looked up the graceful upward span absolutely choked with runners, it is as if the whole world is running as fast as it can to get to see who can get to the gates of heaven first. The span is steep. It is more than a mile, seemingly straight up, to the top of the arch. Only the fittest (or most foolish) try to maintain their normal pace as they strive for that golden moment when you reach the top and know the rest of the course is downhill and then blessedly flat. The calves start to burn, the lungs too. Movements become more labored, more mechanical. Many folks who got off to jackrabbit starts move to the sides of the course, hands on hips, chests heaving. Sisyphus -- I feel your pain, baby. I had thought I would pause at the top, take in the view; smell the roses, so to speak. But, I didn't. I think

I was so elated to make it to this point that stopping was like an insult to my effort. And, senselessly, I figured this was the perfect moment to leapfrog a lot of competitors. Yeah, right. As if this would land me among the first several thousand finishers!

The rest of the way was a blur. Almost anti-climatic. Until the end. With crowds bunched along the sidewalks, yelling their support, whatever reservoir of adrenalin there was kicked in for many as the streets of Charleston slid away under our feet, and the promise of a finish line became a quickly approaching reality. As I'm sure many folks who enter these events will tell you, there is no way you don't sprint to the finish line once it comes in to view, like some sort of oasis in the desert. You've worked too hard to get here and the joy is all the fuel you need.

How did I do? Only some 12,000 or so finished ahead of me. Never had 12,000th place felt so good. Thank goodness for the tortoises and zombies.

Cardinal Rules

We have visitors. No, not the type you think. Not out of town friends or relatives here to soak up some rays or dine in the splendor of Charlestonian cuisine. No, these visitors are far more colorful, more ornate, yet tantalizingly more elusive. In fact, they are birds, two of them as best as I can tell. They are cardinals, or so Lily says. Mr. and Mrs. C, I call them. I'm not sure how long they are staying; we don't seem to have much to say about that. But, their presence is more than just a bit of seasonal charm. They are intruding on our senses and at some point they could prove to be less than charming to their hosts.

The focal point of our concern is that these feathered redheads, predominantly Mrs. C, appear to have delusions of moving in, and by that I mean move IN. The grounds of our home do not appear to be quite enough for these apparently upwardly mobile social climbers. Although for millennia the trees of this world have suited their forebears well enough, Mrs. C has apparently decided to push the evolutionary envelope by house hunting, and ours is the one they've set their sights on.

How do I know this? We have many windows in our home, facing all directions. At this juncture, there is barely one that has gone unpecked on, if I may coin a phrase. Starting almost like clockwork at 7:45 a.m., Mrs. C starts tapping on our bedroom windows. Incessantly. The pecking by itself would be sufficient to awaken us, but the wing flapping -- charming in some circles, I'm sure -- adds a certain note of panic to this morning serenade. She repeats this overture again and again and again. At some point, Lily and I just admit defeat and get out of bed since there is simply no sleeping through this feathered assault. Sometimes, I go to the window next to my side of the bed and stare back at her during those moments when she uses her toes to secure a tenuous foothold at the window's edge. We make eye contact. She cocks her head in 12 different directions never taking her eyes off me while I unwittingly play her game by cocking my own head from side to side as if somehow this will have some meaning for her. So far, this does not appear to be the case. She chirps, however, with a certain methodical cadence straight at me that, I swear, has to mean something. I want to yell at her through the glass, "Dude! Please say it in English." I'm not optimistic.

A word about Mr. C. I hesitate to jump to conclusions about these things, but as far as I can tell, Mrs. C most definitely wears the pants in this family. Mr. C has made a couple of appearances, but only in a supporting role. She does the talking. He flits around a bit, sometimes clinging to the window ledges next to her, but mostly he retreats. Probably back to his man cave. He may be more brightly colored -- he does have that on her -- but if it didn't sound so weird in this context, I'd say he was henpecked.

And so it remains to learn what it is exactly Mrs. C is seeking. Maybe she's just fed up with the way we use our TV remotes. Maybe she'd like to see us eat more organic foods. Maybe she just has designs on the third bedroom. It's so hard to tell. But, I'll tell you this: I'm not loving this early morning drama day after day. I've been consulting with Mojo on possible solutions since it appears, as you might imagine, he has more than a casual interest in this. But, sadly, English isn't Mojo's strong suit either.

Falling Down

As happens so often with most things in life, it begins innocently and without agenda. In this case, it's time to walk Mojo. He's just eaten dinner and his bowels are eagerly pointing him to the great outdoors for post-dining relief. I have him on his leash, poop bags in hand. My flip flops go on with nary a second thought, and we head out to the deck on our way to the mean streets of Wild Dunes. A repeat of a drill done at least a thousand times in the almost two years since the big guy joined our family. It's been raining and everything has a nicely glazed sheen to it. Beautiful. And, then, fate decides to hiccup. As I work my way down to the first landing, my weight distribution shifts just a bit and the combination of the rain-slickened staircase and my less than tenacious flip flops causes me to lose my balance. My feet take off in a direction I had surely not anticipated, my body goes horizontal, and in that micro-mini second of awareness, you know nothing good is about to happen to you. My body crashes downward to be intercepted by the edge of the last step above the landing. I hit very hard and the pain shoots through me as no pain I could ever recall. I am in disbelief but the spectacular pain in my back reminds me every passing second now that what I think has happened, in fact, has.

As I lay on the landing, my right hand spastically and reflexively reaching for my back, my various body parts extend at oddly inconvenient angles. Cattywampus, some might say. Others might legitimately have mistaken me for the damaged scarecrow in "The Wizard of Oz" laying in a disorganized pile by the side of the road. I moan, I scream, I grunt. In my own mind, I am groaning loud enough to be heard on Neptune. Lily, however, is no more than twenty feet away behind closed doors and, apparently, hasn't picked up on the tumult just steps away. My mind is racing: Have I truly damaged myself? Can I get up? Have I severed my spine? Has Mojo run off? Do I still own two kidneys? Do I need an ambulance? The pain is now at DEFCON 4 and not subsiding. Lily does emerge and is aghast. She asks me if an ambulance might be needed, but for a few moments I think maybe I can shake it off. All I need to do, I say, is walk. Lily takes the leash from the amazingly patient Mojo and we head down the street. I don't think we are more than 60 feet from our driveway when the reality sets in that "walking it off" is not the kind of serious medicine that is called for here. We head immediately back to the house and then off to the nearest emergency room.

After three hours of lolling about a seemingly empty ER, the diagnosis is presented to Lily and me: a broken rib. Internal organs: good. Internal bleeding: none. I am sent packing with a prescription for oxycodone and a shrug from the doctor that suggests there's really nothing else to be done. I should be fine in maybe 4 to 6 weeks. What they didn't tell me is that it might also be a good idea not to laugh, sneeze, burp, hiccup, and, for all I know, fart. Those things can set off the kind of shock waves in my way too fragile body that are not to be casually invited.

In the aftermath, when folks learn of my mishap and, naturally, want to learn how it happened, I have the strongest urge to tell them it was an unfortunate outcome from a hang gliding incident, or maybe a spelunking adventure, or possibly a heroic effort to save someone from a burning house. But, life doesn't dish these things up quite so neatly, or quite so romantically. No, I fell victim to the mundane not the sublime, slipping and falling at my own home engaged in the simplest of tasks, and now my life is out of joint for weeks. No golf, no running, no swimming, no running with Mojo, no nothing. Nada, zip, zero.

What was it Robert Burns said almost 250 years ago? "The best laid schemes of Mice and Men oft go awry, and leave us nothing but grief and pain, for promised joy!" Yeah, maybe for the hang gliders and skydivers among us. For the rest of us... I'm not sure we are such worthy illustrations for Mr. Burns' lofty thoughts.

Gator Getters

Gator Getters. You have to think long and hard to conjure up a business name that in just two words so totally sums up what they're about. You know right away these guys are not morticians, nor heating and plumbing contractors, nor money lenders or caterers. No, they have one, and only one, highly targeted assignment: help the world with all things alligator. I suppose they could have named themselves Gators R Us, but, after all, that would have been three words.

So, it was with great delight last week that I learned of a presentation being made by Gator Getters to the folks here at Wild Dunes. Think of it as the oral presentation of the Little Golden Book of alligators. In these parts, as they say, this kind of knowledge is fabulously useful at best, and at least interesting at a minimum. We live in a community that shares its backyards, fairways, and sometimes its pools, streets and beaches with the alligator. They are all around us, apparently about 50 or so of them of the 100,000 currently taking up residence in South Carolina. Think of all the questions you might want to ask these guys if you had the chance (and the potential need to know). For example, do gators see humans as one big amuse bouche? Or, what might be the best way to avoid them once you're squarely in their sights? Is it better to run away in a zigzag pattern -- which is the common wisdom -- or flat out sprint in a straight line? Can you reason with them?

Our host -- a most amiable fellow named Ron. He fits the bill so perfectly he's almost a parody of himself. Attired in a safari shirt, cargo pants, sporting a trimmed white beard and a good ol' boy accent, Ron is the epitome of the TV animal expert a la Jim Fowler or even the venerable Marlon Perkins. Perfect. Ron has been in the gator business for many years and his obvious comfort level with the subject, his wearied humor and phlegmatic style make his lecture pitch perfect.

Ron tells us that, above everything, we must remember that alligators are dinosaurs; they have been with us for 265 million years. And so, they know a thing or two about survival. What we see today are literally the best of the best, bred to foster and nurture the species' best representatives so that now we have a survival guru walking amongst us. In fact, of all species of animals, they may be the most finely honed to survive all the foolishness of 21st century man. Ron tries to convince a skeptical audience that alligators are not really out to get us; well, that is not unless we wander on to their turf which they like to share as much as a four year old likes to share his toys with a younger brother who is about to steal one of them. Gators live in and around the water. This is their home. In our local environment, this means the many lagoons that weave their way through the Wild Dunes community. Should you wander to the water's edge, expect the gator to lunge out of the water like a laser aimed at your jugular. Not out of anger, mind you; only hunger. This is especially the case at night or in the early morning hours when they are the most energized. Ron attempted to contrast this with your being, let's say, 20 feet away from them as they bask on the banks of the lagoon where, Ron promised, the gator will leave you alone. Honest.

I saw two flies in the ointment here. First, it is easy to say to yourself. "ok, stay away from the banks of a lagoon. You'll be fine." But, as it turns out, alligators can meander off their home turf in search of food. Like to the beach or down your street or even under your car where, incredibly, they like to take shelter. Seriously. What are the ground rules then, Ron? Huh? Second, as is so often the case, humans tend not to act so smartly in dealing with gators. For example, a lot of folks think it's cute to feed gators around here even though it poses incredible risks and, oh by the way, is illegal. A fed gator is a dangerous gator because he now sees humans as a food source to be pursued. Great. And, so, when you encounter a gator which you are most surely happy to avoid, your prudence may be rewarded by a 30 m.p.h. sprinting gator headed straight at you in search of the culinary treats he has become accustomed to receiving.

Bottom line: treat these guys with the kind of respect normally reserved for potentates, popes and other heads of State. Check under your car every morning. And, when out walking at night, or maybe enjoying that evening stroll on the beach, take a flashlight with you.

Maybe a bazooka too.

Small Things

I have a story; but, it is a tiny story. No major anthems to be played in this one; no great heroics or drama. No major motion picture in the works. But, in my life, as small a part of the cosmos as it is, I was buoyed by it. And, that's enough for me.

Last week, Mojo and I engaged in what has long been our daily ritual: up at 7 and, with Mojo's near frantic endorsement, down to the beach in scant minutes. A truly wonderful time of the day for me, but a time of exquisite and pure happiness for Mojo who looks forward to it in a way that I'm not sure most humans can fully comprehend. We returned home an hour later. In my usual style, I rinsed him off, toweled him dry, fed him breakfast, and got on with the day. What I had not noticed was that Mojo had lost his tags. All of them. The ocean's rust inducing qualities had, over time, literally severed the metal rings holding the tags to Mojo's collar. These would include his name tag, his Isle of Palms license, and his rabies tag. Unknown to us, Mojo had become -- in a legal sense -- nameless, illegal, and a rabies menace.

How long this situation would have endured, I cannot say. I do not check his collar for these things any more than I check my wallet to make sure my driver's license is there. But, later that day, when I opened our mailbox, there was Mojo's shining name tag laying in there next to the day's mail. There was no note with it. No indication of whom had come upon it at the beach. No hint as to who had picked it up, and, without expectation of reward or recognition, had made the effort to return it to our home, silently and anonymously.

Just a good, unnamed person doing what he or she thought was the right thing to do. A small kindness. How can you not smile at this slight, but warm, gesture of caring?

But, this was not the end of the story. Once I realized that Mojo's name tag had been AWOL, I knew I needed to take steps to replace the others that were now likely on their way to Bermuda, or, more likely, resting on the ocean floor somewhere. The following day I headed down to the municipal offices of the Isle of Palms armed with my IDs and the receipt I had for Mojo's original tag. When I approached the second floor window -- also the home of the IoP police -- there was a fellow on the other side amiably looking at me asking if he could help me. I told him I needed a replacement IoP ID tag for Mojo. He asked me for my name, and I told him, "Golland." He looked at me for more than a normal moment, and asked, "Jeff Golland?" In that moment I stared intently back at the clerk aggressively wondering whether this guy knew me, or, just as likely, whether I knew him and had, sadly, failed to recognize him. Concluding that the guy was, in fact, a stranger, I responded that, yes, I was, indeed, Jeff Golland. Hearing that, he reached to his left and presented to me, lo and behold, my missing IoP ID tag. Not only had the tag not floated to Bermuda nor been surrendered to the ocean floor, but yet another nameless and goodhearted soul had come to the rescue. Someone out there had found this tag laying in the sand and had made the effort not just to pick it up but to take the time (and make the effort) to actually return it to the offices at the Isle of Palms in the hopes that it would find its way back to me, a total stranger. And, it did. And, I was amazed. A replacement tag would have cost only a few dollars, but some kind soul thought enough of my predicament to try to spare me the expense, and maybe make my life a bit easier.

I assure you, no music played. There were no rows of people clapping or cheering in the corridors as I walked back to my car, tag in hand. But, I might just as well have heard music in my head - uplifting, inspiring music. I couldn't stop smiling. Would this have happened in New York or Los Angeles? Not likely. Is this what it means to live in a small town? Maybe. Would it encourage me to do the same if I should come across someone's lost stuff?

You bet.

Looking Back. What I Loved.....

Ahh, our paradise-like time in Southern France and northern Spain!

Herbed olives from the local market; Jesse comfortably speaking Spanish with the locals; sopping up the amazing sauce from the stuffed squid tapas in Barcelona; Dali's mustache; the incredible blue of the Mediterranean; my gnocchi, pesto, pancetta and vegetable dinner; the incredible industry and dedication of the ants who hung out at the pool; the lily pond at our house; the views from the mountaintop Cathar castles; the tree canopied heart of Cerret; the sunsplashed brilliance of Cadaques; seeing the Valmy castle as our beacon guiding us home; the crispy "pork tower" I had in Girona; the croissants and baguettes that Bob Keith faithfully retrieved every morning from down the hill; drinking beers and playing speed scrabble at the beachfront café in Collioure; the low lying clouds that drifted below the peaks of the Pyrenees; Lily's drawings on old tiles she found on the beach or on hikes; the little carousels in Collioure and San Sebastian; Maggie's epic turns as my sous chef; the incredible white wine from the Valmy vineyard; strolling La Rambla in Barcelona with Lily and Jesse; Jamie's earnestness; sweet apricots from the tree at our front door; the all-consuming organ music at the Palau de Musica in Barcelona; the Oreo Express; crossing the Greenwich Meridian in the middle of nowhere Spain; Brendan's ability to swim three laps on one breath; Donna's ipad; the hike above the monastery in Montserrat; Lily and Maggie's homemade hummus; the flea market in Cadaques; Picasso's painted bowls of bullfights; cassoulet; Hannah's incredible energy; the delicious dinner Lily and I had in the cave-like dining room in Montserrat; hearing Matt idly trying his hand at the grand piano; the admiring way women looked at Lily's dresses in San Sebastian; the coastal drive from Cadaques to Argeles-sur-Mer; Donna's wonderfully unrelenting enthusiasm for taking group photos; the death defying cliff hugging hike we took at Gorges de Carança; Lily's blue hat; the fabulous outdoor dinner we all enjoyed courtesy of our husband and wife team at "Le Marilyn" in Cap Leucat; Donna's goat cheese salad; the incredible bells of the Montserrat basilica; magnum ice cream bars; the amazing artistry of Victor Omar Torres; the electrified hair of all those standing atop the Chateau de Peyrepertuse in the (literally) electrified atmosphere; old men playing bocce; Jesse's amazing father's day card for me (and the personally formatted Cds); and....

Mojo's entire body wagging when we arrived home.

Alex and Myles

Alex and Myles

Easy Chair

Katie, Alex and Owen

Laura and Jesse

Laura, Charlie and Oliver

Lily and Jeff

Lily and Owen

Lily

Mojo

Myles

Owen

Alex and Owen

Jeff with Charlie, Oliver, and Owen

Katie and Owen

Laura, Jesse, Oliver and Charlie

Mojo

Basquing In It All

So. We finish up here in San Sebastian along the north coast of Spain. We have never been here before although we did find ourselves in Biarritz 33 years ago just up the coast and over the French border. The two places, sometimes home to the glitterati over the decades, are like bookends -- jeweled, exquisite bookends. Two towns that enjoy a magnificent shoreline and just scream picture postcard. The curve of the wide sandy beach here is ringed by a broad promenade ideal for strolling and people watching, perhaps with a gelato in hand. The luminous blue of the cove is dotted with white boats; throng of people do their beach thing. It is serene, slow-paced, and for us, a stark contrast from the immense energy, speed, crowds, and cacophony of Barcelona which we just left. Here in San Sebastian is a place where you stroll the old city that is not unlike the narrow alleys of so many European cities, and enjoy the shopping, the ubiquitous dog walkers, and the young children who provide a wonderful and stunning contrast to the ancient steps they play on.

And, the tapas! We had read that San Sebastian is a rising star in the culinary world, but the staple here is tapas -- those fabulous small bites that show off the creativity and culinary history of this region. Tonight, we spent an evening in one such place -- Bar Aralar Tatetxea in the old city just up the way from the beach promenade. It has the feeling of an Irish pub in a way -- friendly, crowded, noisy, but lighter and with more color. The ritual here is to work your way through the crowd, find a table (or not), and ask for a plate. The tapas are arranged in platters on the bar like some sort of red, brown, green and yellow jewelry display. You inch your way along pulling on to your plate whichever morsels you care to sample, order your drinks, and then pay before retreating to your table.

And, there the fun begins. Maybe it's stuffed squid in a spicy garlic sauce, or octopus in oil and paprika. Maybe you would like a ball of deep fried mashed potatoes and egg, or cured ham, goat cheese and a plump sundried tomato all atop a baguette slice. Or, as we had tonight, marinated artichoke wrapped in a smoky ham and topped with a shrimp. As the saying goes, it's all good.

Then there is Victor Omar Torres. The world is full of street artists, some great, some not. Tonight we were wildly entertained by Mr. Torres whose gift is to paint scenes - local and imagined -- on pieces of tile. The magic is that this guy does it all without a brush; his fingers and a sharp knife are his only tools. His fingers moving at warp speed, Victor spreads his paint with such assurance, such precision, and so flawlessly, it suggests he has done this thousands of times. He manages to create nuances in shades and texture that are so mind boggling you find yourself either staring agape or giggling. To create the finest lines, as with a tiny boat mast, he merely uses his fingernail to sweep color upwards to create the mast's illusion. By rolling his thumb, he creates depth of color that make me wonder whether a paint brush could ever achieve the same result. He flicks his sharp knife to remove color leaving behind the roll of a wave or a small building on the shore. And, it's all done in literally the span of two or three minutes. I'm telling you, it's brilliant and it's magical.

Lastly, there is the sunset. Sunsets make almost every scene more beautiful, but to fold in the grandeur of a sunset into a scene that is already awash in beauty, is almost unfair. The sun sets late here this time of year. Around 10 p.m. As the sun sets around the town's surrounding hills, the sky turns an electric turquoise and pink with thin strands of rose colored clouds running through it all. The Atlantic waters take on the same coloration especially at the water's edge where the reflected pink is as stunning as the sky's. And, the many boats sitting calmly in the cove become almost blackened silhouettes, a sharp counterpoint to the waters they sit in.

Not a bad way to tie things up.

Dali is Da Man

It is hardly an original thought of mine, but I earnestly believe that Salvador Dali either had more fun than any man alive, or he was seriously in need of deep psychotherapy. I tend to go with the former.

We have been exposed to Dali of late through a museum dedicated to his work in Figueres, Spain -- just a bit over the border from France -- and at his seaside home in Cadaques, Spain, a gorgeous village also just south of the border. What I came away with was this was a man whose middle name should have been "whimsy" and who likely giggled and winked his way through life. In some afterlife, somewhere, he is likely sharing convivial, drug enhanced, conversation with Mark Twain and John Lennon, explaining how on earth he could grow that zany mustache of his that jutted outward like two pencil thin skewers.

His house is so fitting. Its whitewashed, serene exterior belie the mischief awaiting inside. His studio, for example, features a pulley system that allowed him to raise or lower his large canvases to a floor below so that he could sit in an overstuffed chair and never have to move no matter how large the canvas he was working on. The outdoor pool area has a sofa shaped as a set of bright red, puffy lips. Multiple statues of the Michelin Man dot the gardens. And, one room is perfectly round with built-in couches all along the periphery. The ceiling is domed. If you stand in the middle of the room, you can hear your voice resonate as if you were shouting into the Grand Canyon. Yet, if you move two feet from that spot, all sounds normal.

The man was not shy either. It seems as if his image is featured in half of his works, from soaring ceiling frescoes to three dimensional holographs to paintings of himself from the vantage point of his feet so that as you gaze upward you are struck once again by that crazyass mustache.

It is said of Dali that he once had an epiphany that the railroad station in Perpignan, France was actually the center of the universe. In that moment, perhaps in an acid driven fog, he wrote, "Suddenly before me everything appeared with the clarity of lightning."

Really, Sal? Really?

JUNE 14, 2011

Living on the Edge

The day didn't start edgy. Truly. It began as a perfect example of what has become the routine around here. Adults up first; Bob trekking down the hill to pick up our daily delivery of baguettes and croissants; breakfast; check email; read a bit. Kids arise later. Much later.

Today's plan called for the Oreo Express to journey west, this time to Villefranche, an ancient walled town buried in the foothills of the Pyrenees. There we would pick up Le Train Jaune (the yellow train) which would whisk us away closer to Andorra and then return. That was the plan.

But, things happen. The Yellow Train looked great. Like something Charlie Chaplin might have ridden. Maybe W.C. fields. It reeked of Disney. It came complete with an open air car that seemed perfect for optimal viewing as we steamed through the countryside. But, sadly, this train was not the engine that could. Barely a mile or two out of the station, it quit. Finito. We returned to the station, got our money back and drove on. And, this is when it got interesting.

Just last night we talked about the possibility of riding the train for an hour or so, getting off, having a couple of beers, and then riding back. Simple enough. Certainly pleasurable. But, no, we couldn't leave well enough alone. Instead of the beer, we drove to the Gorges de Carança where we were promised "death defying" footpaths. The hike up was steep, very rocky, and, at times, very challenging. But, then, just when the path leveled off, we knew why people come here.

Certainly for Americans it was something you would never, ever find in our country because the liability concerns would be overwhelming; indeed, prohibitive. What we came upon was a narrow path, maybe 3 feet or so across that was literally etched into the side of a cliff several hundred feet above the valley below. And, there was no guardrail! The path was devilishly uneven with large rocks making certain you would never be entirely comfortable with your footing. All that kept you from running away screaming was a cable bolted into the side of the cliff that gave you a degree of confidence you would not hurtle to your doom with one slight misstep. Some of us gripped the cable as a drowning man might grip a life preserver thrown his way. We proceeded, our group of twelve, perhaps gaining a measure of confidence borne out of some weird sense of shared insanity.

As if to taunt us, the gods whipped up a breeze and rain, and, finally, flashes of lightning to fan the flames of our increasing doubts. While a few of us wanted to venture onward if only to see what madness might lurk around the next bend in the mountain, cooler heads prevailed and we headed down the ridiculously steep and rock-filled paths now increasingly slippery from the rain.

Exhilarating to be sure, but not what you might call a day at the beach.

Ces Tours d'Epingle francais; Ils Sont Fous. (Those french hairpin turns; they are crazy.)

It all seems so innocent. You gaze at the map of the French highway system and see all manner of brightly colored strands wending their way through the countryside. Some are denoted in red, some in yellow, others in white. Very pretty. What these merry designations fail to reveal is the mayhem that lies beneath.

The Oreo Express has been in high gear these past several days. Crisscrossing Languedoc-Roussillon in search of castles, wineries, art museums, and walkable ancient towns has all led to an increasing storehouse of knowledge of French roads and the vehicular mortal combat they present. Take yesterday, for example. One of our nominal destinations was the Priory at Serrabone, a 10th century retreat with an excellent pink marble representation of Roman architecture. Sounds refined enough. Looking at the map, the Priory is only mere inches west of our house, a straight shot. As the crow flies. But, we are not crows; we rely on the automobile to get us from here to there. And, cars do not fly. To get to the Priory, we must navigate a road that on the map takes on exactly the same shape as my lower intestine, worming its way through the mountains in every possible direction except straight. As if by some rudimentary law of road physics, the more turns a road has, the narrower it is.

We head up into the mountains joyously embracing the "charm" of the smaller roads. You know, that wonderful elation that can

consume you when you're "off the beaten path." Almost imperceptibly, the road becomes steeper and, again, by natural law, narrower.
The turns tighten. What was once a road that would reasonably
accommodate two cars passing one another now devilishly morphs
into spaghetti width trails, albeit paved. Every turn is now virtually
180 degrees. When an approaching car nears us, our backseat passengers, Hannah (Bob and Donna's daughter) and Megan (Hannah's
buddy), audibly suck in their breath as if somehow this will facilitate
the other car's passing.

The coup de grace for all this is the fact that most of the way the
only thing preventing one's being catapulted down the mountainside
is one's overwhelming drive to live through this. Guardrails are clearly an afterthought in these parts. What started as a joyful jaunt now
becomes a true white knuckling pursuit of staying alive. And, this
is the scene for far too many kilometers. Lily manages to keep her
screaming eruptions to a minimum, which is helpful. The backseat
girls seem transfixed, perhaps traumatized. My white knuckle grip
on the steering wheel goes unabated. When we arrive at the Priory,
Bob immediately lays down on the grass, exhausted. I, semi-franti-
cally, search out the toilette.

Are we having fun yet?

Tales of the Oreo Express

As it happens, we have three rental cars in our group, two black and one white. Striking out for new adventures each morning, we form a small caravan, generally with Lily and me in front, Bob and Donna in the middle, and Maggie trailing. Sort of a black, white, black sandwich which I dub, "the Oreo Express."

On our first day of serious exploration, we set out to find two Cathar castles each perched on a mountain top northwest of here. You might describe the Cathars as sort of a splinter group breaking off from the catholic church over -- how you say -- doctrinal issues. When the pope sent an emissary to quell the spiritual discontent, the poor guy was unfortunately executed leading to 300 years of mayhem as the pope launched crusades to put the kibosh on the whole thing. The Cathars, not to be taken lightly, retreated to their fortresses, lording over the region from the highest pinnacles of land this part of France offers.

What we found were the Chateau Queribus and the Chateau de Peyrepertuse, two of the craggiest, most magestic aeries you're apt to find. Built in the 11th century, these magnificent testaments to human fortitude and dedication are reachable only through great and hair raising effort. And, this is by car! Arriving by a cliff hugging road about the breadth of a fat pencil -- often with no guard rail to discourage an unintentional descent into the valley many hundreds of feet below -- one is exhausted by the mere threat of such danger. For all the ridiculous effort it takes to get up to these retreats, I kept wondering aloud, why didn't the Catholics just let the Cathars keep their castles and take over everything else. I'm just saying.

But wait. Once parked, now you must take on a vertical hike on pathways clearly unchanged in a millennium. To say they are rocky is to say there are a couple of holes in swiss cheese. One must climb up "steps" some of which seemingly require pole vaulting apparatus to be surmounted. And, once in the castles, you must negotiate skinny, spiral staircases that are helpfully assisted by a lighting condition one might best call pitch black dark.

But, the views! Ah, the views! Incomparable. If you cup your hands on either side of your eyes, you can imagine yourself flying. The valley is so very, very far below, the towns reduced to a smattering of red roofs. In the distance one way, the Mediterranean. In the other, the majesty of the Pyrenees that one can tell are even higher than you are. A lot higher. At the peak of the Chateau de Peyrepertuse, we experience the odd sight of seeing strands of our hair sticking straight up. Great gayety ensues. Many photos are taken. We conclude the static in the air is caused by gathering storms clearly visible from our perch.

Perhaps not the safest place to be in that moment.

Living the Dream

How often have you spoken the phrase "living the dream" and meant it to describe yourself? Hopefully, it's often, right? For the next two weeks, we are living the dream. After considerable planning and an avalanche of anticipation, we have arrived in Collioure at the south-western tip of France's Mediterranean coast.

We have rented a house that might even raise the eyebrows of Brad and Angelina. It is located up in the hills that slide down into the Mediterranean Sea and is reachable only by a steep and tortuous ascent up a rocky and rutted path for cars and foot traffic alike with barely any signage that announces its existence. The house was first built in the 1700s and then added on to in the 1800s, and is now gorgeously updated for 21st century living. It is all stone -- the floors, many of the walls, sometimes giving it a cave-like subterranean feel. The many overhead spotlights bring it all to life. There are rough hewn timbers - sometimes entire tree trunks -- bolstering the ceilings. Befitting such an old and quirky house, each of its 5 bedrooms sit seemingly on different levels lending a sort of maze-like quality to the place. The couches are so deep two people can sleep on them (as two of the younger members of our group did). The Steinway baby grand piano awaits those more talented than we are. The stone sunroom has a long, gorgeous table that is cut from one huge slab of a tree complete with a million knots and age rings. It seats at least 13 and is impossible to lift. An apricot tree sits at our front door providing us with its delicious treats. There is a pool steps from the house, its floor tiled in a way that adds to the sparkle already provided by the sun. And, all this sits on a 23 acre private estate providing much room to roam and explore.

Sitting down the hill from us looms the most charming of chateaux, Disney-like in its appearance, rising above the surrounding vine-yards like a mirage. Cinderella's home, no doubt. And, the skies! They are the bluest of blues. As Henri Matisse said a century ago, "No sky in all France is bluer than that of Collioure. I only have to close the shutters of my room and there before me are all the colors of the Mediterranean."

Five of us went to the market today and we returned with twenty bottles of wine and food to suit your every fancy. Lily and Maggie teamed up to create some fabulous homemade hummus which they served to us at the pool with incredibly flavorful local, herbed olives, baguettes, and chopped vegetables.

I mean, really, does it get much better than this?

Monk Business

We have arrived in beautiful Montserrat, Spain -- a small settlement about an hour west of Barcelona, in the heart of Catalonia -- and we find ourselves staying in a monastery, not something we have a lot of experience with. This is a place first built in the 9th century and re-built from time to time as the invaders du jour took exception to the monks' way of doing things. Let me assure you, I am confirming my loosely held belief that monks were not big on such things as jacuzzi baths or room service. No, this place is "monastic" as we tend to use that word. The beds are small, there's no mini-bar, no tv. Hell, there isn't even any soap. And, for what I believe to be the first time in my life, I have to sit sideways on the toilet which was obviously designed for the exclusive use of Toulouse Lautrec. But, all of this is amusing-ly inconsequential since whatever creature comforts it lacks is made up in the oh so continental charm of this place. Montserrat is carved into the side of a mountain which is literally dotted with towering, hooded rock formations that appear for all the world like giant pe-nises brandishing themselves skyward toward the heavens. Seriously. The view from our monastery window is sublime looking down on the cobblestoned main square that is filled with playing children, an outdoor café, and a healthy splash of evergreens. Beyond, down the 4,000 foot drop below Montserrat, lie green valleys flecked with what I fondly imagine are vineyards. Every half hour the soul-throb-bing, richly hued tones of the basilica's bells chime in such a joyous way you'd swear they are announcing the end of war.

Although we've been traveling for more than 24 hours -- through three countries and three cramped airplanes -- we drop our gear at the monastery and head for the funicular which promises even grander panoramas from up the mountain. The path is steep. How steep? As we head up the mountain on the funicular, both Lily and I feel our butts slipping downhill over our seats causing us to use our feet to brace ourselves. Even the locally written guide warns that the mountain walkways are very "steepy." The views do not disappoint as we wend our way back on foot to collapse for a well-earned nap.

Tonight: a visit to the spectacular basilica where we peek in on that night's vespers, and then dinner in a cave-like 16th century building with rock walls and a low-slung arched ceiling. We feast on spinach salad, tagliatelle with pesto, a Spanish rosé, grilled rabbit, and a rich chocolate brownie with crème caramel.

Not a bad start.

Thoughts of Home

Although it was so many years ago, I vividly recall the day my family deserted our home – my childhood home – or, at least that's the way I saw it. Our family car made its way slowly up Ogden Avenue in White Plains leaving behind so many wonderful years as just so many memories rapidly vanishing in the rear view mirror. My mother refused to look back. She was ready to move on to another stage of her life; but I wasn't. I looked back trying to squeeze out as many of those memories as I could in the few seconds while our house was still visible. Maybe I thought they would be lost forever if I didn't lock them in right then. I always suspected my mother was feeling something more intense that day than she let on, but she never acknowledged that. She told my sister and me to embrace the future with my soon-to-be pursuit of a college education and my sister entering the labor force. I do recall not just a general sense of loss, but a jarring blow to my personal universe that I thought, in those moments, would take many years, if ever, to repair.

These thoughts came back to me recently as we traveled back to both New York and, more recently, Washington, D.C. I was not looking for "home," but I was wondering if that old, warm feeling of familiarity and comfort could manifest itself again. With Washington, in particular, I knew that it surpassed even White Plains as the personification of "home" in my life. It was here that I had my career spanning more than three decades. It was here that I forged bonds with such a wide variety of people as lifelong friends. It was here that I had the first thirty wonderful years of married life, and it was here that Lily and I raised Jesse and Alex. As would be the case for anyone else who has had the pleasure of such a longstanding home stand, the memories of that period of my life are unspeakably sweet and, I dare say, never to be replicated. When we left the Washington area, there was a poignancy I felt that here, again, was the loss of "home" as I had known it for so long in exchange for an exciting, but alien, environment.

We are now in Charleston getting into the rhythm of a new life, one without children close by, career, or longstanding friends. Closing in on almost three years into this new adventure, there is so much that is now familiar – even instinctive – about this new place. We love our house and certainly the surroundings of sun, sand, and surf. Through a succession of baby steps, we are meeting people, enjoying new relationships and share an optimism about the future and the choices we have made. We refer to where we live as our "home," but it is not home as White Plains once was or Washington. Not yet. I think that is something that can only feel complete over time, just as it did in those earlier days.

When we were in the process of leaving Washington, I recall Alex's heartfelt lament that with our departure he would not know where his home was anymore. It would not be Charleston even though he had spent four years here in college. It would no longer be Washington despite his extensive social network there because the only home he knew would no longer be his. I explained to him how eerily similar my experience was to his, and that his future would know a home even if he did not know yet where that would be or when. He understood, of course, but it was his head that was agreeing, not his heart.

I sometimes wonder what it's like for those people who live their lives in one place; where their immediate and extended families surround them as well as their friends who they've grown up with. Whatever else might plague their lives, there is no ambiguity about where "home" is. I am not jealous of those folks – I have enjoyed the changes in my life too much to dwell on that – but there is a certain warmth and security that I would think accompanies those life choices.

I have a fantasy that one day I will drive up to White Plains and have Lily, Jesse, and Alex with me. We will drive down Ogden Avenue and pull up to my old home. I will knock on the front door and someone will answer ready to shut the door on what they believe to be yet another unsolicited sales pitch, or perhaps something more threatening to them. But, I will have a few seconds to explain who I am and why I've knocked on their door. They will let us in, resisting their urge to call 911, and I will take in the sweep of what was so long ago my life. It wouldn't matter how much has changed. I would know the rooms; I will recall where the furniture was, and, best of all, I will allow a thousand memories to come washing back over me. I will show my family where my room was, where I would sit in the kitchen learning so much from my Uncle Milt, where I would sit next to my father on the couch as we listened to my mother play the piano after dinner, where I would throw a ball up against the house for hours on end in my own way mimicking my childhood baseball idols.

Maybe some day.

Running Down Memory Lane

It had been planned for months. A weekend getaway to re-ac-quaint ourselves with memories still embedded somewhere, but in need of being refreshed. Rehoboth Beach, Delaware was in our cross hairs. One of those special places we all have where memo-ries long submerged come blasting to the surface like a dormant geyser waiting to be experienced one more time, needing no more of a trigger than just being there. We rented a house in the North Shores section of town mere steps from earlier rentals – familiar turf. The group: folks who have shared these wonderful moments with us over the decades, some for long weekends, some for a sum-mer's term when we would bolt the stuffy confines of Washington and head for the ocean and its promise of clear air, surf, sand and serenity. Friends who will be there for a lifetime. For Lily and me, this was the place where we raised Jesse and Alex in the summer months, and it was where the seeds of the strong magnetic pull to beaches were first born in them.

Just driving into town was enough to get the smiles going, but, for me, the deal was sealed by a run through the old neighborhoods and the town. Like my own personal tour bus with my brain serving as tour guide stimulated often by seemingly nothing but the merest visual cues and the music from my iPod blaring in my ears. I took off from our house on Harbor Road and made the turn on to Cedar Road where at number 9 resided the heart and soul of our times here. Sadly, the old, red, one-story frame house is gone now replaced by a mini-mansion box that I suppose is attractive to someone, although certainly not to me. But, the house didn't need to be there to bring it

all back. Here is where a young Amy DePippo embarked on a deter-
mined course to bake a very young Alex a birthday cake decorated
to look like a pool table, and make it all happen in a toaster oven.
Here was where, on unrelenting rainy days, we would succumb to
the elements and encourage the boys to play in the downpour out
in the backyard, sometimes with the yellow slip 'n slide that was in
perfect shape for rainy day play. It was here that our old chocolate
lab, Hoover, would fight over the orange baton thrown far into the
ocean with Randy and Cathy's border collie, Domino. Their truce
was for each of them to have a firm grip on either end of the baton
as they swam ashore together like a canine synchronized swim team
might do.

Right around the corner was 1 Ocean Drive where our Virginia
neighbor, Mark, saved a very young Markey Mark from cascading
over a railing to the floor below, and where a young Jesse blithely ignored a small army of secret service personnel to walk up and introduce himself to what was then a newly elected Vice President Gore.

On I ran. Where the road passes closest to the beach, just north of
town, there is a stretch of beach where they used to hold the sand
castle competition, a must see for us and the boys. The creations
there were a testament to a kind of creativity and architectural
genius that we could only marvel at. In the evenings, this is where
you wanted to be to see the moon's reflection trip along the water to the shoreline. Magical. And, then there was the boardwalk
running along the beach, through town and on to the residential
area to the south. People strolling arm in arm, dog walkers everywhere, babies in strollers, tattooed people of so many sizes, shapes
and coutures you'd swear you had come upon the world's truest
melting pot. And, there, on the right, was the kite store where on
this day the breezes were strong enough to make everything spin,
flutter and dazzle.

Further down the boardwalk I came upon a statue commemorating Giovanni Da Verrazzano -- a statue unknown to me from our times here -- and a testament to his exploratory forays into this region in the early 1500s. Who knew? Just as this historical reality was sinking in, up loomed the irrepressible sign for Dolle's, a big juicy red, sticky sweet sign that lords itself over the boardwalk announcing to the world its saltwater taffy and other less famous sugary treats. And, then, holy ground: Grotto Pizza where one can clearly identify the soul-melting aroma of a veggie bianco or the fresh basil from its margherita pizzas.

I pressed on. If I could laugh and run, I would have at the sight of Funland. Here was the world's epicenter as far as Jesse and Alex were concerned. Rides, games, food. A juvenile perfect storm. But, Lily and I weaved a fable back in those days advising the boys that Funland was only open when it rained. It's amazing they still talk to us. On this day, Funland was shuttered but I swear the air was filled with the aroma of popcorn and melted butter.

This run was, for me, a wonderfully sweet experience. I wanted more than anything, just this one time, to have the endurance to run forever.

Gorging to the Max

I don't think it's entirely unreasonable of me to expect all-inclusive resorts to liberally post warning signs that what lays in store could be hazardous to your health. I'm thinking maybe some diabolical figure with horns and a rictus grin standing atop a pile of absurdly bloated bodies. Maybe, just maybe, this message might thwart one's overwhelming impulse to eat 1400 times what you normally consume. Maybe. I'm not sure there is a single term or phrase that best describes vacationing in an all-inclusive resort: fabulously indulgent, unspeakable gluttony, guilty pleasure, hedonism run amok, wasteful and wanton consumption, paradise. It's so hard to decide. In the end, it's whatever you want, whenever you want it. Limitless choices, limitless quantities. Think if it as a cruise without the claustrophobia and the company of 380 pound fellow travelers.

This is our lot this week as we indulge ourselves a few miles south of Playa del Carmen on the Yucatan's east coast, or, as it has now become known, the Mayan Riviera. Here at the Catalonia Royal Tulum we are celebrating a birthday for long-time friend, Cathy, who is here with husband, Randy, and their grown children, Travis and Shannon.

We arrived here a few days ago tired from a long flight and a 3:45 a.m. wake up alarm to be met at the airport by a seemingly friendly chap, Carlos, who, in my stupor, I thought was an associate of the transit company that would ferry us to our hotel. But, no. It took us a couple of minutes to realize that Carlos was a shill for a time share resort and was laying on his considerable persuasive powers and charm to seduce us into a presentation by his employer. This, of course, was way too reminiscent of our similar experience in getting our "free" Caribbean cruise about a year ago which was as enjoyable to us as water boarding is to most right minded folks. Free of Carlos, we are whisked away on our one hour ride south past wonderful memories of past visits to this region.

The hotel is most surely elegant. Its lobby is open to the elements protected by a huge conical thatched roof that seems to rise several stories above where we stand. The path to our room is through vegetation lush enough to fairly be called jungle. A curving white-stoned path leads us through the jungle to our rooms and the beach and is not a bad substitute for the Yellow Brick Road of Oz.

But, the recurring theme here is food and drink. Unless you opt for a sensible continental breakfast, you are faced with a buffet that offers more customized omelets, more fresh fruit, more bread and rolls, more sausage, bacon, smoked salmon, and champagne than you see in six lifetimes. It's crazy. Same for lunch where the dessert display alone is ten feet long and one is faced with choices ranging from ceviche to salads to tostadas to pulled pork to sushi. And then, five restaurants to choose from for dinner where once again you engage in the good angel/bad angel debate over how many delicacies (and calories) to inhale. It's a wonder management just doesn't encourage you to lose the pants and go straight to togas. And, the liquor. Oh my, the liquor. It's all included so you find yourself smacking down multiple cervezas at lunch followed by an afternoon (at least in my case) of mojitos (with Cuban rum!) as you semi-absentmindedly await the sunset. I'm already thinking I should maybe ask the flight attendant on the way back for one of those seat belt extenders.

And then, there is the animal life, which abounds. Mammals come in various sizes with various snouts. One creature looks like a large groundhog, not unlike a capybara, but smaller. Coati mundis travel en masse and playfully accost passers-by looking for a handout. They do this in a most polite way standing straight up on their hind legs arms outstretched above their heads as if beseeching you for one more crumb. Schools of fish swim around you in the shallows with a cockiness reflecting their awareness that humans are woefully too slow to threaten them. There are toucans whose beaks are, truth be told, significantly larger than mine. And, then there are the parrots, "Ricky" and "Martin," who seem quite content to pose with me, one cradled in my arms on his back like a baby, the other perched on my shoulder taking a bit too much interest in my hair. Iguanas scurry here and there showing their own addiction to the local red flowers. None of them, however, has been taught to whisper. Their early morning screeching, whistling, cackling and clucking is, I guess, what you might call your daily wake-up call, Mexican style.

I loved this week. Good times with old friends, blowing it out. What's a few calories among friends?

The Gift

It is one our favorite pastimes here in Charleston to go on the "art-walks" they have here several times a year, as do many communities across the country. You stroll from gallery to gallery having a chance to see some wonderful art, drink some wine, maybe have a chat with some of the artists to learn more about their craft. Over time, we have found that our favorite gallery is the Robert Lange Studios on Queen Street, owned and run by Robert and his wife (and fellow artist) Megan. The energy and creativity that we see in this gallery is always stunning, whether it's a depiction of a surging ocean, landscapes that are so razor sharp you'd swear you are really looking at photographs, or portraits that tell a story or offer mystery through a turn of a smile or a laser-like stare. And, this is where the story begins.

One of the artists that displays his work at Lange is J.B. Boyd. J.B. is young, exuberant, marches to the beat of a yet to be identified drummer, and has an incredible flair for creating magic out of the local landscape. Whether it's trees or ocean or lowcountry marsh, J.B.'s work leaps off the canvas in a way that hypnotizes, seduces, and makes your eyes linger. In one of our visits to the gallery some months ago, Lily spotted one of J.B.'s works in particular and was spellbound. It was the lowcountry marsh with an unseen sun low in the sky where the highly shadowed grasses and trees were as dark and serene as the water was fabulously ablaze with the sun's reflection. The water was seemingly on fire and the effect was riveting. It painted a scene that we had observed on many occasions from our own backyard on the Isle of Palms but without the intensity and amped up beauty that J.B. had found. Lily turned to me and, with a plea that can only come from the heart, said how wonderful it would be to own this one. She gazed lovingly at the painting, but in the hubbub of the artwalk and the distraction of so many other paintings, that momentary expression of desire got distracted, and the matter was dropped. For the moment.

I made up my mind. I would buy this painting for Lily. I called the gallery the next morning, spoke to Robert and sealed the deal. It would be a surprise, a Christmas present. Robert suggested that one thing I could do would be to write a personalized note that would be displayed next to the painting, and one day we would walk into the gallery and surprise Lily with her gift. Pictures would be taken. A very personal history would be recorded. Brilliant. The element of surprise, the joy of watching another's joy, and the almost dark pleasure of guarding a secret. The plan was to return to the gallery shortly before Christmas and feel the excitement build.

Months went by. We went on with our lives, happily filled with all the things that have made our days here so satisfying. The painting mostly disappeared from my consciousness and, I believe, from Lily's as well. But, with the passing of Thanksgiving, the painting took center stage. The time was nearing and the moment had arrived to plan the perfect evening. There was an artwalk looming with a terrific new show at Lange and I knew Lily wanted to go, but I did not want the artwalk to be the backdrop for this present. Too noisy, too many strangers. This screamed out to be more personal, more intimate. Luckily for me, we had plans for both weekend nights and I, as nonchalantly as I could, suggested that maybe we could pick an evening for the following week, say thursday, to go pay a visit. She bit.

Thursday came and I was like a nervous schoolboy. I worried over non-existent obstacles that might interfere with the grand plan and blow the surprise. Would Lily change her mind and decide that we should stay home that evening? Would we have a minor fender bender on the drive into town and force us to miss the gallery's closing time? Would Mojo run off in search of deer at just the moment we were getting ready to leave? Despite my best intentions, would I start acting weird in anticipation of all this and tip off Lily's finely tuned radar that something was afoot?

We drove into town. I don't recall ever being so acutely aware of speed limits and stop signs. But, we made it without incident and worked our way the few blocks from the garage to the gallery. I had called ahead and furtively asked where the painting would be displayed so that I would not risk an all too knowing look from Megan or Rob hinting at its direction.

While I was ready to burst at the seams, Lily was in no hurry to make her way to the spot where her gift was hung. And, why should she be? As it turned out, the works displayed in the front room of the gallery were so captivating that it seemed years passed by as I bit my tongue and went with the agonizingly slow pace Lily had adopted in these insufferably long minutes. Painting by painting, wall by wall, we worked our way ever so slowly to the place where I knew drama was in store.

We approached what was at that moment the only wall that mattered. I held my breath. Lily noted with pleasure and surprise that here was the painting she had so admired so many months before. She peered closer. There was a typed note just below the painting, where you would ordinarily find the artist's name, the title to the work, and the sale price. But, on this night, there was another message. It read:

To Lily

Babe – I have long thought that this work of art belongs in your hands and no one else's. Now it is yours to hold forever. All my love, Jeff.

My eyes were on Lily, not the painting. And, then it happened. You could hear a pin drop in the empty gallery, but what I heard were fireworks. Lily's hands went to her face, the fingers trembled, the disbelief turned to awareness and then to rapture. The tears flowed and there were long hugs. Megan was there with a camera to capture it all. Magic. There would be time to tell the whole story, but that could wait. In these moments, all was given over to joyfulness and the wondrous amazement of what I had hoped to be the perfect gift. We sat on the swing in front of the painting and let the moment live on.

I don't always get things right, but on this night I did.

Getting Laid Back, Mexican Style

Yelapa, Mexico isn't an island although it might as well be. Tucked in to a protected cove about an hour south of Puerto Vallarta, it is – for most normal folks – only reachable by water taxi. Technically, you can get there overland, but that would take the courage (or, more likely, insanity) of a dirt bike or the heartiness of an avid and intrepid hiker to traverse the steep and wildly verdant hills that surround it away from the water. But, as we shall see, Yelapa is more than just a boat ride away from Puerto Vallarta; it's decades away. As P.V. is awash in high rises, Starbucks, and a jumble of high octane traffic patterns, Yelapa is – how you say – as distant in character as Neptune is from New York.

We began our journey on the shores of Boca de Tomatlan, a sleepy village with steep cobblestoned streets. It was here that we intentionally awaited our water taxi long enough to enjoy a beachside treat of octopus (pulpo) empanadas and a nifty seafood salad of shrimp, octopus, and avocado that had a freshness that could only come from a concoction created a moment before we devoured it. The water taxi was not much more than an oversized rowboat, if you ask me, but one with a surprisingly hefty outboard that would throw up rooster tails that might be the envy of many a jetskier. Along the way, we pass jungle worthy terrain and the entertaining sight of pelicans perched on idle boats, a man-made respite from the rolling surf. Forty-five minutes later, we landed on the beach at Yelapa and jumped into ankle deep water. I really don't think I had ever had the experience before of dragging my rolling bag through the sand, but that was the only option to getting the bag to our hotel, the Lagunita.

At the hotel reception, a small and preposterously unpretentious outcropping, we meet Luke, the hotel's owner. Luke, like may here, is an ex-pat. He is from the Chelsea section of New York, and is as charming as he is laid back, and he is very laid back. Luke gives me the big picture of Yelapa and I have this sense that he is always just moments away from a yawn. In addition, I can't get out of my head how his hooded eyes remind me way too much of Javier Bardem's in "No Country for Old Men." He gives us directions to our room key, instructions on where to refill our water bottles, and an invitation to breathe slowly and deeply. Our room – our pelapa – is a bungalow about 7 feet from the beach with a thatched, and very high, vaulted ceiling and "windows" that have no glass, just some more thatching that serves as openings to the world, both in terms of climate and animal life, that can come and go as they wish. Our bathroom is tiled with rounded ceilings and an oddly attractive mottled paint job that might well have been done by Jimmy Hendrix in the days before he hit the big time. At night, all that separates you from the outside world is a simple hook to keep the door closed, not what you would normally find, say, in New York.

The bar and the restaurant are in the sand. What we find there is a fabulous assortment of seafood salads, ceviche, guacamole, burritos, enchiladas, fish tacos and a good bit more. And, of course, the Pacifico beer, margaritas, tequila shots and – my personal favorite – the Cuban rums. The sand is very tactile to the touch – a natural exfoliant.

It would be a shame not to share this grand escape with others, and we have done that. We are joined by Jesse and Laura on the lam from Denver and the daily dosing of stress and grind in their lives. They're ready. They meet us a few hours after we arrive, and the party begins.

As P.V. is of modern times, Yelapa is most defintely third world. No streets as such, just walkways. No cars, no banks, no ATMs. Our room at the Lagunita brandishes no TV or phone. Ah, but there is wi-fi, at least if you locate yourself within ten feet of the hotel office. As tourist meccas go, this one is one step above primal. When we walk through town, we are met by quaintness and unadorned local flavor: there is far more hanging laundry than souvenir shops, far more kids playing with homemade toys than glitzy boutiques. There are a few restaurants and a disco, but not the sort that would attract the Michelin Guide. Credit card usage is rare enough here that a few businesses advertise their openness to this form of mercantile behavior as if it's a novelty. As you venture away from the shoreline, you get a grip on how steep the environment is. The paths work their way upward, sharply. At the end of one is a waterfall high and scenic with a pool of clear and cold mountain water. Jesse dives in and gets the full treatment as the fall's pounding onslaught massages his head and shoulders.

There really isn't much to do here other than what Luke advertised: the opportunity for deep breathing and relaxation. A Canadian group from the Yukon we run across at the hotel is there for a week of yoga and, after a fashion, dancing. Amusingly, the signs for dogs to be on leashes is totally ignored as mongrels of a thousand sorts roam the beaches, often playing with each other in the ocean shallows. Horses appear on the beach. Paragliders sometimes appear. For mortals like us, we find contentment in our beach reading, our raucous hearts games, speed scrabble, and dips in the cenote-styled pool which hangs over the ocean like the best of infinity pools.

A person could get used to this, no?

Best in Show.....Almost

We all know what pandemonium means. It's a commonly heard term often used to describe scenes of chaos or mayhem. To those with a literary bent, Pandemonium was the capitol of Milton's hell in Paradise Lost. For most of us, though, the term conjures up images of things run amok, a place of wild confusion often accompanied by loud noise. But, these are all merely calm reflections of book learning, not grounded in personal experience. Well, for us, all that changed this morning when we followed through on my plan to enter Mojo into this year's annual Isle of Palms Dog Show. While we had once attended this event before we had Mojo, that was as observers – neutrals, you might say. This time we were in the trenches, combatants you might say. We now are quite sure we know what pandemonium is.

The lead up to this day was innocent enough. I shampooed Mojo yesterday after returning from the beach, trying with greater zeal than normal to squeeze out whatever sand still lurked in those pesky undercoats of his. I never shampoo Mojo; it just seems like wasted energy since I know he'll be back in the ocean in literally a matter of hours. But, yesterday he got the royal spa treatment: the massage, a fluffier towel than normal, a careful wiping of the face to remove drool and errant sand particles, a good brushing. He was ready. Or, so I thought.

We arrived at the Isle of Palms Recreation Center to be met by an avalanche of canines. They were everywhere: there were puppies, german shepherds, labs, goldens, poodles, dachshunds, pomeranians, ridgebacks, greyhounds, danes, hybrids of all shapes and sizes, and a vast array of undecipherables. All were excited. You simply cannot imagine how many leashes became fabulously intertwined in mere seconds. Some dogs took this all in quite evenly; others less so. There were plenty of growls, but the growls were far outnumbered by the number of wagging tails, including Mojo's. I would guess there were in excess of 100 dogs there. Some were dressed in costumes for the all-important "best costume" category. (A word on the competition's categories. No, this was not Westminster. This was the people's dog show. This is why there were categories such as "most ear resistible ears," "cutest puppy," "best eyes," cutest name," "biggest breed," "smallest breed," "cutest unidentifiable breed," and best male and female rescue dogs, where Mojo would do battle. Trust me, Westminster is safe as a pinnacle in the pantheons of dog showdom.)

Just getting through the registration process was hair raising. Because Mojo was intent on smelling everyone's butt as if it were a time trial to do this, I must have turned four or five lurching pirouettes as I neared the table to sign in and receive my instructions for what was to follow. It was as if the dogs had all simultaneously gotten their get out of jail card and were hellbent on partying like there was no tomorrow. Sniffing, growling, licking, barking, yipping, humping, jumping, rolling were everywhere. I was a bit out of my element.

Somehow the master of ceremonies got folks' attention (less so the dogs') and the competition was underway. Our group – best male rescue – was up second. Ten in the group. The MC came along with a mike and asked each of us the story of how our dog had come to be rescued. I told them all the story of Mojo getting tossed from a truck as a small pup and getting rescued by a hunter who saw it all happen and how Mojo was now the happiest dog on planet earth. A pretty compelling story, but as the MC went down the line, each owner in turn had an incredible story of saving his or her dog from euthanasia in the nick of time or snatching them from an abusive environment. All great stories, all heartening. In fact, when the crowd was asked how many owned rescued dogs, I'd say about 80% of everyone there raised their hands. But, now it was in the judges' hands, the three ladies sitting with clipboards assessing who knows what. They announced the third place finisher, then the second. And, then the winner of the group.....Mojo! Blue ribbon, an inscribed dog bowl, a gift certificate, dog treats – the whole enchilada. I was immediately filled with excitement, and in an odd way, pride. Really, not at all unlike seeing one of your children winning a spelling bee or prevailing in a big soccer game. All Mojo wanted in that moment was another piece of Puppy Crack, the wonderful dog treats sold by our neighbors, Brian and Jan. As far as I could tell, Mojo's zone of interest consisted solely of dogs and treats, and who can blame him?

Because we won in our class we had to stick around for the awarding of the best in show prize where, once again, Mojo and ten others went on display for the judges. By now, most of the dogs were actually quite calm, their bodies now completely drained of adrenalin. They announced the winner, a beautiful German Shepherd from a group I simply do not remember. It was a blur. One of the judges came up to me afterward and said softly, "I was outvoted" as if to furtively suggest that Mojo got one of the three votes for best in show. That would have been great, of course, but after two hours of pandemonium what we wanted most was our exit visa.

Back to the beach tomorrow, big guy. Hopefully, that blue ribbon is waterproof.

Traffic Court

I woke up in a cold sweat. It wasn't yet 6 a.m., but in my night-mare-addled brain it was high noon, believe me. In the dream, I was at a function of some sort with nameless, faceless people, but I knew I would need to leave to permit enough time for me to get home, shower, and change into some decent clothes. I had a date in traffic court and needed to get ready. But, I noticed that way too suddenly I was almost out of time. No time to get out of my running gear, no time to shower. Just enough time to get in my car and drive to court. Feverishly racing around the multi-tiered parking lot, I could not find my car. It was not where I would have sworn I parked it earlier. Incredibly frustrating. Infuriating, actually. The seconds ticked away in my head as if they were gongs from a huge hammer. At some point, I knew I had to abandon the car – which had my wallet and speeding ticket inside – and make a run for the courthouse. As I got to the street, my moves were exactly what they would be if I were trying to run while at the bottom of a pool. Agonizing, slow motion, not nearly fast enough to keep up with the warp speed that my brain was moving. I woke up staring breathlessly at the clock.

Such was the effect my pending court date had on my psyche. It's not as if I was up for grand theft auto; no, just speeding. We've all been there, right? Maybe not in traffic court, but on the high end of the dial, so to speak. I had been traversing the Island of Palms Connector this past January, the bridge that takes you from the mainland to the barrier island where we live, and there wasn't a car in sight in my lane. The radio was blasting its coverage of the South Carolina primary which was going to take place the next day. I was paying absolutely no attention to my speedometer, just stories of Newt and Mitt and Rick. When I noticed a car in the oncoming lane make a whiplash worthy u-turn, and pull up close behind me, I knew instantly I was in trouble. Let's just say I was heading over the bridge closer to warp 3 than to the posted 55 m.p.h. speed limit. When the officer pulled me over as I got over to the island, he strolled up to my car and asked, "Is there an emergency I need to know about?" I couldn't bring myself to conjure one up so I went to Plan B which, essentially, called for a generous amount of groveling. To no avail, of course. The officer advised me this was "an arrestable offense" seeing as how I was clearly trying to take flight without having first filed a flight plan. He wrote me a ticket for a king's ransom, but suggested I go to court to see if maybe the judge might uncharacteristically take pity on me and lower the ransom a trifle.

My court date arrived. I decided not to go in a suit – too presumptuous and, frankly, virtually unseen on this island. I went with a respectable dress shirt and a pair of khakis: Isle of Palms formal, you might say. I'm not sure what I expected, but I was stunned to see the hearing room filled to the rafters with other similarly nervous looking individuals. I roughly counted close to 60. Young, old, white, black, male, female – the gang was all there. My first thought after seeing this almost standing room only crowd was to wonder why I had been obsessing about what I should wear. I'd say a good handful of people looked like they had every intention of going surfing as soon as they could see daylight again. Others were just in shorts and t-shirts. Bluejeans abounded. There was an occasional tie but I attributed that more to the fact these were working folks making what they hoped would be a short stopover on their way to work rather than folks dead set on trying to charm and impress a judge.

As I watched the slow procession of one after another plead guilty and make exactly the same arguments I had painstakingly thought through in my own mind the night before, I realized I needed to understand that: a) this would not be an opportunity for an oral argument as I had known in my legal career, and b) it probably wouldn't matter what I said whether I could have one minute or twenty to make my pitch. Brevity was the key. My nerves danced like a horde of gremlins inside my head and stomach. My heart pounded. When the judge suggested to one lady that she ask for a continuance to get a lawyer since she faced possible imprisonment, my stomach did a nice little jackknife and my heart skipped several beats. He wouldn't do that to me, would he? I did note that all the speeding cases that preceded mine were for violations far milder than what I would have to account for, allowing my head to make all the crazy assumptions of what would happen to me. By the time my name was called, I was fairly certain that I faced exile and that I would be branded a terrorist.

I approached the podium and listened as the officer I had unfortunately crossed paths with this past January recounted for the judge the charges against me. I had a notion that things might not go swimmingly when the first thing the judge said to me was – and this is a direct quote – "Let me get this straight. Were you driving or were you flying?" Thinking it better not to respond with a joke, I assured him I was driving. I whizzed through my story, and the judge just stared at me for too long a moment. He spoke and ruled. My fine would be reduced a tiny bit, but, as a gesture of goodwill, he would lower the number of points that would go on my record. He sort of obliquely mentioned my good attitude and politeness as grounds for his largesse.

Learning in advance from my neighbor, Brian, that payment of any fine in traffic court here would need to be made in cash, I had stuffed my wallet with all the 20s the ATM could spit out. I could not fold the wallet to get it in my pants pocket.

Now I can.

Are We in Heaven?

It was one of those special moments you know you'll always remember even as the moment is barely unfolding. Sitting on a beach gazing out on what most of us would normally associate with a travel magazine cover. You know – the silky white strand of beach arching in a graceful curve around a bay with an array of pearl white boats floating atop a pale turquoise sea. In my case, I was still smiling from the beach bocci game Jesse, Brian, and I had played improvising with coconuts as our Caribbean sporting equipment. Jesse and Laura had strolled down the beach and perched themselves side by side on top of a large volcanic rock in the shallows taking it all in; Lily was out there blissfully snorkeling; Alex and Brian were on the boat seemingly almost within earshot of where I sat making last minute preparations to swim ashore and join us. There was a slight breeze, just enough to take the edge off a hot sun. In a dream world, there would be some really cool music playing, but the visuals were more than ample to create a long lasting impression. The thing of it is, there would be many such moments that week.

It was Lily's idea, really. What we had been looking for was a Caribbean version of the "Blue Cruise," an informal small boat cruise popular in Turkey that hugs the coast line and lets you spend a week in barely more than your swimsuit. We wanted to include Jesse, Laura and Alex and re-create what we found two years ago and almost 6 thousand miles east. Failing to find that, Lily thought why not rent our own boat and sail it around the British Virgin Islands (the BVI)? A great idea, right? Except for the fact that we know as much about sailing as we do about training camels. Yeah, yeah, we know there's a port side, a starboard, a fore and aft. But, it pretty much falls apart after that. And, then came the stroke of brilliance. Let's hire Jesse's good college buddy (and wedding groomsman), Brian to be our skipper. Brian agreed in less time than you can say Cruzan Rum and we had a deal. Brian, among other things, a sailing instructor at the College of Charleston, had no doubts about his sailing skills, but there were these lingering issues of being trusted to skipper a boat he had never sailed in strange waters and with a crew that would never be mistaken as – how you say – knowledgeable.

Arriving in Tortola, we got briefed on the do's and don'ts of boat operation by the folks at Conch Charters who, amazingly, trusted us with their vessel. We learned about battery power issues, motor maintenance, communications requirements, trash collection, and the all-important toilet operation rules. And, then, as if handing over the keys to the family car to a 16 year old, they cut us loose to do our worst in exploring the BVI. I was thinking these guys must have fantastic insurance coverage. Our boat was the 43 foot catamaran, the "Hazelnut," a sadly inadequate name, we thought. Four cabins below, each with its own bathroom. The cabins were tightly structured; some might reasonably call them crypt-like. The bathrooms were about the size of a medium sized phone booth, but complete with sink, toilet and hand-held shower. The deck, however, was perfect. An interior salon with table and wrap around seating, an outdoor seating area of similar design, and a forward lounging area of trampoline-like netting that was strung between the boat's twin hulls. The boat's galley had a propane stove, neatly stored shelving for plates and glassware, and a refrigerator that would prove adequate if not exemplary. There was a nice recessed storage area for what seemed the 900 bottles of rum, gin, tequila and wine that we felt were essential to this journey. And, the food! When our provisions arrived, we surely believed we had enough food to nourish Luxembourg for at least a day. Fresh fish, hamburger, cold cuts, cheese, pate, game hens, an array of fruit, carrots, potatoes, canned goods, celery, coffee, eggs, bread, juices, mustards and mayo, crackers, chips, chocolate, nuts, and so much more. We were literally awash in food that was now spilling over and out of every possible storage square inch. We would not go hungry.

My concerns stemming from our ignorance of all things nautical were vastly overwrought. Brian, with his anxieties seemingly well under control, proved not only to be an able skipper, but the perfect one. Calm and trusting, skilled and incredibly conscientious, Brian had us learning sailing's basic skills quickly. Laura became a first-rate knot maker on the lines. Jesse and Alex did their duty as sail raisers, and Jesse became an ace on retrieving mooring buoys. Each of us would take turns at the helm with Brian diplomatically hinting that maybe we might take it a bit more "left" or "right" as the need arose rather than trying to lure us into his more proper sailing lexicon. Alex and I manned the kitchen with Alex spilling out first-rate breakfasts, and the two of us crafting lunches and dinners that would not disappoint. Jesse learned the idiosyncrasies of the grill in no time. And, naturally, Jesse declared himself "Captain of the Dinghy," a title even less lofty than it sounds.

The days flew by as we made the rounds up the protected channel between Tortola roughly to the north and Norman, Cooper and Peter Islands to the south along with Virgin Gorda. Taking the turn around Tortola , we made our return via Marina Cay and, lastly, Jost Van Dyke, home to the regionally epic night spots, "The Soggy Dollar" and "Foxy's." During the day, it was snorkeling along the reefs, swimming off the boat, reading, the occasional onshore jaunt to visit beach bars or just walk the shoreline. As we worked into the late afternoon, the call went out for cocktails. A word here about what appears to be the national drink of the islands: "the painkiller." A seductive mix of crème of coconut, pineapple juice, a dark rum or two and fresh nutmeg grated on top. It is hard to say how many of these beauties we slurped down in one week, but I think I spotted a palm leaf this morning trying to emerge from my scalp. They are delicious; they are ubiquitous; and, once you start there are easier things than this to stop. We were introduced briefly to the painkiller upon our arrival, but our first real submerging into them was at a curious place called "Willy T's."

Willy T's is a bar that is also a boat. You can only get there by water which means you either tie up there or swim there. Let's call its atmosphere.... festive. Folks are there to have a good time and, at least that evening, there seemed to be several ways to achieve that, enough so that parents who happened upon the place with their young kids pretty much ushered them to "safety" off the boat as things got a bit louder and a bit raunchier. I am told by Jesse and Alex that I overtly declared my intentions to mingle and get to know the crowd better. I have no particular recollection of this. What I do recall is a couple of oaths taken by Alex before we boarded Willy T's that may have set the tone for that evening, if not the rest of the trip. In his best island lilt, Alex announced his plan to go "HAM" for the trip which translates to "go hard as a motherf**ker," and his proclamation that, "I want to be banned on this island by the end of the night." I recall his saying these things as he rolled out his eyepatches, pirate earrings, temporary tatoos, and the always indispensible inflatable pirate sword that he brought with him in preparation for this adventure.

When we were not out for the evening, it was game time: scategories, charades, hearts games. Scategories, in particular, got the juices flowing as we energetically immersed ourselves in such metaphysical debates as whether among the things you see at a circus that start with the letter H could be hippies. Alex strenuously argued in the affirmative; the rest of us said no. Gypsies, maybe, but not hippies. Alex argued that gypsies were only a more contemporary form of hippie, that they were really the same phenomenon; we said no, gypsies are gypsies and they begin with the letter G, not H. And, so it went. I'm sure the painkillers added nothing to the enthusiasm and laughter that accompanied these activities. And, Jesse was always there to pose imponderable hypotheticals. Like, "what would you rather do, spend a year alone on one of these small, unpopulated isolated islands, or spend the rest of the vacation this week in Alex's bathroom onboard?" Hmmm, let me think about that one a bit.

We have been on so many great trips around the globe with Jesse, Laura, and Alex that it is hard to single out one that surpasses them all. But, we seemed to come to a consensus that this one may have been the best. I thought about this a lot afterwards and have a theory as to why this trip was so memorable, so thoroughly enjoyable. With other trips we have done, the focus has always been on where we are whether that might be the Tuscan countryside, the Portuguese coastline, or the exotic offerings of Indonesia. Here, though, while we were in a fabulous environment offered up to us by the BVI, the location was incidental. Rather than being wonderfully distracted by the sights and sounds of these places, we were focused instead on each other. We lived on a boat that created, when you think about it, a very intimate experience where we were never more than a few feet from one another. As a result, far more time was spent in conversation whether it was about jobs, travel, books, movies, common friends or past adventures or misadventures. It was far more personal this way. Second, when on the boat, there is really very little to do. If you're not reading or swimming, you're interacting with someone, and so the focus once again is on who you're with, not where you are. I think we all loved that about this trip whether or not we were conscious of the reasons that enabled it.

On our last night on the boat before returning to Tortola, we all found ourselves laying out on the netting at the prow of the boat that connected the two hulls. There was a full moon, lots of stars. There was a slight breeze, the air temperature perfect. The rum and gin, and a week's worth of incredibly satisfying vacation, had us tired and mellow. In my head I recalled something I had said earlier in the week after a glorious day when I posed to everyone and no one, are we in heaven? I closed my eyes, not to nap, but to take it all in one last time.

Yeah, we were in heaven.

Jake Shimabukuro

Tell me something. When was the last time you listened to someone perform music and you were genuinely excited by what you were hearing? I'm not talking about just loving the music or being nicely entertained -- that's common enough -- but being riveted by what you were experiencing. Enraptured, not merely attentive. Where you would stare unblinkingly and listen without the slightest distraction at what was unfolding before you, allowing yourself an occasional "wow" or "whoa" in a barely audible soft whisper. This is what we experienced the other night listening to Jake Shimabukuro.

And, if I were to tell you that Jake's instrument is the ukulele, you would scoff just a bit, wouldn't you? I know I would were I not familiar with his wizardry. In my life, the ukulele is one of those instruments I have always associated with cutesy island folk tunes, and, for those as old as dirt as I am, the insincere pawings of an old Arthur Godfrey in television's early days. An instrument, fairly or unfairly, dismissed as not worthy in a conversation about serious music or serious musicians.

The setting for this musical magic was this year's Spoleto festival here in Charleston. Jake was slated to appear at the cistern at the College of Charleston, as wonderful a venue as you are apt to find. The cistern is the college's quadrangle, the outdoor space that is draped in the overhanging boughs of live oaks and that holds an ancient building at its head whose façade on performance nights is lit from below in colors arching skyward. On other days, the cistern hosts graduation ceremonies, on others it is a favorite gathering place for students who loll in the shade with friends or books. On this night, however, all this was in doubt as Lily and I took cover from a downpour that we were certain would lead to a cancellation, or, at a minimum, the relocation of this event to somewhere indoors. We wandered over to the cistern under a borrowed umbrella and were surprised to hear that expectations were that the show would go on with the storm front sliding to the east. Towels were handed out by event staff to dry the seats, and, as the rain subsided even further, the crew came out to sweep collected water off the stage, and to set up the lighting and sound equipment. The crowds drifted in, looking skyward, as amazed and delighted as we were to know that the show would, indeed, go on. The event's master of ceremonies pointed to the emerging stars and the moon.

What followed for the next hour was a kind of brilliance that most of us are not often fortunate enough to witness. Jake Shimabukuro, alone on the stage, showed us that this reputedly modest and light-hearted instrument had some secrets of its own lurking behind those strings. Ambitions of greatness. The ukulele (or, as Jake pronounced it, the "ookelele") looked tiny in his hands, just enhancing the image of this instrument as one not to be taken seriously. It appeared as a toy, perhaps a starter instrument for a 7 year old. But, then he began to play.

Whether he was performing Adele's "Set Fire to the Rain," or Queen's "Bohemian Rhapsody" or George Harrison's "As My Guitar Gently Weeps" or the Japanese "Sakura, Sakura," or bluegrass, Jake coaxed sounds out of this little instrument that defied not only expectation but logic. Alternatively, we heard beautifully rounded tones ridicu-lously deep in character, and soaring riffs that made you feel as if you were taking flight just as the music was. Jake's fingers were a blur as they slid among, and up and down, the strings, sometimes sliding down inches from his right hand to produce impossibly high notes that surely would have cocked Mojo's ears. In his rendition of "Sakura, Sakura," the ukulele was once again transformed, this time into the Japanese koto, the traditional instrument used to play this song. Close your eyes and you just knew that was not the ukulele producing these notes. No way. In those numbers where the intensity of the music grew, Jake would slap at the instrument rhythmically while never losing the song, creating a percussive backdrop that -- once again, if your eyes were closed -- you'd swear was the product of more than one instrument. Amazing. Electric.

At the end, the crowd flew to its feet. Polite applause would simply not do. The crowd's whistles, wild cheers, and unrestrained smiles said it all.

Going Home

Deep in the last century, Thomas Wolfe wrote "You Can't Go Home Again," and, of course, he was right. The thousands of pieces of the jigsaw puzzle that was our lives have long since been scattered to the winds never to be reclaimed, at least not in a way that we remember them. Too much has changed, too many people from those days have moved on, too much has been forgotten. But sometimes, if we're lucky, we can catch a glimpse of what was, and sometimes it can seem incredibly real and incredibly immediate. Such was my good fortune recently when I visited my boyhood home in White Plains, New York. What I hoped would be a glimmer of my past turned out to be as close to time travel as anything I am likely to experience in my lifetime.

It has been on my bucket list for some time to return to my old home. I'm not sure why, really. Likely a nice blending of sentimentality and curiosity. As it is for so many, the home in which we spent our childhood has a special place in our hearts. The memories are sweet; there's a certain serenity and warmth associated with it. We were young and felt protected. And, with those thoughts in mind, I wrote a letter to the occupants not knowing who they were. After all, my family left the house a half century ago. In the letter, I introduced myself, explained my interest and included copies of some old photos showing me as a child in front of the house to prove my bona fides. I was delighted with the response which was both prompt and enthusiastic. What I had not bargained for, or remotely considered, was that the folks to whom my parents sold the house a half century ago still lived there. I was stunned. And, that fact added to my urgency in making the visit that I had long hoped for. Lily and I had a long planned visit to the New York area to visit close friends and the opportunity to re-visit the past now beckoned.

We headed up to White Plains with our friends, Tom and Ellen. Our path took us up the Bronx River Parkway, a scenic, bending and generally lush path through Westchester County that I recalled with such great fondness from my youth. We passed through Mt. Vernon, Bronxville, Tuckahoe, and Crestwood each mile seeming more and more familiar to me. When we ducked in to White Plains, there was so much I did not recognize. The city has exploded from what was once a nice suburban outlier to now a thriving metropolis with soaring towers, wide boulevards, and a host of gleaming new buildings. Ah, but the street names were the same, and as we worked our way from downtown to my old neighborhood, I ticked off all those very familiar, but long lost, guideposts: Main Street, South Lexington Avenue, Martine Avenue, Post Road, Bryant Avenue, and then Ogden Avenue. As we approached my old block of Ogden Avenue, I was caught up in a euphoria we don't often get to enjoy. And, when we reached the block on which my old house stands, I realized I was holding my breath. How do you explain to someone what it's like to have memories come to life? To take form and move and not just be imprints that you have held inside for decades.

I got out of the car and was met by Amy, the daughter of Irving and Rita – the home owners. I must tell you that when I entered the house it took my breath away. I touched the walls as if they were life forms, not just wood and plaster. It was all the same as when we left it. Yes, the walls were different colors, but the structure was the same. It was an emotional moment for me. Irving and Rita spoke of Sam (my father) and Susan (my sister) as if they had seen them just a week ago, like time had never passed. They invited me to take the tour, and, as I did, I noticed certain things. There was a wall sconce

in the living room that was there when we lived there. I used to remove the light bulbs when my parents weren't home, use the sconce
as a basket, and would crumple up a wad of paper as a basketball
and play games that were feverishly real to me. I pointed to the old
cabinets in the living room which were still there and laughingly said
that one of them was my folks' liquor cabinet. They advised me it
was theirs as well. In the back, behind the living room, was what
we called the TV room, and it was still called that so many years
later. They asked me if I remembered the dining room wall paper,
and I did. It was coral with images of a white leopard. That paper
was gone from there, but they opened the hall closet and there it
was – the same wallpaper – lining the closet. Upstairs, my bedroom
was exactly the same as when I left it, except for the furniture. The
wood paneled walls, the cabinets, the shelves – all the same, never
altered. I sat on the bed and looked out over Ogden Avenue and a
thousand micro-memories flashed through my head like so many
life-filled electrons jabbing at my memory bank.

Even the bathroom, now one of the most changed rooms in the
house, brought back a memory long lost to me. When I was a boy, I
was plagued by a bronchial condition that often would compromise
my breathing. It provided me with the scariest of moments I can recall from my youth when I was not sure where my next breath was
coming from. In those dark moments, my parents would usher me
into that bathroom where they had turned on the shower to create a
steam room atmosphere in the hopes it would ease my breathing. In
one such episode, I recall being there with my father and I told him I
couldn't breathe. He gave me a long kiss which I realized years later
was because he thought, in that moment, he was losing me; that I was
dying. I hadn't brought back that memory in decades, but there it was.

On the way out of the house, I stopped to acknowledge the Japanese
maple tree in the front yard. We had planted that tree so many years

ago, and, as a child, I watched it grow as I did and marveled when it surpassed my height on its way to a glory I could only imagine. Now, it is fully mature. It towers over the yard with a massive trunk and boughs reaching upwards, far away. In what I can only characterize as an impromptu moment of perfect blending between sentimentality and anthropomorphism, I found myself giving the tree a hug and giving the bark a kiss. Clearly, I was lost in the moment.

I said good-bye to the wonderfully gracious Irving, Rita and Amy and returned to the real world.

But, what a memory.

Walking on Water

Venice is an assault on the senses, but in the best possible way. Yes, yes, tourists crowd the streets and piazzas as ants cover a pool of honey. And, yes, there are more eateries and shops per square inch than anywhere else in the civilized world. But, if your mindset is right, and you've had just the right balance of wine and gelato, you can look past the mobs and merchandise and see the beauty and uniqueness of that Gothic and Byzantine architecture that has moved millions for centuries.

It is often written that Venice was created out of fear that the crumbling of the Roman Empire would leave the mainlanders easy prey to those nasty Huns and Visigoths. Establishing an offshore, less approachable, community would be a good idea, or so they said. What the history books too seldom recount, however, is that there was another scheme afoot, one more subtle and devious in its design. In fact, Venice was created to instill a sense of humility in what was apparently way too many narcissistic and arrogant navigators of the time. Oh sure, these fellows could navigate the Mediterranean with ease; they could do that blindfolded. But, just let them try to navigate on foot from the Piazza San Marco to the Campo della Madonna dell' Orte. Very humbling. Just when you think you've nailed the perfect route, there's a canal keeping you from getting from here to there and, as GPS devices around the world will tell you, you need to constantly "recalculate." There are no straight lines of passage in this bewildering city. One must be nimble and flexible in one's approach if one is to avoid a healthy dose of exasperation. Specifically, the phrase, "as the crow flies," really has very little meaning in this water-filled kingdom.

And so the legacy remains. Today, Venice is a city that among its many wonderful qualities is home to the tourist, head arching upward, eyes dazed, camera lens cap dangling, map unfolded, with an expression of puzzlement and slack jawed resignation wondering, "where the hell are we?" We see all too many shopkeepers being asked for the 14,000th time that same question by these lost souls seeking no more than another Murano glass shop or perhaps the comforts of their hotel rooms. You can tell the shopkeepers immediately; they're the ones wearing the world weary, bored expressions seemingly on the verge of screaming something they might later regret. It is a tableau that M.C. Escher could only dream about. It is all because the city was designed by charter members of the Satanic School of Navigation.

But, I digress. Venice is sinking, we are told. In fact, one recent study concluded that it is sinking five times faster than previously thought. In certain parts of the city, depending on the tides, water overflows walkways and, in some areas, slightly raised wooden walkways have been created to keep everyone's tootsies dry. In autumn and winter, even the Piazza San Marco -- the geographic heart and soul of this city -- is underwater at high tide. To complicate matters, Venice is moving slowly eastward toward the open spaces of the Adriatic in what perhaps may be its own feeble attempt to escape the millions of tourists that possess it daily. When these overflows occur to the ancient walkways of this city, you can reasonably argue you are walking on water, or something akin to that.

And, so, you ask, if the water poses the problem, then make it your friend, right? Inspired by Lily's sister, Ann, we decided to see Venice by kayak. After all, who needs vaporettos or gondoliers? Ann, at least, had credentials for this adventure. The rest of us? Not so much. It was not the city's canals that gave some of us pause; rather, it was (or, at least in our minds it was) the seemingly vast expanse of water we had to cross to get from Certosa, an island across the lagoon from Venice, and also home of Venice Kayak, to the city proper. And, the knowledge that our adventure would have us paddling for three hours. Timing our sprints to dodge the constant onslaught of the high powered vaporettos, we made it to the city, and breathed deeply. From here, the magic began. Wending our way up the residential, non-touristed, areas where the locals live, you could almost hear a pin drop. The only sounds we heard were those of giggling school children and occasionally the sounds of workers unloading goods from their boats. The canal water was not just calm, it was perfectly still allowing clear reflections of the ancient buildings lining the route. Our guide, Loretta, would approach each "intersection" and yell out our approach to potential unseen traffic around the corner lest we be steamrolled. We passed under bridges, some so low I had to duck my head to avoid scraping my nose against the bridge's underside.

As we proceeded through more touristed areas, people looking down on us from the bridges and walkways would gaze at us with amusement in their eyes, or delight, and some with looks of bewilderment as if to say, "you're doing what?" Often we would be met with a chorus of "ciaos" from those ashore. Apparently, this is still somewhat a novelty here. No folks, it's not a gondola, it's not a vaporetto, it's a kayak! And, so it went as we made our way down the Grand Canal, under the Rialto Bridge and down toward Piazza San Marco. We even had to hold up to let a monstrous cruise ship, at least ten decks high and the size of Wyoming, pass by us before we could begin our trip back to base. Did we bump into walls and other boats along the way? Sure. Was it not until we were through at least a third of our journey that I was advised I was using my paddle backwards? Yes. Did my back ache and my hands get scraped by a totally unorthodox paddling style? Sadly, yes, this is true.

But, we were walking on water and it felt wonderful.

The Skinny on Eleuthera

Eleuthera is a topographical string bean. Achingly thin, it stretches its long, green crescent self north and south in the heart of the Bahamas, about 70 miles east of Nassau. With its arched northern end, complete with an extended skinny "nose," and its flared and curled tail at the south, Eleuthera conjures up a seriously anorexic seahorse – if you can imagine such a thing. It is so narrow in width, one is tempted to conclude that not just a hurricane would make this place nothing but a memory, but that a modestly robust high tide might do the same.

Like everywhere, I suppose, Eleuthera has a rich and picturesque history. Folks disagree whether Columbus actually did anything more than a drive-by, but what is clear is that for centuries the island was the home to Arawaks. This was, of course, until the Spanish came, decimated the population and sold whoever was left into slavery – mostly for the mining operations in Hispaniola. Shortly after the American Revolution, British loyalists fled here along with their slaves. As a result of what became a rather insular population, Bahamians who live here derive their last names from the slender roster of those who survived – almost everyone here shares about a dozen names, almost all derived from their British slaveholders.

Eleuthera is really a land divided into three parts: north, central, and south. It's not so much that the three areas are so distinguishable from one another by geography, culture or lifestyle, but rather because the 100 mile long island has pockets of civilization at those various points, like Harbor Island in the north and Governor's Harbour in the middle. The former is a place where money is making its mark. As some have said, it is in jeopardy of becoming "Nantucket-ized." Elle MacPherson, Mariah Carey and Penelope Cruz apparently wander about here, but we did not see them. Perhaps they didn't get the word we were coming. (Or, actually, maybe they did.) In between is a vast nothingness dotted a bit by tiny settlements or a pineapple farm or leftover concrete observation towers from WWII, or, of course, some amazing beaches. Most notable among the beaches are those that revel in their star-like quality as pink sand beaches. Imagine not sand. No, no – that would be far too easy and would render a sensible description of what we found far too mundane to capture its essence. No, imagine instead walking on a surface that has the same tactile sensation one might have by walking barefoot on a TempurPedic mattress: spongy, dense and almost indescribably soft. The granularity one expects to get back from sand on contact is practically gone, especially as one approaches the water's edge. Here, the sand is liberally sprinkled as if with cinnamon powder, but which is instead the remnants of red animal life – formanifera – whose legacy is to create a stunning visual and tactile experience for the ages.

Not all beaches here are like this. It is just as likely you will stumble across a rock-filled beach or one filled with sharp-edged coral. Among the latter is the famous spot nearing the north end that sports what they call Glass Window Bridge. Eleuthera, which is never at risk for being called "wide," narrows itself to the extreme where the island is essentially a few feet from "coast to coast" if I may use that term here. The bridge spans the meeting of the Atlantic and the Caribbean: the sapphire, roiling, wavy Atlantic to one side and, literally a couple of feet away, the iridescent turquoise calm of the Caribbean separated only by a mass of coral heaving out of the water. Depending on the tide, you can picture yourself laying down under the bridge and having your arms span both bodies of water. But, the beach here is not one to be traversed barefoot. Not unless your feet are made of steel – and maybe not even then. The coral is jagged and unforgiving. When climbing the rocks here – in flip flops, of course – it was tempting to occasionally reach out or down to keep from tipping over. Not wise. Unless, of course, you're wearing the kinds of gloves normally found in cooler climes, which we were not.

A word about the roads here. As narrow as the island is, there are not many. The heart and soul of the road system is Queen's Highway which, like a virtual spinal column, threads its way from the north end to the south end. It has two lanes. A very narrow two lanes. For ninety percent of its length, there are no lights. So – should you happen to find yourself out at night to dinner, let's say, you must work your way back to your hotel or house hoping your windshield is reasonably clear while all the while watching for feral cats, clueless dogs, folks who tend to walk inches from the road in dark clothing, and the oncoming brights of the occasional car that leaves you momentarily blinded. All this while trying to remember to stay on the left side of the road. A bit challenging. There are other roads, some of them actually paved. But, the Eleutherans seem to have a love affair with the pothole, some of them crater-like. I'd love to have the monopoly on automobile shock absorbers here. And, the signage. Ha! With the exception of signs for the airports, which are plentiful, any correlation between the map you're holding in front of you and wherever you happen to be is purely whimsical. To be fair, however, I did consider that in the U.S., where we have an instant and unceasing need to know everything right now and often, it is possible that we have become way too accustomed to an overload of signs whereas our more laid back Bahamian neighbors are apt to be pleased wherever they happen to be even if they don't know exactly where that is.

One last word, this time about the food. We have found over the years that Caribbean cuisine is often not the best. Maybe a bit too tilted to the black bean or the heavily fried whatever, I'm not sure. But, we were practically ecstatic over what was laid before us in our stay on Eleuthera. Yes, there is an entire culinary universe based on the conch: conch chowder, conch salad, fried conch, grilled conch, and, of course, conch fritters. I am surprised there is no conch marmalade or a conch-tini on the cocktail list. But, there is so much more. The place we stayed, the Sky Beach Club, had a kitchen that killed. Everything from vegetable risotto to barbequed pork ribs and an array of fresh seafood dishes, including lobster and crab. Other places had sumptuous salads for lunch and tapas for dinner. Very elegant and very varied and very professional, I must say.

You can go to Eleuthera for the snorkeling or diving or fishing or surfing. Or, like us, you can go for the beaches, the sunshine, the Cuban rums (Ahh, Matusalem) and an escape from the crowds. You decide. There is no wrong answer.

Swimming With The Jellies

I don't know who created the notion of the "bucket list," but I love the idea. It says so much about us – our dreams, our idiosyncrasies. For many, it's the pursuit of an experience that is so at odds with our daily lifestyle that we think of certain goals as almost unattainable. Maybe it's a trip to an exotic location or an epic meal at a world-class five star restaurant. Maybe it's getting onstage and starring in a community theater production. Maybe it's learning to play the piano or, for others, skydiving. At the risk of over dramatizing it, a bucket list provides, in its own way, a tiny window into the soul.

In our case, a shared bucket list item for Lily and me has been a visit to Palau, an emerald green bejeweled set of islands that sits millions of miles from everywhere in the western Pacific Ocean. Why Palau? Because it is the home of Jellyfish Lake, a volcanic lake up in the hills that is home to millions of jellyfish – the non-stinging variety. The idea is that you jump off a pier with your snorkeling gear and find yourself surrounded by teeming, pulsating jellyfish which create a tickling-like massage experience that may be unique on planet earth. That's what we had read anyway.

For the life of me, I don't know how I came to become so enamored with this idea. As a kid, my family would travel to south Florida from time to time. It was here that I was introduced to the Portuguese Man O' War, a beautifully translucent blue jellyfish with, what I led myself to believe, was an excruciating and mortal sting. My father and I would walk along the beach, he with a piece of sharp drift-wood in his hand and me with a look of abject horror, as we went out on a mission to kill these outwardly beautiful creatures – to literally pop them like a balloon – before they got us. Later in life, both Lily and I would experience the painful, red striations that are the universal tattoo of the jellyfish that just added to their legend as things to be avoided at all costs. Kind of like the plague. And yet, despite this uninterrupted history of freakish fear and terror at the thought of all things jellyfish, I not only begrudgingly tolerated Lily's idea, but I embraced it with a passion. Life is so strange sometimes.

When we told folks of our plans to swim with the jellies, the reactions were both amusing and predictable. Most folks would instinctively curl their lips and wrinkle their noses and let out an extended "eeuww!" Others would hurl epithets like "weird" or "creepy" or some colorful combination of both. Our neighbor, Jan, said (with just the slightest hint of exasperation), "Why don't you just fill your bathtub with jello and jump in? Why go halfway around the world to do this?" Okay, okay, I get it. It's not for everyone!

Our visit to Jellyfish Lake was part of an all-day excursion to the southern region of Palau. It would be our boat with a guide and just the two of us. We would visit three or four snorkeling sites, apply soothing (and comical) ocean-bottom mud at what they call the "Milky Way," and wander secluded beaches. But, in our minds, this was just prelude to the unchallenged star attraction of all this, Jellyfish Lake. To get to the lake, we needed to hike up steep steps, climb over some volcanic rock, and then do the same down the steep path to this mysterious and secluded lake sitting in a totally uninhabited primeval jungle environment. When we arrived, we were the only persons there. We got our snorkeling gear straightened out, and we jumped in.

I expected, of course, to be immediately engulfed in a blizzard of jellyfish. But, we weren't. The water on this day was bathtub warm, but seemingly without any visibility beyond our noses. And, no jelly-fish! Joe, our guide, had told us that the jellies move around and are mysteriously affected by changes in the lunar cycle. He urged us to press on and swim to the center of the lake. As we neared the center, everything changed. At first, it was just the spotting of a jellyfish and then two or three. The water cleared. And then, it was as if the curtain rose and we were permitted to enter a region of planet earth reserved for a select few. The handful of jellyfish we had seen now turned to hundreds and then thousands. They were everywhere. And, they were so beautiful. With the sun's rays reaching down well below the lake's surface, it was as if some of these jellyfish were in a celestial spot-light eager to perform. There were different sizes, none much bigger than the spread of the fingers on one's hand. They were domed on one end with their thick tendrils laying underneath. Imagine a large mushroom cap with stunted multiple stems reaching down below it. But, instead of the mundane earthiness of the mushroom, see instead a translucent figure that lets the sun shine through and which gives it a most definite feeling of lightness, delicacy and grace.

I was giddy and I was awestruck. I felt stoned. I would reach out and gently touch these marine life wonders or cup them in my hands. They were soft, softer than a baby's cheek. They were tinged in a brownish orange, but you could see right through them. And, when we found ourselves surrounded by thousands of these lightly pulsating life forms, I felt like we were in the midst of an incredibly choreographed ballet that, in that moment, was just begging for a soundtrack.

Did we ever get so invaded that we felt the massage-like experience we had read about? Sadly, no. But, what we saw and what we felt was nothing short of magical – even spiritual -- that will forever be hard to replicate.

We'll have to dig deeper into our bucket list for that.

Off the Grid: The Tao Experience

How do you know when home is far away? I mean, really far away. Distance is important, for sure. But, it's not all about distance, is it? It's also about a taste of alienation and uncertainty; it's about a culture shift and a departure from all the sensory benchmarks we have in our day-to-day lives. It's something that transports us far beyond the realm we know and take for granted.

Such was the case for us in the Philippines recently as we ventured not just out of Manila, but further and further up the west coast of Palawan, a slender reed of an island southwest of Manila in the lower region of the South China Sea. To get here, at least for some of us, required six flights, one van ride, and three boat rides. To the ends of the earth, I'm telling you. The boat rides were courtesy of the "bangkas," essentially narrow wooden boats with bamboo outrigging and two wooden benches facing each other to carry their six or seven passengers. The sounds the bangka engines make are not unlike those of a 1994 Camaro whose muffler has long been missing – only louder. From Puerto Princessa to Sabang to Port Arthur to El Nido. And, all this was merely by way of prelude to our jumping off point to lands that, for all we knew, had been officially mapped for the first time just yesterday. There were no people along the way. No towns, no cars, no planes. Nothing. All we saw en route was the occasional flying fish rocketing across our bow earnestly in search of something. The landscape was primeval: small, heavily treed islands, some with jagged cliffs jutting out of the sea. It would not take much imagination to feel like you were back in the Mesozoic era. I would not have been shocked to see a dinosaur lurking on the shore.

Our hosts call themselves Tao Philippines, a group that takes hardy souls beyond the resorts, the restaurants, the conveniences and creature comforts that satisfy most tourists. We would climb aboard their own much larger bangka that could accommodate two dozen guests and a small staff and head generally north through virtually uninhabited islands in search of good times and memorable stories. As the Tao literature openly suggests, this trip is not for everyone. I mean we're talking no toilet seats here, no towels, and electricity as a novelty, not a given. We're talking sleeping in open air bamboo huts with pads for beds and mosquito nets to crawl through. And, hot water? fuggedaboutit.

And, our guide for all this? An irrepressible fellow named Ollie, a former fisherman from the area, now transformed into part jack rabbit and part entertainer. Relentless energy and good humor flow through Ollie's veins pretty much the way blood flows through ours. Ollie could leap around the boat in hair raising fashion whether over and around the outriggers or from lower deck to upper deck. Gravity is not his enemy.

Our shipmates were an apt assortment of just the kinds of folks you might expect to find on a venture like this one: Brits, Germans, South Africans, French, Dutch, Norwegians, and one Filipino. Everything from teachers, to business managers of various sorts, to IT systems or sales personnel, a TV producer, and one former prisoner. Eclectic. Most of us intermingled to trade personal histories and travel experiences, and share commentary on what we now all faced. Given the fairly limited space available to us on the boat, we would get to know some of these folks far better than your typical fellow hotel guest.

Our days were awash in leisurely amblings about the Palawans, stopping for snorkeling or strolls around empty beaches, as we meandered through our 150 mile course to our end point, Coron. Snorkeling was without fanfare or ceremony. When we stopped for snorkeling, you would just find some fins, mask and snorkel and jump overboard. And, what you might find was amazing. Take Secret Beach, for example. Aptly named. From the sea all one could see was what appeared to be a very small island ringed with tree-covered towering limestone walls. What you did was swim to it from the boat and find a small tunnel to squeeze through and then swim your way to the bright sunlight beyond. Emerging from this darkness revealed a place that many could justifiably mistake for the Garden of Eden: a rounded interior surrounded by the same towering walls we saw from the outside, but with a level of quiet inside at odds at with what we had left behind moments before. Raising your head, you could hear the echos of your voice and others'. There was no breeze, no sound, just a pristine beach and placid water with a wild assortment of coral formations underneath.

Other times, we would find ourselves snorkeling in distractingly shallow water seemingly barely escaping the beautifully colored, but razor sharp coral beneath us dotted with the gorgeous but deadly black spiny sea urchin with their sharp needles unmistakably aimed at our bellies. We would slide by holding our breath, afraid to breathe lest we invite painful scrapes and stings.

Back on the boat, the time would pass with reading, dozing, or chatting, with everyone finding their own comfortable niche on the boat. Lily would find endless inspiration for painting. Chef Toto and his staff, working out of a cramped walk-through kitchen in the rear of the boat, would ply us with three meals a day and mid-day snacks. And, Toto did not disappoint. We're talking squid adobo, fried calamari, curries, beans, rice, watermelon, suckling pig (with its incredibly crispy skin), all washed down with a spicy ginger tea or a cold San Miguel. Other times it might be carved out coconut with papaya, mango and porridge or an amazing assortment of vegetables and fruits. The succulent and sweet mango alone was worth the trip. Whatever we might not have in the way of creature comforts was quickly forgotten when Toto's dishes were wheeled out for us.

Civilization did make an appearance every now and then, mostly in the guise of tiny fishing villages that would appear sporadically. When we would stop at these villages, the boat would get close to shore, and we would either swim or get ferried ashore. At one such place, we were greeted by groups of young, impossibly cute children who would flock to Ollie as kids might to the Pied Piper. When their attention turned to us, they would giggle and swarm to see their images shared with them from all the photos our group would take of them. For the younger ones, these photos were like magic. They don't see too many of these. At another site, we were invited to play in a volleyball game in which the young ladies of the village were on one side and us on the other. Alex, sensing damsels in distress, gallantly took their side. When his spikes won points for the girls, the girls would start chanting, "handsome, handsome" at their new hero with equal parts squealing and laughter. Later, in a basketball game on a rough hewn court, every time Alex scored a basket, the same chorus would break out from the sidelines. I have a feeling Alex won't let us forget this any time soon.

On our last night, in a fitting burst of craziness for this adventure, we were treated to a homespun disco complete with karaoke. They had a book so weathered you'd swear it had been through wars and countless typhoons that listed thousands of songs you could choose to cause you maximum embarrassment. And, select we did: No Woman No Cry, Don't Stop Believin', Viva La Vida, I Want It That Way, Wonderwall, and, of course, Sledgehammer. The ensuing cacophony – and, really, there's no other term that better describes it – roared through the night in a manner worthy of frightening all but the most intrepid children and cats. All of this was nicely fueled through a heady mix of rum and pineapple juice. Nothing was held back. It was great fun and only embarrassing the next morning.

Karaoke aside, what Tao Philippines offered us was special. What we lacked in creature comforts was made up in full measure by some astounding sights, tastes, and, best of all, memories. We were far from home, for sure. As Dorothy once so indelibly remarked, "Toto, I have a feeling we're not in Kansas anymore." I thought of that line more than once on this adventure.

We were off the grid, alright. But, there was no place we'd rather be.

The Final Curtain

It was our last full day on what had been one of the more amazing adventures of our lives. We had returned from the Philippine wilderness to the mayhem of Manila. Our flight out would be the next day, but first we had an afternoon to wander through this city and we got to do this with Jesse and Laura. In the considerable heat and searing sun, we walked through city parks and gardens, ventured up to the old walled city, and headed back in the hopes of catching the sunset. We took in the beauty of this place and tried to make sense of it against the ever present backdrop of poverty that punctuated the scenery. With every lush promenade came the homeless sleeping wherever the shade permitted. Beautiful monuments and charming horse-drawn carriages were balanced by small, naked children wandering with no apparent connection to anyone or anything.

We headed toward Boulevard Raxos, a broad avenue teeming with life both from the crazy quilt of suffocating traffic and the ubiquitous vendors selling whatever might catch your fancy. We thought how cool it would be to watch the sunset from a rooftop bar in one of the shining towers dotting Raxos and, just steps beyond, Manila Bay. Our search was fruitless, however, and we went to Plan B: find a 7-Eleven, buy cold beer and snacks, and head to the sea wall that runs along the promenade overlooking the Bay. With our cocktail supplies in hand, we sat four abreast atop the wall, our legs dangling over the edge, and stared out over the armada of fishing boats as the sun slowly set. Cold beer, pringles, oreos, and pizza flavored chips. Perfect.

Pictures were taken, memories were rehashed: three weeks, 11 flights, 22,000 miles covered. Swimming, diving, snorkeling, hiking, adventuring. The happy hour supplies vanished, and the Bay turned from blue to orange. We would have an absolutely delightful evening that night in Chinatown with Colin and Shanti, but it seemed as if the curtain on our trip fell as the sun did over the Bay. The orange and red sky and the now orange streaked sea were not unlike our own solar fireworks display – a wonderful exclamation point on some everlasting memories.

In the Hothouse

For many years, folks who know me well sometimes refer to me as the reptile. While I have not encouraged this nickname, I have come to understand that it is not wholly inappropriate. I don't tend to sweat very much. I tolerate very warm temperatures without great effort. While others are swimming in body soaking perspiration, my body tends to dampen only slightly even during intense physical activity which has prompted my friends – out of jealousy I am quite certain – to liken me to a lower strata of animal life. Which is why I was curious how I might respond to a taste of Bikram Yoga. Bikram is that version of yoga that requires you to spend 90 minutes in a room heated to 105 degrees and 40 to 50% humidity while you twist and turn and bend your body in ways that make you feel like a first cousin to a pretzel. Its benefits are legend ranging anywhere from stress reduction and enhanced flexibility to a sense of well being and injury repair. This is, of course, if you can steer clear of blacking out, crumpling over from dehydration, or succumbing to fits of nausea. I'm just sayin'.

I confess to being a bit wary of this experience. Lily has done it for a long time and, while she returns from class looking like she's been for a marathon swim, she swears she feels like a million bucks afterward. Since I have all the flexibility of a telephone pole, I concluded my time had come to turn over a new leaf and get my body to do things not previously witnessed by humankind.

We arrived at the bikram yoga studio and Lily, perhaps sensing my less than robust confidence at what would follow, generously found me a spot for my mat at the rear of the room where I could do my contortions in relative anonymity. And, as a bonus, there was a slight leak at the rear door that permitted the merest suggestion of cooler air to extend to my ankles. The room filled with persons that I immediately concluded were seasoned veterans of this discipline. I announced for all to hear that my goals were limited: don't die, and try beyond all measure not to leave the room, no matter how close to fainting you might be, no matter how nauseous. That latter issue is sort of an unwritten rule.

Our instructor was Amy Lane, a petite and energetic young lady who does several of these classes daily: a pro's pro. Amy Lane speaks at a pace that would shame an auctioneer. She belts out direction and helpful guidance at an alarming clip which, at first, seems so at odds with the uber-tropical atmosphere. But, Amy Lane is monitoring everyone with an eagle eye and a finely balanced sense of humor. Sadly, for me, I am so focused on just breathing and trying to bend my body in oh so unfamiliar ways, that I find myself watching other classmates to see what it is I'm supposed to be doing. I'm just trying to keep up here.

As my body swoops and stretches, bends and creaks, I find that I only feel like blacking out every now and then. My lightheadedness comes and goes. Man, it's hot. The trick is to stay under control keeping your breathing even and slow and not give in to open-mouthed gulps of air which, let me tell you, can be very tempting. Amy Lane says it's far better to suppress this urge for open-mouthed breathing lest your body lunge into a panicked fight or flight mode. Comforting. And, I find that whatever reptilian habits I may have inadvertently developed over the years are briskly out the window. Gone. I am shvitzing as I never have in my life. Even my ankles are sweating. When I reach down to grab them in one pose, they simply slide off my already liquified hands. Sweat is flying off me. My shirt, once a light gray when I entered this place, is now almost black and drenched. I reach for my water bottles and gulp what I can without losing the rhythm of the program.

When the clock strikes twelve – the moment when the 90 minute session is reportedly over – I suppress my almost overwhelming drive to urgently advise Amy Lane that she can stop now. But, I swallow that urge and melt into shavasana or corpse pose where you can lie still on the floor giving full surrender to your exhaustion. Amy Lane passes out chilled washcloths which, when resting on one's forehead and eyes, provide a sort of outsized pleasure that, in that moment, is pretty much what you want in life above all else.

I have survived! I am not dead; I did not black out. I am not nauseous. True, I am wondering what the quickest route to the North Pole might be, but I am more than relieved; I am energized by my modest success.

I will return! Isn't that what reptiles do?

THURSDAY, MAY 23, 2013

A Brush With Reality

Much to the disdain, dismay, and even disgust of my family and some friends, I have been a devotee of certain reality TV programming for the last decade or so. The eye rolling and tongues in cheek of these loved ones is so exaggerated at times in reaction to this foible of mine that, I fear, could lead them to permanent disfigurement. Yes, truth be told, I have been a huge fan of Survivor, the Amazing Race, American Idol, Top Chef, and others for years. And, yes, I have often been forced into seclusion to give full vent to my fandom or risk expulsion from the family Golland/Matheson, but I have done this without flinching, without complaint. Sacrifices are sometimes necessary. After all, I have even applied and auditioned for more than one of these shows. My devotion is beyond reproach. But, let me be quick to say that I am, I believe, selective in my viewing choices. Kim Kardashian and her ilk will never cross my TV screen, nor will the unhappy housewives of Beverly Hills, Atlanta, or Mongolia, for that matter. I will not indulge former football players or over the hill entertainers as they prance across the stage as dancing "stars."

But, watching these reality programs on TV and being there in person to bear witness are two different things, however. Which is why I lunged at the chance to attend a screening of The X-Factor, the johnny-come-lately to the singing competition universe, courtesy of erstwhile American Idol judge – Mr. Simon Cowell. I saw this as a way to immerse myself in the experience, to have my own brush with reality, you might say.

The lines were long at the North Charleston Coliseum. While I got there an hour before they recommended, the place was already crawling with sun-dressed young ladies replete with fancy sandals and the ubiquitously displayed cell phones, sometimes in the company of an occasional adult chaperone. The male species was represented too, but with only a slight sprinkling throughout the lines. A very slight sprinkling. Hazarding a guess, I would say the median age of attendees was maybe 16. Folks of my ancient ilk were few and far between. Let me just say that there weren't a whole lot of folks who could lay claim to being born in the first half of the last century.

After standing outside the arena for more than an hour, we were blessedly ushered into the arena away from the searing sun and the avalanche of Facebook traffic, where I took my seat seven rows back from the stage, about 15 feet from where the inestimable Mr. Cowell would be seated along side his fellow judges. The host of the event – a very able and amiable fellow named Frank – guided us through the pre-program do's and don'ts, encouraging us to boo what the judges say, but not to boo the contestants who were, after all, already exposing themselves to public ridicule to millions of viewers. Frank also directed us in a walk-through of how we should execute our standing ovations, which, he enthusiastically intoned, would be done in waves depending on one's birth date. Who knew? We were also advised never to stare into the camera and warned us that cameras were everywhere – that nothing would go unnoticed. A nice lady named Amy – one of the crew – came out to test the sound system while simultaneously getting the crowd warmed up through a rousing rendition of "Rolling On The River." Her skills were passable, but would never pass muster with these judges were she a contestant, but you had to give her props for her energy and enthusiasm.

The tension mounted. When would the judges appear? The pre-pubescent teens would scream whenever they sensed the judges' appearance, and, through the cacophony they created, they could get the entire audience to swivel their necks at all manner of awkward angles – much like the Linda Blair character in "The Exorcist" – whenever they thought the moment of their arrival was at hand. And, finally, an hour after being seated, they did arrive amidst all the fanfare normally reserved for national heroes or epic pop icons. In they walked to swirling lights and deafening screeches: Demi Lovato and new judges, Kelly Rowland and Paulina Rubio (apparently a mega Latina star). But, wait. No Simon? No, no Simon. Where was he? Demi announced to the crowd that Simon was "running late" and would arrive....uh...."soon." In the meantime the three "awesome" ladies, as Demi humbly described the lady judges, would carry on. And, so they did. For an hour, performer after performer marched on to the stage trying to look their perky best and sound the most professional they have ever sounded. Some had success, some did not. Country singers, hip hop artists, church singers, groups, you name it. Judges got booed, contestants did not. One husband and wife team performed, and it was clear to the judges that the husband had a terrific voice while his spouse most definitely did not. When the husband was asked whether he would consider going on as a solo act, he said "in a heartbeat" whereupon the judges passed him on to the next round. I'm thinking, my oh my, that should make for an interesting, if awkward, ride home for the two of them. One lady, a professed hip hop artist, said she was 38 years old, but I wasn't buying it. Notwithstanding her metallic mini-skirt and stiletto heels, she was 50 as sure as the sun sets in the west. She didn't get the judges best wishes although the crowd tried its best to convince them otherwise to send her on as they chanted her key lyrics and stomped their feet to no avail. As was true for all the contestants, as they sang, you could watch the judges for their attempts at seeking a conspiratorial consensus off camera. Their smiles or frowns, their nodding heads and winks spoke volumes as they tried to minimize their own embarrassment at appearing fragmented and without support.

With an hour left, Simon Cowell entered the fray appearing in his traditional white t-shirt. He blamed his late arrival on Demi's erroneous advice that the afternoon session began at 4 rather than 3 hours earlier. Right. Simon's apparently been eating way too well and seriously needs to consider upping his shirt size which, given his outsized ego, may be hard to do. But, I must say, his one line zingers to the contestants were vintage stuff, and he very quickly asserted his dominance over the panel.

After almost four hours in our seats, Simon announced the afternoon session was over. A break would be taken and the evening session would begin. I would not be there for that. I couldn't wait to get home, pour myself a nice helping of rum and put my feet up. I had no idea this day would prove to be so taxing.

The X-Factor season on TV is coming this Fall. Plenty of time to perfect my couch potato credentials.

And....so much for reality.

Music To My Ears

Bob Marley once said, "One good thing about music, when it hits you, you feel no pain." The man knew something. Is there anything that soothes without physically touching like the tones, rhythms, and lyrics of music? Is there anything that transports you a zillion miles from wherever you are and yet, at the same time, paradoxically, drives you to live in the moment? I readily acknowledge that arguments can be made for other artistic expressions whether it's poetry, a movie or even a breathtaking work on canvas. All of these have the potential to strike us in a way, at both an emotional and even visceral level, that is disarming, revealing about our inner natures, and a source of wonderment. But, music – at least for me – is a cut above other art forms in its ability to move, to turn on the emotional faucets. It stands alone. Many have said over the centuries that this is man's greatest gift – the ability to move one's soul through a progression of notes that, in the abstract, are just random sounds that, when laced together in a certain order, create the ability to have one experience the deepest joy or sorrow, energy, euphoria, reverie, or love.

And, so it is with me. As with most folks, my yardstick for musical magic is a fluid one. What drove me to run five miles once or to dance with unabashed abandon years ago doesn't necessarily do that for me today. I'm not sure why. Have I tired of the old classics; have I heard them too many times? Greatness is greatness, right? Whatever the reason, it is an unending joy that there is seemingly always something new to transport us, to lift us to new heights, to make us want to get out of our chairs and just move. I say these things knowing that what strikes a responsive chord in me is likely musical gibberish to others. Or worse. Just like tastes in food, clothing, friends, or soul mates, we all march to our own drummers that often bear simply no resemblance to another's tastes in the same things.

Take "Red Hands" by Walk Off The Earth, for example. (http://www.youtube.com/watch?v=1bt-FHaFVH8). Here's a tune that no doubt goes unnoticed by many barely raising an audible ripple to the casual listener. Or, just as likely, the song falls on almost deaf ears and disappears as a thousand other forgettable songs do. But, for me, I hear the first few bars and my head is already nodding, my shoulders almost imperceptibly start moving up and down, my fingers unconsciously tapping. If I'm running, "Red Hands" makes me feel like my feet are moving perfectly in time with the music. My feet are transformed into metronomes. I feel I am moving forward effortlessly. Whatever fatigue I might have been experiencing vanishes. For three minutes plus I am transported, flowing with the music forgetting where I am. If I'm cooking, "Red Hands" unconsciously leads me to wave, baton-like, whatever spatula, knife, or tongs I may be wielding in those moments as if I'm leading a phantom musical ensemble or hitting those drums with a fervor that anticipates every beat. And, whether I'm running or cooking, I'm glad I'm standing because I could not be sitting down for this one. No way.

In a much deeper way, I am seriously awestruck by Per Byhring's "Mr. Wednesday." (https://soundcloud.com/perbyhring/mr-wednesday). Perhaps like no other piece of music in my memory, "Mr. Wednesday" takes over my soul. Completely. I'm not sure where it takes me, but I know it's not where I am. It is evocative; it is uplifting; it allows me to think back in time over my life and ahead to wherever it is I might be going. It starts slowly, softly, hypnotically. But, at the two minute mark, it opens up with brassy pronouncements and, if you close your eyes, it does not take great imagination to see the gates of heaven or to imagine an epic moment in one's life filled with all that is important. Indeed, I often say to myself that when I listen to "Mr. Wednesday" I feel something important is happening. For others to whom I have introduced "Mr. Wednesday," this piece of music often strikes them as slow, repetitive, even boring. I get that. I'm okay with that. Maybe I would react to their own choices in similar fashion; that's not important. And, I also feel that, although it would be interesting to me, I believe it is irrelevant what Mr. Byhring had in mind when he wrote this piece. I know what I'm getting from it, and that's plenty.

And, for crying out loud, if you listen to these musical moments, turn up the volume!

A Close Call; Way Too Close

We hear it all the time: how would you really react in a moment of crisis? Would you react sensibly or would you do things that you would heartily scoff at in a calmer, more deliberative moment? Are you really prepared to act in a rational, constructive manner when all your instincts are flailing around in total chaos? I remember a few years ago watching in abject horror as Mojo dove into the ocean to confront a shark as the saner dogs and people scampered in the opposite direction. As Mojo mounted the shark and rode on the back astride the dorsal fin, I found myself marching into the water armed with my "chuckit," the device I use to hurl tennis balls far out into the ocean for Mojo to retrieve. In that moment of crisis, I foolheartedly concluded the chuckit was the ultimate anti-shark weapon and went into the surf to do battle. Stupid, ill-conceived, not helpful. Fortunately, the shark was as freaked out as I was and made haste to return to deeper waters leaving Mojo behind wondering where his ride went.

But, Saturday morning presented a different sort of events. For a couple of weeks, Lily and I had been hearing odd, loud puffing noises coming from the kitchen. For some totally inexplicable reason, we both attributed these noises to a new device we had which makes club soda with the assistance of a bottle of compressed gas. These air gun-like sounds were surely emanating from this new fangled kitchen gizmo. On a couple of occasions, we even went so far as to take the device outside thinking that if it were to explode at least it would be outside where the harm would be less traumatizing. Sadly, we were mistaken, and hugely so. The club soda device had been improperly accused and was blameless. At ten past seven, when even Mojo is still asleep, the loud puffing noise re-appeared, but this time in earnest. It awakened me with a start. Why? Because the now more urgent puffing actually blew open our bedroom door! In a stupor, I went to the door thinking that maybe it was our guest, young 6 year old Marley – our niece – visiting for a week from Florida. Maybe Marley had gotten up early and had opened our door just to see if we were awake yet. I went out of the room and, thinking I was looking for Marley, headed to the kitchen. There, everything changed. As I stumbled into the kitchen, still half asleep, the smell of gas was overpowering, and it was not the kind that emanates from a club soda making machine. It was the gas cooktop. How did I know? Even in my stupor I could see that the cabinet doors below the cooktop had been blown open and there, underneath, were large blue flames shooting out left and right from the junction box like some kind of demonized, blue-haired Medusa.

What to do? They say that the mind sharpens in its most trying moments. I'm not so sure. Coming out of my stupor at warp speed, my first instinct was to go for the fire extinguisher which, naturally, was buried somewhere in one of our kitchen closets. Hadn't seen it in years let alone have any notion of how to operate it. As I turned toward the closet, seemingly a thousand micro-thoughts crossed my brain: do I immediately awaken everyone in the house and get them out; do I put in a quick emergency call to the fire department; do I just try to blow out the arching flames; do I try to smother the flames; do I have time to read the fire extinguisher instructions should I find the damn device; how many seconds or minutes did we have until the house exploded; do I scream?

Somewhere in the midst of this frenetic exercise in weighing my options, my mind screamed at me, "turn the gas off, stupid"!! Of course, kill the problem at the source. The source in this case is a propane tank that sits outside our house, seemingly miles away in those frozen seconds that I thought could spell the difference between life and death. Clothed in nothing more than my underwear, I sprinted for the door, threw it open, descended the steps and ran around to the side of the house to the tank. I opened its lid and – not having much experience with this mechanism either – looked quizzically and impatiently at the various knobs on top in urgent search of the main shut off valve. I figured which one it should be, turned it viciously, and then spun around to make my way back into the kitchen. Bursting through the door again, I saw instantly that the flames were still having their way, snaking their way around the kitchen cabinet beneath the cooktop. Why, I thought. Had I turned the wrong valve? Do I run out there again? Do I hunt for the fire extinguisher this time?

Don't ask me why, but I decided the better course was for me to dive my head into the endangered, flame-filled cabinet and attempt to blow the flames out. Maybe the flames were still thriving solely on whatever remnants of gas remained in the lines and could be subdued as one might blow out a match. A very large match. I dropped to my knees, stuck my head into the inferno and started blowing. Only later did I reflect on this strategy and, as I have in the past, said to myself: stupid, ill conceived, not helpful. Certainly, this would have been the case had the system decided to explode in my face in that moment, but, then again, I wouldn't have been around to hear the scorn heaped upon me for making such a misguided judgment. Once again, we never know how we're going to react in those moments of crisis. One tries to be level headed, but being level headed is often a function of dispassionate analysis – a luxury, methinks, at times.

As luck would have it, my efforts at a manual solution worked. I got the flames to stop. I stared at the junction box certain it would ignite again. I waited. And, blessedly, nothing followed. Just the sounds of my gasping for breath, something I believe I had neglected to do in the previous minutes. At this point, I returned to the bedroom where a still sleepy Lily listened in horror to my little drama. Marley, in the next bedroom was wonderfully oblivious to all that had transpired. Mojo wondered what the hold up was in heading for the beach. I walked to the beach with Mojo still shaken, still wondering what might have happened. I second guessed almost everything I did.

Upon our return from the beach, I found the fire extinguisher, found a readily accessible place for it, and read its instructions. Now, that's something smart, well conceived, and helpful.

A Two-Wheeled Dream

Back in the days when I could legitimately say I was young – somewhere this side of the Mesozoic era – my "Leave it to Beaver" neighborhood rejoiced with the sounds of kids. There were many in the streets around me, and the shouts and taunts and laughter emanating from us all provided a steady soundtrack to our lives. Oftentimes, it was street games of various sorts that would raise the ambient decibel levels, but just as frequently it would be the incessant chatter one would hear as groups of kids on bikes would streak through the neighborhood. Kids would be on their way to other kids' houses to play, or perhaps be riding to pick-up baseball or football games, or maybe just a casual sortie down to our local store to pick up a pack of baseball cards or, perhaps, a candy bar. But, my participation in these events was limited. I did not own a bike.

I wanted one, of course. It would have provided me with a level of social acceptance which I dearly would have loved. It would have enabled me to become one of the group and to participate first hand rather than as just a drop-in on those sporadic occasions when I would walk to ball fields or the store and catch up with the others. The reason I did not own a bike was not a mystery to me, but it was no more satisfying knowing the reason. My mother made it known to me that I would never own a bike because of the sadness she still harbored from a point in her life long past. In her youth, her younger brother had been killed in a cycling accident, and, understandably, that loss left an indelible mark on her – one that would give life decades later to an indomitable fear of having a son who would be out on the streets facing, in her mind, constant mortal risks. My mom was upfront about all this. She fully conceded that her fears were irrational and overblown by the power of memory and time. But, the bottom line was no bike for me. End of discussion.

My best friends, Leah and Greg, both had bikes. They knew of my desires and encouraged me to try riding their bikes on the street in front of our houses. But, my efforts were hopeless. Once I was finally able to get rolling, I had no clue how to steer, let alone stop before I faced an inopportune obstacle like a tree, a street curb, or a fire hydrant. I still recall rolling down the gentle slope of Ogden Avenue, gaining speed, and having no idea how my ride might finish. As if in surrender, I would take my feet off the pedals and let the bike go where it wanted. It controlled matters, not me. I felt equal pangs of exhilaration and terror. My screams, I'm sure, could be easily identified with either emotion. Most frequently, my brief rolling adventures would end with me involuntarily grabbing the trunk of a tree I had just unceremoniously crashed into, or would end with me laying prone on a neighbor's front lawn after a curb had insidiously intersected my path and thrown me clear of my ride. My mother knew none of this.

We now flash forward several decades. I have had an absolutely wonderful life but it has been virtually bike-free. I am now Medicare eligible and am ready to take on life's new challenge: to successfully ride a bike. That is to say, to complete a ride without serious injury or worse. Yes, I have had a few misshapen adventures with bikes over the years, none of them ending well. I have a clear memory of the bruises and indignities that have served only to reinforce my logical side that I should consider other pursuits, ones less grounded in the needs for balance and sharp reflexes.

But, I have a specific reason to turn my attention to this decades-old mission of mine. We have a trip planned to Tuscany this summer and our stay will be in Lucca, a fabulously charming old walled city. Atop the walls is a park, complete with greenery, folks strolling with young children, and animated bocce games. Best of all, you can rent bikes and circumnavigate the city from above taking in all the wonderful sights of the park and the city below. But, as I sit here now, I am seriously ill-equipped to even think about doing this aboard a bike lest I have an unscheduled run-in with a bocce participant or, perhaps, a turret.

For this reason, I have acquired a bike. It's a basic beach cruiser – no gears or other paraphernalia that might mistake it for serious hard-charging wheeled pursuits. But, it is a bike and, as is true for all bikes, it must be ridden with balance and without the wobbling and tentative decision-making that is my current signature for this activity. I bought a helmet. Smart. Now that I have learned which end of the helmet faces which part of my skull, I feel oddly protected. Fortunately, our community is relatively deserted this time of year which means I can wobble my way down neighborhood streets without an ever present fear that I might have to dodge oncoming car traffic or innocent civilian pedestrians. With each episode out on the streets, I constantly remind myself of the helpful advice given to me by Lily and others: look up, don't look down at the wheels, and when attempting to turn, lean into the turn with my body, not a turn of the front wheel. Sounds easy, right? In the two days that I have ventured out to ply my new craft, I have only crashed twice. One incident was entirely my fault, but the other was clearly due to a tree that rudely got way too close to me.

On to Tuscany, I say. Just please do me a favor and don't alert my insurance carrier. I'd appreciate it.

Defending Mojo -- A Short Story

Last night, as I always do, I let Mojo out to do his business before we all retire for the night. It was pitch black dark out there. As Mojo -- who, as you know, is also pitch black dark -- got to the bottom of the steps he took off like a rocket in pursuit of some moving object. I suspected a deer. Although I worry about his dashing out into a dark street and go unseen by passing motorists, I knew he would return -- at some point. And, sure enough he did, about ten minutes later. Seemed innocent enough. He came in to the house without any indication that anything other than an innocent chase had occurred. He slept well.

This morning, as we were about to head to the beach, I got to the bottom of the steps from our deck, and there at the bottom was a dead squirrel. I looked at Mojo who just looked back at me with a clueless, vacant stare. As if he were suggesting he knew nothing about this incident. Could he have done this? Dare I consider the possibility that this loving dog, this tail wagging, lighthearted creature could have committed cold blooded murder? I tried to banish the thought. Maybe the squirrel had fallen to the ground from the bird feeder we had attached to our living room window which I knew from first hand observation was a very popular place for the local squirrel population to hang out. Maybe this one had lost his footing and landed awkwardly killing him instantly. Maybe, in a fit of piggishness, the squirrel had gorged himself to extreme at the bird feeder buffet and had died from over consumption. Or, was there another, darker, explanation?

We walked to the beach, Mojo seemingly without a care in the world peeing to his heart's content, pulling me onward knowing where we were going. But, in my head, I kept going back to the scene we had just left wondering, wondering. There were no witnesses to this incident. Evidence was merely circumstantial. There were other plausible explanations. No jury could convict him, could it?

I hesitated, but upon our return home, I decided to bag up the squirrel and toss him in the garbage. But, I agonized. Was I covering up a crime? Was I tampering with state's evidence? Was I now an accessory?! I decided not to tell Lily. Some things are left better unsaid.

But, I am left to wonder.

Paris is.......

They call it the City of Light. Whether you subscribe to the theory that it was named so because it was the epicenter of learning during the Age of Enlightenment, or because it filled the night sky with light, is immaterial. Both have meaning; both tell us something about the character of this place. For me, there is another meaning of "light" for this wondrous place: it has a levity to it, a lightness of being, a certain buoyancy to it. I'm sure there is a certain amount of self-induced imagery playing with me here, but it is hard to deny the beauty, the elegance, the energy, and the gaiety of Paris. It is hard to know where to begin.

Paris is Sundays at the Jardin du Luxembourg where the feast for your eyes includes glimpses of a variety of exercise classes like tai chi or kick boxing, people picnicking on the grass, impossibly cute kids using long sticks to push their sailboats around the central man made pond. Or, folks just settling back in the many chairs and benches that dot the scene taking in the sun after a long, chilly winter.

Paris is the hot chocolate at Angelina. To be fair, it is almost an insult to call it that because the label of hot chocolate conjures up images all of which are woefully inadequate to describe what it is that is served there. It is far better to think of it as molten chocolate – a rich, thick, hot, sweet, aromatic concoction that explodes with chocolateness as you let it swirl in your mouth now replete with a dollop of fresh whipped cream. They call it Le Chocolat Chaud d'Africain. I call it heaven.

Paris is Rue Mouffetarde, or, as some smilingly call it, The Mouff. It is a street that dates back to Roman times as the beginnings of the pathway back to Rome from Lutecia, as Paris was called then. It is a narrow street that wends its way down a gentle slope from La Place de la Contrescarpe to the Square Saint Medard at the bottom. In between is a narrow street often blocked off to car traffic that is lined with open markets, cafes and small shops. On weekends, it must appear from a height as we view an ant colony: a narrow path ablaze with chaotic pedestrian traffic that darts from market to market, shopping bags overflowing with baguettes, cheese, produce and wine. It was also the location of the apartment we rented, a small but amazingly charming place in a 400 year old building overlooking the Mouff. A pied a terre in the truest sense of that phrase.

Paris is Saint Sulpice, the city's second largest church where on Sundays one is treated to an organ recital that fills the chambers of that edifice with music so full and so rich it seems to take on its own shape, its own visceral identity. Close your eyes and swim in it.

Paris is fashion. The women in their tight jeans, tall boots, Hollywood-esque sunglasses, and scarves perfectly looped and knotted. And the men? Tight jeans, pointed shoes, Hollywood-esque sunglasses and scarves perfectly looped and knotted. I'm telling you, if you're looking for a wise investment, think scarf industry. Don't say I didn't tell you.

Paris is where Lily's heart lies.

Paris is the Ile de la Cite and Ile St. Louis, the beating heart of this city. It is where it all began here more than 2,000 years ago. One is dominated by Notre Dame, allegedly visited by more than 14 million persons each year. It is grand; it is imposing; and it has a wonderful park behind it where one can pass the time reading, people watching, listening to street musicians, or just leaning back and taking in the periodic chimes from the towers. The other is a far quieter universe marked by narrow streets, beautiful residences, epically good ice cream, and one of our favorite restaurants, La Reine Blanche.

Paris is, of course, the Eiffel Tower. As touristy a spot as it is, it is nevertheless as awe inspiring now up close as it was when first erected a hundred and twenty-five years ago. It stretches up over a thousand feet and, with the vast clearances around it, it stands alone eagerly accepting its role as an icon of the city. As we dined at a nearby bistro, we were entertained by the tower as it came to life with thousands of blinking lights that seemed to fill the night sky with a silent fireworks display. The blinkies, as our friend Wayne calls it.

Paris is baguettes, croissants, cheese, wine, creme brulee, mussels, croque monsieur, salmon terrines, truffles, falafel, escargot, onion soup, steak tartare, cassoulet, crepes, and soufflés.

Paris is Blue Bike Tours, which, as the name implies, takes you around the city on two wheels. Having started riding a bike barely five weeks earlier, I embraced (potentially foolishly) the chance to take on the craziness of this city when my only prior experience was on the deserted streets of the Isle of Palms. It was as if I subliminally thought that when you're on vacation, nothing counts – not the calories, nor the possibility of getting steamrolled by a Citroen at a particularly busy intersection. But, on we went on a four hour journey through the Latin Quarter, Le Marais and delightful points in between. All seen before, but never quite this way. As luck would have it (and I can't emphasize that enough), my ride was mostly error-free, crashing only once. In between, however, it was hard to avoid the conclusion that Parisian motorists and pedestrians alike have a very firm grip on who has the right of way, and it was almost never me.

Paris is the Place des Vosges, as elegant and picturesque a town square as ever was. As you scan the early 15th century architecture, once home to Victor Hugo and Cardinal Richelieu, it is impossible not to want to stop and just gaze. Maybe sit on the grass nibbling on your falafel letting it all seep in. Slowly.

In Woody Allen's "Midnight in Paris," the Owen Wilson character, Gil, says it all.....

You know, I sometimes think, how is anyone ever gonna come up with a book, or a painting, or a symphony, or a sculpture that can compete with a great city. You can't. Because you look around and every street, every boulevard, is its own special art form and when you think that in the cold, violent, meaningless universe that Paris exists, these lights. I mean come on, there's nothing happening on Jupiter or Neptune, but from way out in space you can see these lights, the cafés, people drinking and singing. For all we know, Paris is the hottest spot in the universe.

Well said, Gil. Well said.

Cuba Si!

They say it lies just 90 miles away. And, by most conventional measures, this appears to be the case. But, for all its geographic proximity, Cuba might just as well be on the far side of the planet. It is a land of startling contrasts, of head scratching inconsistencies, and a land of joy and optimism amidst a sea of poverty and disintegration. It is sometimes so elusive to figure it all out, to make sense of it. As one Cuban economist would tell us, "If you think you understand Cuba, you're wrong. If you are confused, you get it."

In my life, Cuba resonates in a way that few countries do. We have, after all, a history. For me, Cuba conjures up the Cuban missile crisis in 1962. That was a time when in my heart of hearts I felt life as we knew it was about to disappear. I recall vividly the nervousness, indeed panic, that was creeping through me as I watched the accounts of the impending head to head confrontation between the Soviets and the U.S. Navy barely more than a stone's throw from our coastline. There were missiles there; the kind that could in a flash arch upward across the Florida Straits to destroy all life in my country and, specifically, in my neighborhood in White Plains, New York. In school, we regularly practiced our "duck and cover" drills as if our flimsy wooden desks would miraculously protect us from radioactive fallout. But, I remember as well an earlier time when my parents visited Havana and stayed at the legendary Hotel Nacional, a place also frequented by mafia royalty, Frank Sinatra, and Mickey Mantle. I have some recollection of their stories of that stay which sounded so glamorous, so cool, so elegant.

So, when I got a call from my nephew, Peter, many months ago telling me of his plans to travel there, inviting me to come along, and to do so with a group as legendary as National Geographic, I didn't see an option other than to say yes, I will join you. It is true that the rum I had been drinking that evening helped spur the mood, but this was, in my eyes, the chance of a lifetime to bring these memories of mine to life – to look behind the veil of secrecy that has shrouded this place in mystery for more than a half century, at least to Americans.

What followed was, in my personal experience, epic. I would go to a Cuban baseball game. I would join on stage a choral group to sing with them. I would sit in the engineer's seat of a 109 year old locomotive as we steamed through a sugar plantation. I would play the horse jaw with a Cuban band. I would drink freshly squeezed sugar cane. I would dance with a 6 year old girl and a 70 year old woman. I would ride in a '51 Lincoln and a '54 Dodge convertible. I would be moved to tears by the performances of young adults dancing to programs they had choreographed. I would enjoy endless conversations with artists and locals of all stripes. I would visit a cigar factory and lean closely over the desk of a worker there and watch, mesmerized, by his skill in rolling cigar after perfect cigar. I would have a chance at humanitarian acts that were unanticipated just moments earlier. As a group, we would interact with artists, musicians, historians, architects, sociologists, economists, journalists, religious figures, and, yes, a horse whisperer. And, all this just scratches the surface.

Havana is a prime example of the Cuban puzzle. Old Havana is gorgeous. The grandeur of Spanish colonial architecture is proudly on display from the various plazas to the beautiful tree-lined Paseo de Prado to the Malecon, a walkway that follows the sea wall for five miles along the waterfront. The beautiful archways, multi-colored buildings, the statuary, and high energy that you find here convey a rich heritage that takes little imagination to see. Against this backdrop of picture perfect buildings, toss in a dollop of the armada of brightly colored vintage cars from the '50s, many looking like they just came off the assembly line. And, just to add spice to the mix, picture neighborhoods where there is music literally every block whether from a live band, street musicians, or a radio blaring from somewhere. Even Disney could not replicate a scene like this.

And yet, peel away this veneer and stray a couple of blocks off the touristed beaten paths, and a different story is told. Here, the buildings are dark with decay. Roofs and walls are crumbling; colors are absent. The streets are quieter. At the risk of hyperbole, there are moments when you think you are looking at a post-apocalyptic world shunned by civilization for way too long. We are told that 3.1 buildings collapse every day in Havana and, as wild a statistic as that is, it is not at all difficult to believe.

But then, just as you want to conclude that Old Havana is just a ruse propped up by the government to fool tourists, you come across a community action project in which artists, sculptors and musicians devote half of their earnings to the effort to reclaim their neighborhood from ruin. Buildings are being refurbished; streets are cleaned; art spreads out along the walls of the community. It is beautiful and it is moving. It is here that I meet Nivia, an attractive artist who captures the hope and drive of so many here. Her paintings come alive with brilliant colors and whimsical themes. I find myself buying one of her works: a depiction of tall, multi-colored buildings swaying against a moonlit evening sky as if they are made of jello, smiling. Nivia tells me they are the buildings of Havana doing the salsa. How can you not smile at this? I tell her I want this painting because this is the picture I want to take home with me as the essence of my experience here.

Cubans love their baseball. They are passionate about it. We are fortunate to be in town during the playoff season. Five of us rush off to catch a game that features Industriales, the local favorites. As we approach the stadium, the sounds emanating from within are already loud, but that only serves as a warning of what is to follow. We take our seats down the right field line and take it all in. The noise is deafening, painfully so at times. There are more horns blaring from the fans here than in a Times Square traffic jam. And, it doesn't stop. Ever. Along the walls of the stadium where in the U.S. you are apt to find billboards trumpeting all manner of commercial products, there are only signs proclaiming "dignity," "strength," and "freedom." There is no huge screen in centerfield showing replays or readings of pitch speed. Only the bare story told through inning by inning scoring and the totals of runs, hits and errors. Nothing fancy here, just baseball in its purest form. It's a beautiful thing to watch. And, the ride home? A '51 Lincoln, of course.

Cubans love their music. Schools abound from coast to coast that encourage young musicians to hone their craft, whether it's the piano, the flute, the guitar or the violin. The same for dancers, artists and sculptors. We were treated to a show of this on several occasions. At one school, young adult dancers moved to the strains of soulful music and told stories of longing and despair. Beautiful and pure. A young female violinist, who was just inches from my chair, made her instrument into a most personal extension of her emotions as she stunned us with her incredible talent. At another site, we were entertained by a show of youngsters from about five years of age to maybe fourteen who pranced about the stage with energy, talent, and good humor that reflected childhood honesty at its best. At the conclusion of the show, the kids filled the aisles and pulled members of the audience from their seats to dance with them. One young girl squeezed through our long row to the middle where I was seated. She grabbed my arm and pulled me along to the aisle where we could dance with the others.

And, in Cienfuegos, we were treated to a recital by a choral group, the Cantores de Cienfuegos, a mix of nine males and nine females who sing world-wide an intoxicating mix of spirituals, baroque and classical music, and even American folk classics. The room we gathered in was sparse with precious little to absorb the sound. When the group marched in and started singing it was like an explosion, a most achingly beautiful explosion. The room literally filled with their amazing voices. It was so overpowering and exquisite, that you could just stare and feel their music literally surging through you. After a few numbers, Honey, the group's leader, asked our group if any of us would like to join them up front and join in their singing. Without giving it a moment's thought, I raised my hand. Let me be clear here: I do not sing. To my recollection, I have not really sung more than a couple of notes since the fourth grade. And yet, in that moment, it seemed instinctively like such a magical thing to do. So, up I sprang, took my position with the guys, was briefly tutored in the lyrics I needed to know, and....started singing. It was magical. I felt connected. A moment I likely will never forget.

I truly did not know what to expect from the Cuban people. Given the American embargo of the past half century, the rabid mistrust between our two governments, and the economic fallout that has been extreme at times, I thought we might be met with anger, hostility, or, at a minimum, skepticism. I could not have been more wrong. Time after time after time, we were greeted with surprise, enthusiasm and curiosity. Whether it was the lady selling me a t-shirt, or a taxi driver, or the guy behind the desk at the rum museum, or total strangers who would just say hello, the interaction was incredibly heartwarming. Take Erwin, for example. Here's a guy who was sitting in the shade near a park, and, as we exchanged glances, he smiled and said hello to Peter and me. When he learned we were from the U.S., he said, "Really? That's amazing! How did you get here? This is wonderful!" Or, the guy at the rum museum who, learning of our origins, simply leaned back, eyes wide open, and softly said, "Oh wow." Or, the lady who sold me a t-shirt who stood up, came around the counter, and held my arm while telling me about her family in Hialeah.

And then there was Juan. I met Juan while strolling down the Paseo de Prado one morning. Like many Cuban taxi drivers, he called out to me inquiring whether I needed his services. I declined, but we started talking anyway. In the span of a few minutes -- he with his broken English, me with my even more limited Spanish -- we were trading stories about our families, our lives. He showed me pictures of his young children. After a few minutes, he looked at me and asked whether I might help him buy some milk for his family. I told him I would. We embarked on a search strolling through neighborhoods well off the tourist grid. One store, then another, then another. No milk. At last we found a store that had the large bags of dehydrated milk Juan was looking for. He sighed, looked at me, and asked if it would be okay to purchase four bags. I told him yes. We made the purchase and Juan's lips started trembling. Tears came into his eyes. He told me that these bags would provide him and his family with a two month supply of milk. He threw his arms around me and gave me a huge bear hug, and told me he could never have afforded to do this on his own. I felt like a million dollars.

On the last day of our journey, we had lunch at the Hotel Nacional, the place where my folks had stayed more than half a century earlier, just prior to the revolution. As time was winding down on a miraculous trip, I strolled the grounds of the hotel that overlooked the water. At a far corner of the property are tunnels built during the missile crisis fifty-two years ago. As I descended down the steps, I found myself alone with the fellow who monitored this parcel of underground terrain. Eduardo, as I soon learned. We nodded to each other. As he started showing me the charts on the wall that depicted the Soviet missiles Cuba had at the time and how their range would impact the U.S., he drew me closer and locked the doors behind us. He beckoned me to follow him deeper into the tunnels. His English was passable, again better than whatever Spanish I could muster. He pointed out the placements for the artillery that once were there, the uniforms the soldiers wore, and where the ammunition was stored. When we re-surfaced to our starting point, I explained to him the impact that crisis had on me back then and, in particular, the terror I felt as nuclear war seemed far more than just a hypothetical quandary. I explained our "duck and cover" drills, and the non-stop coverage of the crisis on American television. He smiled and his look softened. Eduardo was about my age during that crisis, and he explained to me the terror and near panic he felt in those days for exactly the same reasons. He feared losing everything and everyone. We had a moment of true understanding. A shared memory. I told him how wonderful that here we were a half century later able to discuss this event together after so many years of mutual mistrust and hostility between our countries. When we shook hands and smiled, it was a knowing smile. We both got it.

Not a bad note to end on.

Dreaming Italian Style

When a dream is realized, it is a miraculous thing. It is uplifting in a way that few things are. In those giddy, almost spiritual, moments, all is right with the world. Happiness is all you know. Some dreams are large, others small, but when they become a reality size does not matter.

I had such a dream and it has been hibernating for eight years. Back then, almost a decade ago, we rented a villa outside Lucca – in my mind, the quintessential distillation of all that is Italian. It is beautiful, scenic, charming. Big enough to offer variety, small enough not to overwhelm. It is a walled city dating back to the Etruscans and was rolled into the Roman Empire more than two thousand years ago. At our last visit, Lily, Jesse, Alex and Laura rented bikes so they could tour Lucca and, in particular, bike the ancient walls of this city. With some sadness on my part, I was left behind. After all, I did not know how to ride a bike. Off they went and returned with smiles and stories that I so much wanted to be a part of. I dreamed of gliding along beside them sharing in their laughter and maybe having a few stories of my own to tell.

When plans were made last year to return to Lucca, I knew what I had to do. And it just wasn't learning how to say "where's the bathroom" in Italian, or boning up on the wines of the Chianti region. No, I needed to learn how to ride a bike. Being left out again was simply not an option.

With both a sense of accomplishment and a healthy dollop of happiness, my road to bike proficiency is now smooth, or mostly so. At

least now, having practiced for several months, I can reasonably expect not to be roadkill when I venture forth. I have my moments of
uncertainty but they are dwindling and I have developed the good
sense to generally anticipate potential trouble spots before they take
me down. But, for almost a week after our return to Lucca, while
we talked about renting bikes, nothing happened. Too many things,
wonderful things, got in the way. At the end of our first week, however, the trigger was pulled and we headed for town to do the walls.
Bob and Donna, Jim, Ivy and the kids, Maggie, and Lily and I found
our way to Poli Bike Rentals just behind the northern Santa Maria
portal to the city. We made our way up the ramp to the top of the
walls.....and we started peddling.

The area at the top of the walls in Lucca is not what you might
imagine. Rather than a narrow parapet where there is just enough
room for an archer to aim his arrows at a marauding enemy, there is
instead a relative vastness. The path is wide and paved and on either
side of the path is enough room for tables, benches, and greenery.
One could literally ride six abreast were it not for the competing
forces of cyclists coming the other way, dog walkers, baby strollers
and runners. The walls are a place to socialize; there were seemingly
endless combinations of folks – some young, some old – lolling in the
sunshine swapping stories, reading a book or just staring out at the
beauty below.

Making our way around the walls was not just invigorating, it was
euphoric. At least for me it was. To the left, you could look out over
the town peering down on the reddish orange terra cotta roofs, the
narrow bending streets, the rising towers, and the occasional piazzas.
To the right, looking out into the distance, you could see the verdant
mountains, the forests, the one-time moat that protected this place,
and the hint of car traffic beyond. Above it all, the fantastic cloud
formations breaking up the sun at seemingly just the right intervals.

I found myself saying "ciao" to folks on the path or at the nearby benches as if they were long-time neighbors. Often, especially among the older folks along the way, I would be met with the kind of blank stares normally reserved for seeing aliens from some far away place. In between "ciaos," I would indulge myself in singing aloud no doubt what appeared to be a strangely atonal chorus from "Funiculi Funicula," that iconic Neapolitan tune from the 19th century. I mean, what else do you sing when biking in Italy? Ok, so maybe I didn't compare favorably to Pavarotti.

Mid-way we stopped and glided down the sloping ramp so that Marley and Piper could ride the small, but oh so charming carousel. A perfect resting opportunity. But, soon enough we moved on. [If I may, a word about Piper here. Although it's possible I'm mistaken about this, at 18 months Piper appears to be the world's youngest stuntman. Fear is not a concept familiar to her. Nor is moderation. This is the same child who routinely closes herself into kitchen cabinets, would walk off a cliff without hesitation, and has been known to stand innocently in the kitchen nonchalantly chewing on a caterpillar. On the bike ride, Piper was firmly ensconced in a child's seat attached to the front of Jim's bike, facing forward. Her face was barely visible under a Star Wars-like helmet. As we moved forward along the walls, Piper would scream her excitement and make the clearest of gestures suggesting that we move faster. Shortly after her carousel ride, when back on the walls, Piper would grab her father's hands (which were tightly clutching the handlebars) and, as forcibly as she could, tried to pull Jim's hands clear of the bike. She could not have more eloquently said, "I got it, dad. I'll take it from here." Jim, in an effort that even one day Piper will be grateful for, resisted. I'm telling you, this little girl is extraordinary. Watch out for her.]

We continued on. Some of us circumnavigated the wall twice. This was an experience long in the anticipation and not one to be shortened. At the end when our bikes had been returned, and we settled in for a gelato and beer, I realized that the only part of my body that hurt was my face. At first, I wondered why. Then it hit me. This is what happens when you've been smiling unrelentingly from ear to ear.

Dreams can do that to you.

Vroooom!!

Ok. Let's be honest. You're out on the road. Alone. A country road: curvy, isolated, inviting. You're driving anything other than a 1966 Ford Falcon or a dump truck. You know, something that has some degree of performance creds, some potential. A smile creeps across your face. You say to yourself, "I wonder what this baby can do." You tap the accelerator, gently at first, but then – as you get caught up in the moment – a bit more vigorously until the trees are a blur and all you know are the road's white lines that are now your sole moral and survival compass. Your smile turns wicked, your eyes narrow, and you become someone you don't recognize except that you're too busy leaning into turns to realize this. Yes, yes, I know; we've all been there. Or, most of us have.

The quest for speed tempered only by the law and, yes, common sense is widespread, if not ubiquitous. It's the excitement, the challenge and perhaps even the danger that focuses the mind. And, it is most certainly a break from the normal – almost everyone's normal. For many, it begins in their youth with a roller coaster ride or even a mildly out of control skateboard, but the emotion is always the same. There's an intensity there borne of an element of uncertainty reinforced with the promise of sheer joy.

So, last year, when Lily and I were at a charity silent auction, I couldn't help but notice an offering by the BMW Performance Center, just upstate from us in Spartanburg, South Carolina. It offered a chance to drive the BMW model of your choosing through obstacle courses and speed sprints and wet track wipeouts that seemed, well, irresistible. I was not alone in having that spark, and it was through some auction sleight of hand strategy that made this opportunity mine. I couldn't wait. A couple of folks at the event, who had already experienced this, told me that it didn't matter how macho you thought you were. Once you got in a car with a professional driver there, they said, you'd be screaming like a little school girl.

Our opportunity came a few days ago. Sure, the BMW folks threw into the deal a tour of their amazing 5.6 million square foot robot-driven production facility, but the big prize was your time on the test track. Everyone knew that. And, while they said that the purpose of the exercise was to familiarize you with the performance capacity of your car, guests were there for the thrills. Everyone knew that.

We left the orientation area and were introduced to our cars. I had chosen a new X6 model, the one with a 4.4 liter engine producing 550 horsepower. MSRP: $93,000. I mean, why settle for less, right? It would be the only way I could ever get behind the wheel of one of these. This baby has acceleration attributes exceeded, I do believe, only by a Saturn rocket or possibly the legendary warp speed of the Enterprise. We broke off in to groups with a few of us lined up in our cars caravan-style. Our guide/instructor had each of our cars armed with walkie talkies from whence came barks of instructions as we lined up at the track for our first exercise – the obstacle course. One by one we entered the track, a safe distance apart, and, following explicit directions, hit the gas with much the same gusto as one might squash a large bug with one's foot. Game on!

The idea was to accelerate rapidly and forcefully and head into the tight turns offered in quick succession by the traffic cones lying ahead. Because of the dramatic acceleration, and the incredible demands on your reaction time as you dodged one set of cones and then another with contorted, body-jarring sharp turns, the effect was significant and immediate: exhilaration and giddiness. Although we were doing things behind the wheel that you would likely never attempt under any other circumstances, I felt oddly immune from danger. I think this is what the dictionary refers to as foolishness, or perhaps insanity. Notwithstanding the ocean of waivers we had to sign absolving BMW and their employees and their great, great grandchildren and succeeding generations from any liability regardless of their possible negligence, I was calm, focused and happy. Unfortunately, not everyone felt the same way. Within the first minute of riding shotgun, absorbing the rocket-borne body throws and white-knuckled grips, Lily had squealed and screamed enough to realize she was getting very nauseous. She simply had to get out of the car. That very second. In fairness to Lily, it is a vastly different experience being behind the wheel and riding shotgun when your car is lurching everywhere as if the car is suffering from violently spasmodic seizures. There is something about being "in control" behind the wheel – no matter how delusional that might be – that completely alters your perception of whether you're going to die in that instant or, conversely, have the time of your life.

On we went. One exercise had us accelerating rapidly to sixty miles per hour and then hitting the brakes as hard as you could. You know – an innocent lesson in braking distances. No pumping the brakes here; just a vicious slam of the foot down on the pedal. Despite the tight grip on the wheel, you could still feel your body announcing its intention to bolt through the front windshield, shoulder harnesses notwithstanding. Something about inertia, right? And then on to the "wet" track where, once again, warp speed was being recommended by the disembodied voice from the walkie talkie. Once launch speed was achieved you would aim your vehicle into very wet pavement and then hang on as your car did a series of 360 degree spinouts as it eventually came to a stop. This exercise had something to do with traction control, but, frankly, I wasn't paying any attention to that.

That would have required a level of attention my psyche, in that moment, was simply not willing to provide.

Lastly, there was the "off road" experience where, among other tasks, we were asked to have our cars follow along a steep, boulder-strewn path that would, at times, place our cars at what felt like a 45 degree angle with two wheels completely off the ground, spinning aimlessly. Again, as they say, not something you would try at home. But, here, it seemed more like an amusement park ride than something that threatened our well-being. After all, they kept telling us that if we followed their instructions, we were in no jeopardy. Hmmm, and if we weren't that compliant, then what?

When we returned home and were relating our experience to friends, the most frequently asked question was, "how fast were you going?" The funny thing is that these various drills required such intense concentration – whether it was to avoid a collision with an obstacle or making sure you didn't launch yourself through the windshield or trying to keep your head clear as you spun in circles – that the thought of glancing at the speedometer is laughable. What I should have told them is we were traveling at the speed of fun.

Memo to Captain Kirk: We're ready for you, baby. We're ready.

The Mean Streets of Hanoi

We Americans are so spoiled, aren't we, when it comes to navigating our streets? Yes, yes, we endure our traffic snarls, the occasional erratic or rude driver, the road construction. But, we have a certain expectation, almost always validated, that certain norms of behavior will be honored. We have rules about lane usage, right of ways, spacing, and what we blandly refer to as common courtesies. The same can be said for life on the sidewalks. There are rules here too: pass on the right, don't obstruct passage, restrict the walking lanes to pedestrian traffic. I think you know what I mean.

Well folks.....welcome to Hanoi, or at least the Old District of Hanoi where, fairly said, it is a world gone mad. Here, chaos reigns. The only rule here is that there are no rules. None that I could discern anyway. All I can say is that Charles Darwin would be chortling with glee were he to witness this.

Imagine you are in a video game. The object of the game is to avoid bumping into anything that moves on the street or sidewalk: cars, buses, trucks, scooters, bikes, other people. To get bonus points you have to cross the street. Safely. Sounds simple, right? But, what you face? Oi zhay oi, the Vietnamese would say: Oh my God! Imagine an unending, relentless wave of motor vehicles carpeting the streets. Kind of like a lava flow of motorized traffic. The traffic moves in all directions. And, here, I'm not talking about left to right traffic all going in one lane and the reverse in the other. No, no – that would make it far too easy a game. No, here, the traffic streams in both directions regardless of lane assignment. There are painted lines in the streets, although for the life of me I'm not sure why. For decoration, some locals suggest. Scooters merge into this maelstrom without hesitation (and without so much as a casual glance) from alleys, side streets and sidewalks. Factor in the occasional truck or bus backing into the street at random intervals and you can only watch the ensuing melodrama in slack jawed awe.

The sidewalks pose less of a mortal threat, but a most challenging one nevertheless. Here, you learn quickly that sidewalks are really not designed for flowing foot traffic, but are instead areas designated for functions of daily living that apparently cannot be contained any longer in the buildings they front. It is the sidewalks where scooters and bikes are parked. It is here that merchandise of all sorts is displayed and sold. Haircuts are given here; women's hair is styled. Laundry gets done here as does the cooking of family meals. Kids play, adults sit on dwarf-like stools and play board games or just chat. Essentially, life plays out here. Which means there is barely, if any, room left for the individual who is merely trying to get from here to there without daring to step into the already chaotic streets. This "situation" leaves the average pedestrian between the proverbial rock and a hard place.

But, back to crossing the streets – the epicenter of our game. Given our Western mindset, we presumed at first that the safe bet to avoid a run-in with the "lava flow" would be to find a crosswalk at a traffic light, and wait for the light to turn green. Sadly, our naivete was grandly on display. To our befuddled consternation, we soon learned that traffic lights are, apparently, mere suggestions, not the moral and legal imperatives we observe at home. At first, given the almost insurmountable obstacles we faced, we relied on our guide, Young, to lead the way. We would watch him with unadorned adulation as he would step off the curb in what at least he thought was an appropriate moment, and calmly hold up his arm to signal our intentions, and just as calmly lead us across the teeming streets in a manner that was oddly reminiscent of Moses parting the Red Sea. It was magical. The cars, scooters, trucks – they all worked their way around us almost as if a collision would hurt them more than it would us. Amazing!

But, the question remained: how would we fare when Young was not with us, when we had free time to roam the city? At first, we would tiptoe ourselves off the curb and made sure our bodies were as tensed up as we could muster. Then, we would take a couple of steps forward and freeze, certain some guy on a scooter with a mountain of bags, boxes, children, and God knows what else aboard would smash into us. We would ultimately make it to the other side muttering that we should have taken greater care in making sure our life insurance policies had been updated.

After many attempts at this suicidal folly, we began to understand that the secret was to "let go." The sooner we could achieve a zen-like state, the better. You'll be fine, I said to myself. Just take a deep breath and refuse to let any thoughts of impending doom enter your psyche. We'd wait for what we thought was an auspicious moment, and calmly step into traffic like we owned it. Unlike before, there were no backward steps; our muscles relaxed. Just a forward glide. Arm extended high, eyes fixed on the oncoming stampede, confidence the controlling emotion.... and then go. Well....it worked. Pretty soon it was as if we were almost daring scooters, cars and buses to hit us.

Of course, in hindsight, the confidence – indeed, the cockiness – we developed was downright scary. When we look back on the experience we will know we temporarily lost our minds.

But, brother, were we piling up the bonus points!

Con Cuidado, Senor. Con Cuidado

Do you ever get caught up in the moment, decide to do something, and then almost immediately question your logic, or, more likely, your sanity? We all have, right? This is a bit overly melodramatic way of describing an outing we had recently in the Andean hills outside of Otavalo, Ecuador. Otavalo is a lovely town maybe two hours by car north of Quito and sits just above the equator at about 8500 feet. It is known for its markets and was a destination of our intrepid group, Jesse, Laura, Alex, Lily and myself. In anticipation of our visit, we agreed that we would indulge in a horse back riding outing at the hacienda where we were staying. Seemed innocent enough. After all, Lily is an experienced rider, and wouldn't it be nice to accompany her and share with her an impassioned pursuit she has and make this a family-filled, fun-filled activity. But, mind you, I am not an equestrian. I am about as close to having the requisite skills for such an undertaking as I do for performing brain surgery. Maybe less. The last time I was on a horse was nineteen years ago in New Zealand. Let's just say it was a bumpy ride which did not encourage me to pursue anything smacking of equestrianism bar the occasional carousel ride. (Interestingly, despite the passage of time, both Jesse and Alex remembered the names of their horses from that time long ago – Fat Boy and Tank – which should suggest to you that they were not exactly astride former Derby entrants.)

With helmets now giving us the illusion that we were well protected, we headed off with our guide. At first, the experience was actually rather bucolic. We slowly roamed through neighborhood streets, at first the cobblestoned variety with our horses clip clopping past small residences. The locals waved, the dogs barked. Cobblestones soon gave way to rocky roads and then rutted dirt roads as we headed further up into the highlands. Gazing at the humble, time worn communities and now dust-filled roadways, you almost expected Butch Cassidy or Wyatt Earp to appear, smilingly tipping their hats to us. The Andes were often shrouded in clouds; the sun was intense. Occasionally, when the clouds thinned, we could spot a volcano.

As we headed further uphill, the scenery became more wooded, more mysterious. The air felt cooler. My horse was named Ganador, which Jesse advised me meant "winner." But, given the clouds we seemed to be entering and the steep rise of the mountains around us, I kept thinking Ganador sounded more like a name you might find in Lord of the Rings. You know, something Gandalf or Bilbo Baggins might have named their steeds. Anyway, let's just say that Ganador and I had some issues. He had his own notions of how and where he wanted to travel, and, perhaps sensing my utter lack of equine understanding, concluded he needed to be in control. He was right, of course, but that didn't prevent me from erratic stabs at "showing him who's boss" if you know what I mean. For example, Ganador would often turn 180 degrees from our intended path, apparently deciding he had a better idea of how to navigate our route. He'd wrench his head left or right and head in some odd direction or in the direction of a near-by field no doubt lured by the green "salad bar" that awaited him there. I would grab the reins and pull left or right trying to lurch him in the right direction. Sometimes we went in circles. Calls from the group would yell out, "you're holding the reins too tight," or "you're not holding the reins tight enough." While I would have been more than happy to get a tutorial in reins management, spinning in circles is not always the best time for that. Or, I'd hear helpful admonitions like "lean back" or "heels down" which I'm certain were the right things to say, but are hard to put into practice when one's head is spinning.

The coup de grace, however, were the body blows I endured when Ganador started feeling a little peppy. Sometimes, he decided he didn't want anyone passing him. Sometimes, when his road-side munchings would leave him behind, he would take off in spirited fashion to catch up with his buddies. In both cases, the toll one takes on one's lower torso makes waterboarding seem like a Disney fun-fest. Hurtling downhill in the last segment of our ride, one could hear the screeching voices and wails of the male members of our group as each endless set of bumps made us desperately wish there were several layers of tempurpedic mattresses beneath us. I was, in one spastic movement, trying to keep my sunglasses from stabbing me up my nose, trying to keep my helmet from dropping over my eyes, and trying to keep the lens cap from flying off my camera. As Alex would describe it at one point late in the ride, everything below his waist was dead. I would put it slightly differently. The only sensations emanating from any region below my belt were intense pain, numbness or paralysis. Why the folks at the hacienda did not issue steel jockstraps along with helmets is a mystery to me. I'm pretty sure I was speaking in a soprano voice as we arrived once again at the hacienda.

Despite the bumps and bruises and my brief experience as a soprano, seeing the Andean highlands through less than well traveled paths was worth every minute. It presented to us a world vastly different than the one we had left behind, one beautiful in its differences to ours. As Dorothy once alluded, we knew we weren't in Kansas anymore.

Adios Ganador!

Floating Away. Far, Far, Far Away

I left the planet today. No, not for long. Only an hour or so, actually. And, no, no, I was not rocket assisted. It was so much easier than that. I went to a float spa. And, right there, at a place called Glowspa, in the heart of Mt. Pleasant, I found other worlds. Or, perhaps they found me.

Up until recently, my knowledge of float spas was formed by the most misplaced of impressions, thanks to Hollywood. Back more than three decades ago, there was a film called "Altered States" in which a Harvard scientist, played by a young William Hurt, experimented with what was not so invitingly described as a "sensory deprivation chamber." In this chamber, all sensory perception was removed: nothing could be seen, heard, or felt other than what your brain felt like composing. With Hurt's character, Eddie Jessup, fortified by LSD, his experience in the tank took on frightening, if not outright terrifying, dimensions such as his mutating into other, never before seen, life forms. Lily and I, with a group of friends, went to see this film in something of an altered state ourselves. We were so utterly fixated, indeed hypnotized, by what was happening on the screen that none of us noticed that Lily was so completely freaked out by what she was watching that she desperately sought an exit from the theater and blacked out – not once, but twice – in the aisle as she attempted her escape. Only when the theater lights later reappeared, did we turn to one another and inquire what had become of her. She still sternly reminds me of our complete oblivion to her absence until the film was over.

With that said, when our friend, Cathy, recently told us about modern day float spas where one could experience complete sensory deprivation, I was intrigued. (Lily less so.) What I learned was that the concept of the float spa has been in development for more than a half century. A fellow named John Lilly experimented with these back in the 1950's to explore the workings of the mind when it was deprived of all sensory information. And, interestingly, this experience has become popularized not just as a casual outlet for one's meditative endeavors, but also as a course of treatment for those with PTSD as well as those suffering from depression and a range of anxiety disorders.

In my case, I first stopped by Glowspa and conversed with the owner, Steve, to better understand what it was that might be in store for me. Steve told me that the tank was the size of an oversized bath tub completely enclosed to shut out the sounds of life coming from anywhere outside the flotation tank. The water in the tub would be about 10 inches in depth and would be infused with about 1,100 pounds of epsom salts, providing about double the buoyancy of the Dead Sea. You would lie in the tub which would be pitch black dark, be wearing earplugs, and have water temperature at 93 degrees so that your skin and body would have no sensory perception whatsoever other than the sound of your breath and, perhaps, the vaguest sensation of your heart beating, pushing blood around your organic self.

The day arrived for me, and I stepped somewhat gingerly into the tub. I was 90% excited and curious but about 10% apprehensive based totally on the decades old, but indelible, impressions left on me by "Altered States." Hollywood, could not have been more wrong.

I leaned back and immediately realized that, no matter how hard I tried, I could not sink. Impossible. I was weightless. The dark was so complete that I had no sense of whether my eyes were open or shut. I heard nothing but the sound of my breathing. As the minutes wore on, I became aware that the intervals between my exhales and inhales became longer and longer. That is the sound of relaxation. I also realized later that the relaxation I was experiencing was no doubt the greatest I had ever felt short of sleep which, after all, we do not really consciously experience. And, to add to the Twilight Zone element of it all, I felt nothing as the water temperature was so parallel to my body temperature that it precluded any sense of place. I might as well have been in outer space weightless as an astronaut would be. I settled back, realized that I was not going to freak out, and let my mind wander.

And the places it would take me! We sometimes refer to those situations in our lives where we are "alone with our thoughts." Sometimes, it's when we are swimming laps in a pool. Other times, we feel this is the case when we are sitting alone on a secluded beach perhaps at sunset. Very meditative. But, even in those scenes, we have at least a subliminal sense of the world around us. Maybe it's the breeze we feel touching our skin. Maybe it's the sound of waves breaking or a seagull screeching. And, of course, there is the ever present daylight. In the pool, maybe it's just the end of the lap or the coolness of the water that always keeps us centered with the notion that we are on planet earth; that there is an environmental context to what we are doing. But, in the flotation tank, we have none of those stimuli. We have nothing but our inner thoughts.

In my case, I took a journey into my past. I did not intend for that to happen, but that's where my brain wanted to take me. I saw myself sitting around the dinner table a half century ago looking at my grandmother, an image that has not occurred to me in decades. I saw myself toting around a 2 year old Jesse in our beach house in Rehoboth, Delaware introducing him to the artwork on the walls. I saw Lily and me on the beach in Phuket, Thailand almost 40 years ago. I saw Lily, Alex and me on safari in South Africa a few years ago watching an elephant spray dirt on our jeep while protecting her baby. I saw my father in his dressing area in our home in White Plains, New York as I looked up as a youngster in adulation. I have no idea - none - why these images came to the forefront of my consciousness. But there they were. And, while I could not be sure of this, I believe I smiled. It was too dark to tell.

I realized at some point that I had absolutely no idea how much time had elapsed. 7 minutes? 27 minutes? 47 minutes? No idea. But, at some point, as promised, soft music started infusing into the water. I knew my time was up.

And, I knew I would be back.

Adam's Big Mistake

How silly of me. Here I am a citizen of planet earth for multiple decades always believing that the fable of Adam and Eve and the Garden of Eden were just that – a fable. An endearing story to be certain, but not one grounded in reality if you ask me. Written more to educate, you might say, than to have any grounding in fact. Mythical but clearly delusional. And, just then, we landed in French Polynesia and I had to rethink everything.

Like so many exotic, far away places, French Polynesia sits near nothing. It resides in the belly of the huge Pacific Ocean. Draw a line southeast from Hawaii, west from Peru, and East from Borneo and you will find it, an aggregation of 118 islands and atolls among four archipelagos. When viewed island by island, they appear on the map to amount to essentially nothing. But, if you were to draw a line around them connecting the archipelagos, they would constitute an area akin to the main part of Europe. But, the hugeness of the Pacific swallows up everything making any visible land mass seem inconsequential, even presumptuous. What it gives us is an array of islands that offer a lushness of multi-hued greens, and soaring razor-topped mountains that loom over volcanically created jungle island after island after island. It has that primeval look to it, as if you might expect to see a dinosaur pop out at you at any moment. And, the water! Imagine a blue rainbow, each segment projecting a luminescent shade of the lightest turquoise to the fiercest sapphire blue. And, a clarity so great that from fifty yards you can still clearly see the ocean bottom and the explosive colors of the coral formations below. You may call this place French Polynesia, but, if you don't mind, I will call it the Garden of Eden. Adam, you just had to go ahead and bite that apple, didn't you, and then face expulsion from this place? Huge mistake, my friend, huge.

Our travels would take us to three islands: Moorea, Bora Bora, and Vahine. In Bora Bora, we would stay at the Continental, one of those resorts that offers over-the-water bungalows. Part of the magic is that part of your living area is floored in glass allowing you a constant view of the coral beneath and the ever-present sea life that is drawn to the coral as we are drawn to chocolate. Want to go for a swim? Well...just climb down the ladder and immerse yourself in the warm, translucent waters and explore the shallow depths below in your snorkeling gear and exchange greetings with the multiple sea creatures there. In Moorea, we would go on a tour of the interior on ATVs, lurching ourselves forward up the one-time volcano's heights. We would pass dense forests of towering bamboo, arching palms, and greenery so lush it is almost an insult to refer to it as merely lush. Who knew that the color green could take on so many assorted, so richly diverse, spectrum of personalities? Up on the surrounding mountains, clouds would invariably snake around the peaks in thin tendrils almost as if to embrace them.

We would devote a significant amount of time exploring the snorkeling possibilities here in the Garden of Eden. Whether it was drift snorkeling (where our boat would drop us off and then anchor down the current allowing us to literally drift to the awaiting boat after our exploration of the coral reefs below), or an excursion where we would sample an array of different sea-life environments, the result was always the same: magic! First, the water is so spectacularly clear that you believe what you're watching is in high def. The coral reefs were often alive with color: purple, red, white, pale green. And, joining us down there would be a vastness of sea creatures. It might be the 12 foot wide manta rays who would swim at us with their mouths open revealing an impressive inner chamber that would (they hoped) soon contain an array of plankton or other micro-sea organisms. Or, perhaps the groups of black-tipped sharks who hopefully had received the memo that their diets did not include humans. Or, barracudas, moray eels, eagle rays, majestic lion fish, or box fish. At one point, I was offered a small octopus to hold in my hand and found that he stuck to me like velcro! The explosion of black ink that followed led me to believe he wasn't nearly as interested in us as we were in him. And, then there was the "aquarium." Our guide referred to a place that was named that way although it wasn't clear to me what he meant exactly until we jumped in off the boat. As we dropped below the water's surface, we were literally surrounded by hundreds of bright, multi-colored fish who were barely inches from our face masks, and who were apparently as curious about us as we were about them. Ahh, the aquarium! I get it! Seeing this seemingly endless menagerie of fish so close to us made me instinctively giddy. Laughing actually. (By the way, have you ever tried to communicate with someone with your mouth mostly occupied by a snorkel? The emanating sounds really are quite humorous as you carry on a "conversation" with your snorkeling neighbor in a series of screeches and grunts. Tone of voice conveys quite nicely what the articulation does not.)

Then, there was Vahine Island, not just an easily overlooked atoll off the nearby coast of Tahaa, but a destination that we almost overlooked ourselves as we prepared for this trip. What we discovered as we arrived there by water shuttle was that Vahine is a private island. There is literally nothing there but a hotel with nine bungalows that hug the shoreline. There are no stores, no cars, no roads. Nothing. Well, almost nothing. There is a two hole golf course that one plays barefoot and only after consuming a suitable amount of the local Tahitian brew, Hinano beer. The bungalows offer you a deck overlooking the water, walls decorated with shells and they don't even come with keys. A sliding glass door is all the security you might want or need. Our host? A fellow named Terrence, an amiable Frenchman who, not coincidentally, is a gourmet chef. Terrence plied us with meal after meal that begged not to be eaten lest you undo the amazing visuals provided in his presentation. Whether it was his foie gras, grilled octopus, sushi, roasted duck breast with polenta, eggplant caviar and goat cheese in a tomato and basil coulis, or his crème brulee flambe or lemon tart with meringue, our taste buds and eyes swam in ecstasy. This was simply too good to be true. Our traveling friends, Randy and Cathy (but especially Randy), would start a daily chorus of "mmmmm" followed moments later with the same commentary. Lily and I would soon find ourselves lapsing into the same language. I have to admit, the "mmmmm's" pretty much dominated the breakfast, lunch and dinner conversations. But, after all, as they say, words do not do it justice. It is no wonder that this resort was voted by Conde Nast Magazine as one of the best retreats on the planet. While I suspect this resort was not around when Adam and Eve roamed these parts, Adam must nevertheless surely be shaking his head somewhere at his misfortune of not being able to stick around long enough to enjoy it.

There was an overwhelming serenity about this place. And, this atmosphere was underscored by the temperament of the local Polynesians. Almost to a man or woman, the local populace exhibited a gentleness and sweetness that was too common, too noteworthy, to be merely a coincidence. Whether it was hotel staff, or snorkeling tour guides, or shop owners, or just people you'd pass in the streets, people were soft-spoken, and quick to smile. Even one of our snorkeling guides, Roy, when whistling softly from our boat would cause, magically, a flock of terns to swoop out of nowhere to hover over us in the hopes of a feeding. And, all this with a willingness to help whether it was to teach us something about the local physical environment, find us something we needed, or just chat about life here.

Terrence told me at one point that Polynesians, as a general rule, always speak softly. Except when they laugh.

Adam, baby, you gave all this up for a bite of the apple. You know you're a fool, don't you?

Darwin's Hustle

We all know about Charles Darwin, don't we? You know – the Emperor of Evolution, the Grand Master of Natural Selection. We have been led to believe all these years that Charlie was a most serious sort, an academician of the greatest rectitude. But, I have another theory. I think Charlie was bored. He lusted for something a bit more exciting than the medicine he was studying, probably bullied into that by his physician father. So, Charlie dabbled in natural history a little and then hoodwinked Captain Robert Fitzroy into believing that he was a "naturalist," all so he could hop aboard the H.M.S. Beagle for a five year fling around the globe. Who can blame him, right? And so the twenty-two year old went on the trip of a lifetime. A Spring break without end, you might say!

And, what did he find? Darwin would experience much, but it is the Galapagos Islands where he left his immortal mark. Here, in an island group of 13, roughly 600 miles off the western borders of Ecuador, smack dab on the equator, Charlie made history. As we approached the islands from the air, the Galapagos seemed so inconsequential. Just tiny brownish droplets of land so small against the Pacific you had to remind yourself that these droplets were not weightless floating things but rather the protrusion of mountains and volcanoes anchored to the bottom of the sea. And, at least the islands we saw from the air were mostly brown dotted with touches of green with slender threads of sandy beaches rimming the islands. This would not be the jungle exploding with green vegetation of a thousand sorts, but largely a semi-arid, cactus-dotted environment.

Upon arrival, our bags were closely examined to assure local officials that we were not carrying with us any alien plant or animal life that might threaten the fragile ecosystem we were about to explore. This theme would emerge time and time again as we learned of the lengths to which the locals strived to protect the local environment. No doubt the motivation for this was driven in part by the paramount need of the locals to protect their only viable source of income – tourism -- but there was no questioning the sincerity of their effort as they advised us constantly of the things we needed to be mindful of to protect the flora and fauna from potential threats to their well being. Even our plane was generously sprayed, including the overhead luggage bins, to further these objectives.

We found our way to our catamaran, our intrepid group of seven (Alex and Katie, Jesse and Laura, Maggie, and Lily and me) and were introduced to our guide, Oswaldo (who, for some strange reason, I kept thinking in the early hours was named Pablo. My bad.) We would join about eight others from Australia, England, Japan, and the U.S. and together we would begin our exploration.

And, what an eye opener! We were advised to never touch the animals which I took as perhaps a bit of over cautiousness. But, soon enough we would see that was not the case. Our daily routine was generally to do two walking tours around the various islands and two snorkeling adventures. What we discovered was that the animals of the Galapagos have NO fear of human kind. None. There were moments when I was sorely tempted to reach down and touch that blue footed boobie or that sea lion or that pelican or marine iguana or that giant tortoise. But, I didn't. None of us did. (Speaking of blue footed boobies, by the way, please forgive me if I tell you that it was just too tempting to say from time to time, "wow, that's a nice set of boobies over there!") Since natural instincts, I would think, would give these animals some trepidation at human presence, I have to think it was because of the consistent and firm instruction to visitors over many years now not to touch the animals that this fearlessness has become so imbedded in these creatures.

Nowhere was this characteristic more amiably on display, and wonderfully so, than in the water. For sure, the multitudes of brightly colored fish kept their distance; apparently they hadn't gotten the memo. But, the sea lions....oh my goodness! These guys, especially the young ones, were more than just idly curious about us. They wanted to play! One morning, for example, while casually snorkeling in the shallows alongside a stone jetty, minding my own business, a young sea lion spotted us and swam straight at us, no doubt to personally introduce himself. He would swim right up to my mask, looking me straight in the eye. If sea lions could smile, this fellow would have one ear to ear. Without any effort, he swam within an inch or two of my face and then, in a most coquettish way, would flip himself upside down and spiral away. Moments later he would return, this time with his mouth wide open – no doubt laughing – and come within a couple of inches of my wiggling fingers. You know, the kind of wiggling of fingers one might do when talking to a six month old baby. I'm not sure whether he was playing tag, or keep away, or whatever, but this young dude was having a great time. And, so was I.

And, so it went. A wonderful flowing mix of interactions with people, both familiar and unfamiliar, and daily encounters with animals who, clearly, were on a first name basis with us. The Galapagos were a wonderful discovery for us. And, I have to say, Charlie Darwin may have bamboozled Captain Fitzroy, but I admire his chutzpah.

As Mary, Katie's mom would say, "carpe friggin' diem!"

Jungle Rules

We were in search of a wilderness -- something wild, remote, dense and warm. Something far away from TVs, a spa, and swim up bars. And so we headed east from Quito by car, the five of us (Jesse and Laura, Maggie, Lily and me) with Jesse behind the wheel. We headed down into lush valleys, and then up the next layer of the cloud enshrouded Andes, and down again. We progressed over nice highways to bumpy roads and, finally, several hours later, to a turn off that looked like a rough hewn parking lot on the edge of a river. We pulled in and almost immediately were spotted by someone knowing our need to complete our journey. He pointed us to a covered canoe that would take us the rest of the way. We loaded our stuff onto the canoe and headed down the river yet further into the wilderness, finally arriving at our destination: The Anaconda Lodge.

Arriving at the lodge, we meet Francisco, the owner. Francisco is a story teller, and a good one. He is of Chilean descent, his father once the Chilean ambassador to England, and himself a former director of a major Spanish bank doing business in Chile. Some years ago when the economy crashed in Chile, and the banks along with it, Francisco and his wife made a command decision to journey in the opposite direction in almost every respect. They came to the Amazon basin and took over the site of what had once been the only lodge in this region. It once boasted visits by President Ford and later President Carter. But, when Francisco arrived, the place was crumbling and in disarray and in need of a complete reconstruction. Now, a much smaller lodge, the Anaconda has about 14 bungalow type units and accommodates fewer than thirty guests.

When we arrived, however, Francisco tells us that we are the only guests! We are led to our rooms which have no air conditioning, no TVs, no phones, and no glass in the windows. And, a hammock. Perfect.

We are soon introduced to Cesar, our guide. Cesar is a native of Anaconda Island which boasts maybe 400 people. Francisco describes Cesar as an encyclopedia wearing boots. He knows everything about the local flora and fauna in addition to the local culture and history. We have barely unpacked when Cesar leads us into the jungle for an amazing three hour walk. The vegetation is dense here. Very dense. If you step off the rocky, dirt path you cannot venture more than a few steps without being consumed by a wall of vegetation. And, Cesar opens our eyes to things only moments earlier we could not have imagined. He shows us plants and trees, some of which you can touch, others to stay away from. We learn of the leaves of which trees we can eat (like the delicious leaf from which cinnamon is made) and those that would kill us. We learn how each plant or tree figures into the lifestyle of locals and which figure into the various rituals of the local shaman throughout history. Cesar speaks to us in Spanish with Jesse and Laura very ably serving as translators.

Cesar leads us to a home carved out of the jungle. We visit with the family that lives there. The house is up on stilts and is very rudimentary: no windows, just open air. Two impossibly cute, barefooted kids give us a cautious eye, but almost immediately resume their prancing around the house. The young boy swings wildly on a hammock; his sister almost bouncing off the walls with an over-brimming energy. We sat on a wood bench and were treated to a drink made from fermented yucca and sweet potato. Not exactly a mojito, but dripping with authenticity. And, then we are treated to some freshly made chocolate served on a leaf.

But, before entering this home, Cesar introduces us to the art of using a blow gun, not something that we folks tend to have had much experience with. There is a target, a wooden carving of an owl sitting atop a tall stick, that will be the focus of our efforts. Let me make an observation first on the use of a blow gun. First, the wooden flute-like tube is incredibly long – like about 8 feet. Picking that thing up and trying to balance it while focusing on a distant target is quite the challenge, one that I cannot say I marveled at. And, it's heavy. I felt it was a moral victory just to lift it and aim it in the general direction of the owl. Beyond that, there is the challenge of managing the dart. Cesar prepares them and tucks them behind his ear. He stresses to us the absolute importance of breathing in through our noses when preparing to shoot lest we inadvertently suck the dart down our throats! Good to know. He smilingly tells us that if any of us hit the target we will be treated to a free drink back at the lodge. Two hits would get us a dinner and drink, and three hits would earn us a drink, dinner and dessert.

(By now, Cesar, who spoke Spanish with a much greater mastery than his English, decides to give us nicknames which would make it easier for him to remember us over the next few days that we would spend with him. Somehow, while we believe Cesar meant to call me Juan, it became muddled in the translation, and I became "Iguana," not Juan. The name stuck.)

Lifting that eight foot long blow gun was like lifting a midget telephone pole. Very hard to keep balanced and steady and not drooping. And, as I said, for god's sake don't forget to breathe through your nose. And then, blow hard!! At first, all of us missed with Lily making a credible attempt at sounding either like she was playing the trumpet or farting. In subsequent attempts, Jesse, Lily and Maggie would actually hit the target. Iguana, on the other hand, was a bust.

And so our days would go. Sometimes it would be hikes with Cesar up incredibly steep hills through jungle so thick the notion of getting lost was no longer an abstraction. At times, we would be serenaded by the chaotic screechings of tamarind monkeys apparently arguing over who was getting which insects (or, so Cesar theorized). At other times, we would swat at both real and imaginary bugs who apparently found us to be a tasty novelty. Once, we stopped for a respite and Cesar, using a local plant sap, painted ceremonial warrior faces on each of us that, astonishingly, did not make us look even a tad bit more fierce.

And, then there was the tubing down the river. We were told to bring our swimsuits with us, so when our canoe came ashore Cesar indicated this would be our changing area. We looked around. Uh, where does one change exactly? No, no – no cabanas here, just a rocky beach and a shrub or two. When in Rome.....

But, the ride downstream was epic. Riding the currents and occasional rapids, it would have been a serious challenge to wipe the smiles off our faces. "Steering" the tubes was, at times, a challenge, but we all ended up where we were supposed to. The rumors of crocodiles and snakes in the local waters quickly evaporated. And, that was a good thing.

Back to the lodge for lunch and more stories from Francisco. And a nap.

Yes!

Eat, Drink, Sail, Repent!

We called ourselves the "Haightful Eight." We thought "Hateful Eight" might suggest a far more darkly sinister and angrier mood than was so clearly the case with our lighthearted group. No, this group would be far too merry, too mirthful to be bothered by any negative vibe. We thought "Haightful" more reflective of a euphoric era, one now laced with unending gallons of wine, beer and rum if not certain leafy herbs of days gone by. Together, we would walk, dine, drink, swim, dance and laugh our way down the Croatian coast. Our vehicle? The 50 foot catamaran, the "Indian Summer" which somehow I kept referring to as the "Endless Summer." No harm there.

To assist us in our journey, the wonderful Sanja ("Sah-nyah") and, at the helm, Ivan ("E-vahn"). The former served as an amazing jack-of-all-trades: cook, adviser, guide, Croatian language instructor, and occasional disc jockey. Ivan, the steady hand at the helm, would perform his duties as easily and without fanfare as one might open a wine bottle, if I may use that as an analogy. Our group? Eight friends associated by random streams of shared personal histories some dating back forty years and, in one case, more than sixty years. We gathered from California, Montana, Colorado, New York, and South Carolina. What a fabulous blend!

We would sail the azure blue waters of the Adriatic from Brac to Hvar to Korcula and other destinations which, I must confess, at this moment, I simply cannot remotely recall. On a daily basis we would stop at a variety of locations and experience the beaches of Croatia. And, what about them, these beaches? They are singularly beautiful, but, if I may say so, lacking in one meaningful way. It seems Croatia was near the back of the line when they passed out sand. What we have instead is a spectrum of rocky beaches some of which boast stones as smooth as a baby's bottom and others clearly designed by the Marquis de Sade. None that we encountered were especially foot friendly. But, we didn't care.

At these beach stops, we would simply jump off the boat, take off in any direction, sometimes aiming for the shoreline, sometimes not. If we did reach the shoreline, we would mostly sit (gingerly) on the rocks, gaze out at the sea, drink in the secluded beauty, and decide which smooth stones were worthy souvenirs. We would agree to disagree whether the waters of the Adriatic were "bracing" or "refreshing" or "chilling," but we could all agree the waters were crystal clear and "invigorating."

One of our stops was Hvar. We would toodle around the island but finally make landfall at Hvar Town. I felt a special connection to this place because it was a decade ago that I visited this place with Jesse and Alex. At that time, we hiked up to the fortress overlooking the small city so that we got a rapturous panoramic view of the city below and the shimmering sea beyond. I remember thinking, as I looked out over the ramparts, that it was like looking at the gates of heaven and I always wanted to return here. Sanja had advised us that over the intervening years, Hvar had become quite the tourist destination. She referred to it as the St. Tropez of Croatia. And, indeed, the place had become quite trafficked and blanketed by one cool cafe after another serving smartly dressed men and women. But, I didn't care. We hiked up to the fortress where I put on my headphones to listen to Per Byhring's "Mr. Wednesday," a tune that resonates with me like no other. Staring out at the sea and listening to this tune had been an ambition of mine for years. My bucket list is now a tad shorter.

I cannot let our Hvar visit pass without one more story line. When I was here with the boys long ago we happened upon a restaurant that featured what we all thought were the best mussels on planet earth. Mussels perfectly cooked in a broth rich in tomato, garlic and enough spicy heat to make it interesting. Perfect for being soaked up by a crusty bread. Here I was ten years later standing outside the very same restaurant. And, did I go in to re-create that epochal culinary experience? No, I did not. Why, you ask. Truth be told, Sanja and Ivan were about to pick us up and serve us lunch featuring a spaghetti carbonara with lobster crafted by Sanja. When we advised the boys that I had passed up this shot at mussel heaven, they were aghast. What? You travel thousands of miles and go to a place you are likely never to revisit and you pass up the best mussels ever created? Are you mad? Ahhh, I will never live this one down, and I will graciously accept the criticism that has not yet ceased to be piled upon me. (P.S., the carbonara was awesome.)

Back on the Indian Summer the party continued as we sailed between islands. Hours would pass as we read, swam, chatted, stared at the beauty of it all, ate and drank. And, what would we talk about? Well, we would delve into the momentous issues of the day of course like, what's the difference between a mule, a donkey and a burro? If only males can be jackasses, would a female be a "jill ass" or a "jackie ass?" Sometimes we would delve intensely into the riveting and earthshaking ramifications of a Brad and Angelina break up. And, then sometimes it seemed the group might add to the list of nicknames for me. At varying times I was referred to as Rasputin (even though I disavowed any physical resemblance) or T.C. (trans century) for my alleged simultaneous resemblance to Rasputin, Marco Polo, and Einstein. Or, sometimes it was merely Yeff.

In the evenings, we would go ashore to find ourselves some dinner, often following Sanja's recommendations. One such evening, we were in Trpanj, not far from Dubrovnik. (Yeah, Trpanj is spelled correctly, I promise. Just another funny example of this vowel deprived language!) In a town of 871 people, it was not terribly hard to find a place called the "Tuna Beach Bar." Here, we enjoyed epically good tuna sashimi and carpaccio among other fresh morsels. What followed was a spontaneous eruption of dancing joined in by our whole group. I mean, we held nothing back. It was fabulously enthusiastic if a bit spastic, but since there were literally no other people at the Tuna Beach Bar I can't say we fell prey to embarrassment. Michael Jackson, the Stones, the Pointer Sisters and other icons led the way with Sanja excelling as disc jockey. Since we were the only patrons at the place, we sometimes asked the manager if he wanted to close it down for the night. He would shrug and tell us he was obliged to keep the place open until 2 a.m. anyway. Good to know!

Poor Sanja. She was so earnest in her efforts to teach us some of the rudiments of the Croatian language. But, seriously, how does one try to learn such things when vowels appear about as often as sand does on Croatian beaches? Take the days of the week, for example. How about Monday, Wednesday and Thursday, to name three. What we have is: Ponedjeljak, Srijeda, and Cetvrtak. And, let's not forget Sunday: Nedjelja. Really? In this vowel starved universe we were severely challenged. But, Sanja persevered and occasionally would connect with our less than graceful attempts at compliance. Sadly, whether it was Sanja's howls of laughter or ours that accompanied these tutorials, we made little progress.

Upon arriving at the boat at the outset of our journey, Randy surprised us all with a gift of t-shirts to commemorate the occasion. On them, it said, "Eat, Drink, Sail, Repeat." A few days in when we were threatening to consume about 15% of the world's wine reserves, Randy suggested a slight revision: "Eat, Drink, Sail, Repent."

He knew what he was talking about.

Almost a Bird

Mark Twain once said, "The air up there in the clouds is very pure and fine, bracing and delicious. And, why shouldn't it be? It is the same the angels breathe." Similarly, Wilbur Wright once remarked on flying, "More than anything else, the sensation is one of perfect peace mingled with an excitement that strains every nerve to the utmost, if you can conceive of such a combination."

Haven't we all looked skyward some times in our lives and looked in wonderment at the flight of birds whether it is the effortless gliding of a group of pelicans above the ocean or perhaps a soaring eagle so high up it boggles our minds. We have all wanted to take flight or to know what it feels like to be a bird gazing down at us. Certainly, I am no different. And, by flying here I am not including skydiving which, when you get right down to it, is merely an extended act of falling. Nor do I refer to those who engage in parasailing when, after all, they are still tethered to the earth. And, while I would like to include those individuals who engage in wingsuit flying -- you know, those intrepid souls who wear outfits that make them look oddly like flying squirrels -- who jump off cliffs and then try not to crash, most of us do not comfortably pursue that level of lunacy.

And, so, there we were: Jesse and Laura, Alex, and Lily and me arising in what seemed the middle of the night in Mexico City, all so that we could get to Teotihuacan, about an hour's drive northeast of the city. There we would experience a sunrise flight of a hot air balloon that would take us above the Pyramid of the Sun, a pre-Aztec construction that dominates the surrounding landscape. I won't say we were nervous; that would be misleading and overstated. But, we were in a highly anticipatory mood, that's for certain. In part, this emotion stemmed from the fact that we didn't know what to expect once we got airborne. Would we be terrified? Would we be ecstatic? Could we remain calm? Who knew?

As we walked out to our designated balloon, we could see the propane flames slashing the air inflating the many balloons around us. They were hot those flames. We could feel them. We arrived at our balloon and learned that we would need to climb up into it and take our positions in the four corner quadrants of this large woven basket which, upon further inspection, seemed a bit delicate to be entrusted with the weight of eight passengers, propane gas tanks, and our pilot, Enrique. Nevertheless, we stumbled our way over the edge of the basket and received our twelve second "safety briefing" from Enrique. The sum and substance of this was to advise us to bend our knees upon re-entry. Good to know.

And then, we left mother earth. Rising so slowly, so gently that if you had your eyes closed you might be totally unaware you were now floating in the air. But, how could you have your eyes closed when your brain is spilling over with excitement, anticipation, and, yes, a spoonful of fear? The sun had not risen yet and so the only real light was that projecting from the propane flames which seemed so close to my head my hair sometimes felt like it was about to burst into flames. Enrique smiled and assured us the flames would not pose a threat to us. When I asked Enrique what direction we were headed, he shrugged his shoulders and said the wind would take us wherever the wind wanted to take us. We would have no control over that. Hmmm, really? He made a stab at assuring us about this uncertainty by telling us he would try to land in an open field somewhere and avoid houses or other buildings or cactus fields. Alrighty then!

And, up we went. At first, we were close enough to the ground to feel like we were a human Google Earth, focusing on buildings, trees, the headlights of moving cars. But, then, we were too high for that. Even the pyramids below seemed hopelessly insignificant now. Then, the mountains in the distance took over. And, then the clouds. The air cooled. At times, we were so surrounded by clouds you could see nothing else. And, what a sensation that was. I could say, I suppose, that we were experiencing the same view one might have gazing out of an airplane window. But, what we saw and felt was so strikingly different. We were not surrounded by metal or sitting in an upholstered seat. We were floating outside in the air with nothing between us and the clouds but our ecstatic smiles. So -- THIS is what birds see!

The sun rose and filtered through the clouds in an epic way. There were nineteen other balloons aloft with us and each caught the sun's rays and brightened the already colorful patterns on each of them. Seeing them all floating so easily out there made for an extraordinarily breathtaking wallpaper. Photos were shot by all of us at a rate of about thirty per second, or so it seemed. Enrique told me we were up around 3,000 feet (or 10,000 feet above sea level). It looked it. We rose above the first cloud layer and then had the weird, but endearing, sight of nothing but the clouds beneath us, the sky above us, and our fellow balloonists all around us, seemingly miles apart.

When the clouds beneath us disappeared, the act of leaning a bit over the edge of the basket came into play. It was here that you got the best sense of how fragile all of this seemed; how the only thing we had between us and the ground thousands of feet below us were this basket, hopefully enough propane to keep us aloft, and Enrique's steady hands at the controls. Yes, it did give us that funny feeling you get in the pit of your stomach when facing some potential fate you want nothing to do with. Giggling helped offset the fear that so badly wanted to take control.

After forty-five minutes or so, we floated slowly and gently back to earth. When we got close, we hovered over a cactus field, the kind Enrique assured us would not be under our feet when we landed. And, sure enough, we elevated a bit again and found a perfect landing space in an open field. Within moments we were joined by a "ground crew" that would help us anchor the balloon and provide us with a ride back to our starting point. As Lily and I got in to the truck's cab, what music was playing on the radio? Why, "Safe and Sound," of course. Really.

The ride back would enable us to sit back and think calmly about what we had just experienced. Memories that will last a lifetime. Twain and Wright knew what they were talking about.

The Wild Way

Imagine that you're dreaming. In this dream, you find yourself in a car. But, wait, something's wrong. You are sitting on the right hand side in what you normally consider the passenger seat. But there, smack dab in front of you is the steering wheel jutting out from where one might normally find the glove compartment. Your tension mounts; you unconsciously twitch. As the dream progresses, you are now driving but on the left side of the road. Your every impulse is to get over to the right hand lane before something very troublesome happens, but other cars around you are following the same contrary rules that you are. You are about to turn on to another road and are gripped by great anxiety thinking and re-thinking in a succession of nanoseconds where you should aim the car. You suddenly awaken with eyes wide open, gasping for breath.

Welcome to Scotland and Ireland where the rules of the road pretty much lead you to the conclusion that it's a world gone mad. When planning our trip to these destinations, we knew, of course, that driving could pose a challenge. I had driven on the left side before: once many years ago in New Zealand and eight years ago in South Africa. But, this trip posed a different challenge. In Scotland and Ireland, the roads are narrow. Very narrow. And, they are often winding with seemingly an infinite number of blind curves where in the next moment you could be confronting a bus, a truck, a car or wayward sheep. I spoke to random folks I met on the beach before we left to see if any of them might have had this experience, and to see if they had any insights. Conservatively, 80% of them said they lost at least one of their outside rear view mirrors. They reported banging into oncoming cars, or parked cars, street signs or sometimes even buildings on roads that are barely wider than angel hair pasta.

So, when we got to Scotland -- Lily and me and good friend, Maggie -- I was ready to pay for whatever insurance the rental people would offer me. I did, however, manage to constrain myself from inquiring about renting body armor suits that would liken us to a team of Pillsbury dough boys. We had an agreement, Lily, Maggie and I that as we hit the road they should never be shy about yelling out to me, "STAY LEFT" just to keep my mind focused. I told them that no matter how many times they might do that I would never, ever feel irritated by it. Our plan was for me to drive, Lily to be the navigator, and Maggie to do her best impersonation of Miss Daisy from the back seat.

Leaving the airport, naturally, I was confronted with a series of roundabouts which, to the untrained motorist (i.e., me), posed immediate brain wracking challenges. Hearing the animated guidance of the "stay left" crowd, I tried to focus on entering these circles going clockwise, not counter clockwise as I had been doing my whole life. Okay, easy enough, but what about exiting these circles? Do I stay in the left lane or right? What about the guy rapidly approaching the circle from another direction? Do I stay to his right or push myself to stay in the left lane to ease my exit further along the circle? Remember, these are not decisions you can mull over leaning back in a reclining chair sipping a cognac. No, decisions like these are split second experiences. Hopefully, you choose wisely.

The first day was marked by my hitting the left side curb eight times and by me happily having only one near death experience when, at a turn, I instinctively looked right for oncoming traffic instead of left, narrowly avoiding getting t-boned by a not so happy driver who was approaching from the left (of course). Our time spent in the car over this two week period would present Lily as the in-car sound effects lady as she would alternately screech out "eeks" or "yikes" or yowees" and other exclamations that frankly are too difficult to spell as we would barely miss an oncoming car or street sign or building.

These dramatic outpourings were never more in evidence than when we encountered the most insane of Scottish and Irish driving realities: the one lane road. And, by this I mean one lane roads designed for two way traffic. I mean, seriously, what were they thinking?!? I never realized I'd be engaging in the game of chicken whereby you are zooming down a road and see an oncoming car zooming right at you and wondering who would flinch first. It turns out that on these roads there are small carved out spots where one may pull over to avoid head on collisions, but you're pretty much on your own in determining when and if you do that as opposed to seeing if the other guy might pull over first. Like I say, a game of chicken, Irish style. (I thought it so thoughtful that these roads, which are barely wide enough for one car, would actually sometimes provide a painted line down the middle as if there might be plenty of room for two cars side by side on this noodle width causeway.)

As the days passed without incident, my confidence grew and Lily and Maggie greatly diminished their helpful guidance tips. Even Lily's outbursts of indecipherable exclamations largely vanished from our adventure's soundtrack. There came a time when I could actually enjoy the amazingly beautiful and lush landscapes. To describe the steep landscapes as merely green is almost an insult. The intensity of the color is transfixing. The hills were routinely dotted with hundreds of sheep who often managed to escape from their already lush pastures to nibble at road sides oblivious to traffic. I convinced myself it was sheep that were responsible for inspiring the phrase "the grass is always greener on the other side of the fence." Notwithstanding my increasing comfort with the whims and eccentricities of local driving, there were certainly times when I would do a double take when the occasional approaching car would have a golden retriever in what I would normally consider the driver's seat. For a microsecond I could hear myself think, oh my god, that dog is driving!

Along the southwestern coast of Ireland, we would see many road signs that would label our route as "The Wild Way." Yes, it is I would say to myself. Yes, it is.

Incident at a Pub

How many times in your life have you heard someone start a joke with, "a guy walks into a bar"? Pretty often, right? Frequently, the guy described in the joke is apt to be hoodwinked in the few minutes following his arrival. Well...let me introduce you to one of the newer guys in this category. That would be me.

When we were planning our trip to Scotland and Ireland, one of the adventures that called out to me the most was having the "pub experience." Whether it was through movies, stories from travelers, or just my imagination, I have always wanted to be immersed in the local pub atmosphere of these two countries. It was in these places, I had imagined, that the gaiety level is incredibly heightened, the live music promises a most believable soundtrack, and the beer wonderfully amplifies the mood. Getting down with the locals; that was the goal.

It was one of our first nights in Scotland, in Oban to be precise. Oban is a very picturesque and charming example of Scottish coastal towns. This one is a bit northwest of Glasgow. There was a block in one of the local streets that seemed reserved for pubs there were so many of them. We decided to go in to one whose name I cannot remotely remember. It was Lily, Maggie and I. We found a table near the back of the place sitting directly across from a couple of elderly gents who were providing music, one on an accordion, the other on some kind of drum. Empty beer bottles were amply on display in front of them.

We could see soon enough that to get a beer one needed to get up to the bar and get the bartender's attention which I volunteered to the ladies I would do. I got to the end of the bar and found myself staring at a display of the many beers on tap none of which were at all familiar to me. To my left was a huge guy seriously working on his beverage. I looked over at him and asked him what he might suggest as a choice in beer. He gave me a frowning look and said, "Well, what kind of beer do ya like"? I shrugged and offered that I often like a pale ale. His frown deepened and he looked down at me and said, "Oh no, that's a fookin' girlie drink! You can't be a man and do that!" I'm not sure what was more pronounced, my laughter or my embarrassment. So, I figured a follow up question was in order and I asked the fellow to recommend a beer to me. He pointed to his now almost empty pint and then pointed to the tap where I might find more of his favorite. Quickly getting caught up in the moment, I gestured to the bartender that I'd like one of what the big guy had suggested. A glass was filled and placed in front of me.

Almost immediately, a fellow to my right tapped me on the shoulder. He looked at me and, gesturing at my newly poured beer, asked me if he might have "a wee sip." Caught up in the mood and a desire to fit in with my new cronies, and definitely caught off guard, I said sure. Well, the guy takes my glass and drains it!!! Every last drop of it! He lets out a satisfying sigh, nods his approval to me, and places the empty glass back on the bar. I am not sure whether to be howling with laughter or deeply offended, but I could see immediately that a number of folks in the immediate vicinity were falling down laughing. I was exclaiming out loud, "Whoa! What just happened here?" Welcome to pub life, I concluded.

Turns out that the fellow asking for merely a wee sip, but whose ambition far exceeded his request, was the owner of the pub. When the laughter died down, he calmly went behind the bar, got a new glass, and gave me a full one. That's getting your chain yanked, Scottish style. Lily and Maggie found it quite entertaining.

And, I knew this trip was going to be pretty special.

Safari So Good

You're sitting in an open air Land Rover moving slowly along a wild looking plain. The morning breeze is cooling, nicely offsetting the growing humidity. As you lazily gaze around the local scene, you smile thinking it reminds you a bit of something out of Jurassic Park: primeval, promising things out of the ordinary, filling with feelings of anticipation. Out to the horizon is a suggestion of hills and the beginnings of many miles of sand dunes that hug the coast. The Indian Ocean lies just beyond.

Just as you're settling in to this relaxing vibe, you spot some activity up ahead. There's a group of female lions grouped together. As you draw closer, the lions pay you no mind because they are so focused on tearing apart the body of a wildebeest they have recently killed. The meal is being shared by the mother, her not quite fully grown young ones and their Aunt (so we are told). Your guide slows the Rover and creeps to within a few feet of the ongoing feast. Now that you are so amazingly close, you can smell the wildebeest meat and hear the lions tearing pieces of it away. Their subdued growls are oddly similar to those you might hear from a group of Harley Davidsons at a low throttle. You realize you're holding your breath.

But wait. As crazily engrossing as this scene is, drama is about to increase. Approaching on the right is a herd of water buffalo, large beasts not to be trifled with. The lions look up and carefully watch the approaching horde. The buffalo slow their pace and stare at the lions. They are now just a few yards away from the lions and you are sitting in the front row almost uncomfortably a part of what appears to be looming combat. The younger lions break away from their meal, and their more sensible adults, and face the buffalo. Heads lowered, tails slowly and menacingly wagging, they seem interested in exercising their still evolving machismo. A tense stare down begins.

Welcome to the safari experience here at the And Beyond Phinda Game Park. Located about a three hour drive northeast of Durban, it provides the epitome of the South African bush environment with terrain that varies from the densest of woodlands to hills that allow fantastic overviews of the game reserve to seemingly endless miles of open plains that oftentimes provide the stage for the hunt and kill by the large beasts here.

We have a cottage here with a nice front porch that sometimes provides all manner of passing animals and weird but amusing animal and bird cries. In the bedroom the large windows allow for staring contests with baboons who are sometimes mere inches from you. We are advised to keep our door firmly hooked since otherwise the baboons pose a real threat to ransack your place looking for food. To walk to the common area our path is sometimes blocked by large nyalas who lift their heads and stare as if to ask, "who the hell are you?" We are under strict orders not to leave our cottages after dark since all of the animals here have access to where we sleep. This is also a place where everybody knows your name from the guide and tracker to the managers and wait staff. They've got us labeled it seems almost immediately while we're still struggling to remember just some of their names. This adds such a pleasing boost to the already significant hospitality we receive and the warm welcoming feeling we get every day.

(Speaking of names, it is clear we are dealing with an art form, or better yet, a culture that is rich in imagination and daring. There are no Bobs or Bills, no Anns or Nancys. Oh no, no. Here in Phinda and elsewhere in our travels nearby, the locals' names pop with adventure and emotion. We meet Wonder, Lucky, Happiness, December (born on Christmas day), Justice and our favorite, Shamiso Sibanda which translates to Amazing Lion. Appellation-wise, we Americans are so hopelessly boring and simple minded, aren't we?)

Our guide is an amazing fellow named Matt. He's only 27 but he has the encyclopedic knowledge and game world experience of a David Attenborough or a Jane Goodall. Or maybe Tarzan. The guy knows everything and shares it with us in a vibrant, upbeat and humor-filled way. We receive wonderfully endless tutorials on the animal realm from the idiosyncrasies of the dung beetle to the mating habits of the bull elephant and the hierarchical geography of everything in between. From time to time as we are ambling through the bush, Matt pulls our open air Land Rover off the path to show us a leaf, sometimes a lethally poisonous one, other times a most beautifully fragrant one. He teaches us the tell tale smells that can tip off the presence of a hidden animal. This can include the popcorn "fragrance" of leopard urine or the nutty urine profile of the genet.

Accompanying Matt is Muzi, our Zulu tracker. Muzi sits in a seat mounted just above the left headlight binoculars in hand (or floodlight at night). This guy, too, is amazing. He spots animals magically in an almost zen way. While he has a devilish sense of humor and a most infectious laugh, Muzi is at heart a very calm person. From his perch he ever so subtly signals to Matt turns we should make into the dense bush as we continually track the animals here. And tracking is what this is all about. Matt and Muzi might just as well be lions themselves in a constant hunt for prey. For the lions, of course, tracking is a matter of survival. But for Matt and Muzi it is a game of passion that they play with a wonderful combination of intensity, grit and glee. The art of the pursuit relies on so many clues. Sometimes it's the tracks of the animals and the direction they lead. Are they so fresh that they make an imprint above the latest Land Rover tracks? How fresh are the animal droppings we see along the way? Not just smell, but color can be probative as well. Urine smells can take us left or right such as the popcorn-filled air of the leopard. And, of course, the noises coming from the bush are clues that must be minded. This is not a case of "Where's Waldo." There's just too much knowledge and awareness being exercised for successful trackings to be considered random or lucky. I asked Matt if he could foresee a day when chips might be imbedded in animals so that GPS could assure the accuracy of animal pursuits. He shook his head slowly and said, no, he hopes that day never arrives. And, I soon enough realized why. It would rob the exercise of its clue-pursuing, puzzle solving element that is at the heart of animal tracking. The passion would be gone.

Over the next few days our twice daily game rides would allow us close-up viewings of lions, elephants, giraffes, rhinos, hippos, baboons, zebras, wildebeests, and a host of birds whose names I will likely never recall. Matt's tutorials would continue. Seemingly, with each animal sighting we would learn the proper titling of the groups of each type. We all know of a herd of cows or a pride of lions. But, did you know we refer to a "parliament" of owls, or a "dazzle" of zebras, a "coalition" of cheetahs, a "murder" of crows, or an "implausibility" of wildebeests? No, I didn't know either.

On our last day in Phinda, the day would start dramatically enough with our closing in on two male lions who had eluded us until then. We were headed in one direction when Muzi casually pointed to the right. As was often the case, when Muzi pointed one way or another, Matt would chime in with, "let's give it a bash." Or, as others might say, let's give it a try. And soon enough, there they were. Although lions are often referred to as the king of beasts, they are not that. The elephant reigns supreme. No creature of sound mind takes on one of those dudes. But, there is an unquestionable majesty to the male lion with his massive size, his almost deadly calm demeanor, and, of course, that incredible mane that might just as well be a crown. Once again, we pulled to within about four feet of this guy. I challenge anyone to say that their minds don't do cartwheels when a lion is that close to you and his head turns so he can stare at you squarely with those calm, or perhaps menacing, eyes. It is wonderful to think about in the aftermath, but not so much in the moment it's happening.

But, later came the coup de grace. Once again, Muzi spotted a few female lions off in the distance. It was clear from their slowed, measured pace and laser-like stares they were tracking something. Because we were a distance away, Matt got the Rover into high gear and tore through the bush to get closer. The path was incredibly bumpy as we skirted large rocks and mini-excavations done by aard-varks which surely would have cost us an axle had we landed in one. We would learn later that this rough ride is often referred to as an African massage.

As we got closer, we could see, amazingly, that one of the adults whisked away the young ones off to a place far from the path of the warthog we now saw. Matt advised us this was an important move because the young ones, if left to their own devices, would reveal the lions' intentions in a fit of youthful exuberance and thereby tip off the unsuspecting warthog. The remaining two lions separated, laying out a masterful plan to ensnare the warthog as they closed in on him.

The unevenness of the terrain plus our distance from the looming drama deprived us of being eyewitnesses to the kill. But, the kill did indeed occur. As we came over a slight rise, there was the lioness standing calmly with her jaws firmly draped around the warthog's neck. The warthog was still alive judging from its screeching voice and madly scrambling but airborne legs. Darkly fascinating but hard to watch as well. But, there we were telephoto lenses stretched to the max, binoculars providing more detail than one might want. One of the lionesses veered off to bring back the young ones who had dutifully remained on the sidelines.

Our time in Phinda was up leaving us with memories that will be etched into us for the rest of our lives. The immediacy of it all, the vivid reality of it and, yes, the savagery of it are not elements that typically dot our lives. And, to share it all with Lily, Maggie, Jesse and Laura just heightened its meaning. If you have not had this experience, I implore you to embrace it. Get it on your bucket list. Or, as Matt might say, give it a bash!

Farewell Captain Matheson

I remember the first time I met him. It was about 43 years ago, but for some reason I remember elements of that encounter vividly. Back then I was a fledgling attorney trying to make my way in the world. We had a paralegal in our office named Betsy (later to be known as Lily) who had told stories of her father that would fill the pages of a movie script: tales of adventure, accomplishment, and fortitude. One day, he decided to visit his daughter at the office, and Betsy showed him into my office to make the introductions. He was wearing a khaki safari shirt and had the look of a man of the world. He strode in to meet me, arm extended in what would prove to be a most firm handshake. The look on his face and the meaningful eye contact could not disguise the obvious confidence he had. In that moment, combining the almost legendary stories I had previously heard from Betsy along with that most impressing spirit about him, he could easily have garnered the title of the "most interesting man in the world" that we see in TV ads these days.

What I learned about and from Jim Matheson, Sr. was stirring and memorable. From an education at the Naval Academy, the University of Chicago, MIT, and Harvard to serving in a submarine off the coast of Japan in World War II, to working with Admiral Hyman Rickover in the dawning age of the nuclear submarine, to his skills as a Deputy Director and then Director of the Peace Corps in Jamaica and then Ecuador, to his directing of the Fermi Lab in Chicago, Jim was, to put it mildly, a most accomplished fellow. Amidst all this, he even found time to get a law degree. And, most importantly, he helped raise a family of four children: Ann, Lily, Susan and Jim. As was so often the case with military families, they wandered the country from Massachusetts to Key West to New Hampshire to New York to California and ultimately to Northern Virginia.

Over the decades, once I became a member of the family, I would get beneath the surface and learn in greater depth more about Jim. He was an avid debater. Nothing spurred him on like a vodka martini and a debate of all things political. He was not always the easiest man to contend with; his views were drop dead strong and even closer held. He would hear you out, but it was not a commonplace thing for him to change his views after hearing the other side of the issue. But, having those discussions were great fun if only because of his energy, passion and extensive knowledge which he freely shared. While they were sometimes trying, they were always stimulating and energized discussions, a profile he would carry with him for the rest of his days.

Jim was a man who relished the open waters. Starting with the navy, and then later as boat owner and sailor, it seemed to me this is where his heart was at its fullest. And, Jim was no casual sailor. When he took his boat out on Chesapeake Bay it was all business. No margarita-filled lazy cruise here. The few times I was aboard, we'd hit the waves and beat into the wind for hours on end making me think I was actually racing in a marathon, not out for some laid back afternoon dalliance with the sea. But, again, this was a pure reflection of his passion which he so avidly embraced.

Jim died last year at the age of 96. A life in full by any measure. Because of his military background, Jim was entitled to be buried at Arlington National Cemetery. Although I had lived in the Washington, D.C. area for almost four decades, I was never privy to share in such a poignant tradition. As is true with so many things in life that are understood only in the abstraction, I had no idea the impact the ceremony would have until I experienced it myself.

It was a brisk day, at least for Lily and me. Temps in the mid-40s, but with a clear and sun-filled sky. As we entered the gate at Ft. Meyer, we were instructed to proceed straight to the Colonial Chapel where there would be a memorial service for Jim. When we were all gathered, the organ music began. If, in the preceding moments, we might have momentarily lost sight of why we were there, the music changed all that in a heartbeat. There is something so penetrating, so resonant, about the organ music that filled the chapel, the spare decorations of the building allowing the music to fill the room and echo in it like it was alive. After some opening remarks, the chaplain explained that since he had not personally known Captain Matheson he thought it appropriate that all of us focus our thoughts on him as we listened to the sentimental strains of "Amazing Grace." In those moments, my memories of Jim darted through my head in no particular order and with no hierarchy of importance. Just random thoughts about a life led and the impact he had on so many people.

At the end of the ceremony, we headed outside to now witness the caisson waiting for Jim. His cremated remains were carried solemnly, one gloved hand above and one below the box. At the curbside, the box was ever so carefully set into the casket which would be taken by the six horse drawn caisson to the grave site. It was an eighteen minute walk from the chapel to the grave, and it was along this walk that we witnessed something extraordinary. There were many people at the cemetery that day, many just tourists but undoubtedly some visiting departed close ones of their own. As we moved along trailing the caisson, people would line up along our path. All stood facing us. Many stood with their hands over their hearts; others stood and saluted to what they knew was a fallen veteran. It is one of the images I will take with me forever.

At the grave site more words were spoken, but what brought the undeniable air of finality was the playing of taps, the firing of the guns, and the band's playing of the emotionally laden "Going Home." A most memorable day by any measure.

Rest well, Jim. You have earned it.

Serenity Now!

Even just saying the word relaxation can, by itself, sometimes create a calming experience. Maybe it's because of all that term conjures up: deep breathing, lack of stress, endorphins on the rise, simple pleasures. You get the idea. And, when we think of relaxation, the beauty of the concept is that it translates into an almost infinite variety of possibilities wholly dependent on the personality and psyche of the person engaged in the contemplation. For some, it means just leaning back in a most comfortable chair or couch and contemplating nothing. For others, it's the closing minutes of a yoga class when you can hit the floor and devolve into savasana, or "corpse pose" as it is widely known. Often, it's sitting on a secluded beach and staring out at a most calming ocean. Or possibly, just sitting back, feet propped up, and listening to the music that soothes your soul. As I say, the possibilities are nearly endless.

But, when you're in Paris -- well, at least for me -- another possibility presents itself. And, that's sitting at an outdoor table at one of the gazillions of cafes and taking in the world as it sidles past you. There is something zen-like here, maybe even meditative if I want to lean towards the hyperbole. It is a place without time limits, without interruptions, but one that offers a cinematic view of local life with all the color and diversity that life offers.

When Lily and I are in Paris, it is often the case that Lily loves to spend her mornings sleeping late and then engaging in her wonderful pursuit of painting until early or mid-afternoon. That means for me that I get up earlier, have breakfast and then hit the streets in search of nothing in particular except drinking in the local vibe. That entails walking the neighborhoods for hours -- the streets, the parks, the river walks. But, I confess, not an insignificant objective on my part is not just the walk, as wonderful as that is, but the breaks from the walk where I can stop at a café, lean back, bask in the sun, and order up a café crème or glass of rose depending on my mood.

While it is hardly unique to Parisians, I love the pace of those strolling by. These folks are not running off to meetings or worried about some deadlines. At least not in a way that Americans do. Rather, they are wandering albeit with an eventual destination in mind. This is particularly true of people sharing their stroll with someone else, whether a spouse, dating partner, or friend. Invariably, the spirit of the conversation is positive. No one is yelling at each other; no melodramas are unfolding. Many are walking amiably with a baguette tucked under their arm, the end of the loaf already nibbled clean. Being a quintessentially cosmopolitan city, Paris offers up a wide variety of languages that one can discern as strollers pass by. Mostly French, of course, but also English, Spanish, German and a variety of eastern European and Asian languages that I am utterly unable to identify. But, it doesn't matter. I admit that I sometimes overhear the conversation of English speakers passing by that can be entertaining. Like the American guy strolling by telling his friend that when he was in Portugal he kept forgetting to say "obrigado" -- which is the proper way to say thank you -- and kept saying instead "avocado." Amusing, right? But, by far, the better course is to allow the chatter to simply become background music, part of a soundtrack that in sort of an existential way serves as a substitute for a soothing mantra. Think of it as one very long "Ommm."

So, what's to look at? Just about everything, I say. Fashion is interesting which surprises me since I pay no attention to that anywhere else. But, it is interesting, even amusing, to see how many different ways someone can wear a scarf, for example. Scarves are ubiquitous and the assortment of color and design is seemingly endless. I could be wrong about this, but I believe to be legally a French citizen one must wear a scarf no matter what the season. Then, an ongoing inquiry is how tight can your pants be? In Paris, both men and women seem to be finding new benchmarks for eliminating any airflow that might make contact with the lower half of their bodies, almost as if there is some health hazard there that hasn't been shared with outsiders. And, the shoes! How some of these women stay on their feet as they come prancing by with footwear whose heels are so thick and so high that for all the world they resemble very artfully crafted cinder blocks is a mystery to me. On rainy days, one can take in the bombastic array of bright, multi-colored umbrellas and crazily designed raincoats that shimmer and add life to what might otherwise appear to be a dreary day.

Then there are the dogs. Certainly, there are many who are average in size, but they are vastly outnumbered by breeds so small they, in my mind, barely qualify as canines. Let's just say many would fit comfortably in a Louis Vuitton handbag. And, let's not forget the wonderfully energized kids. Like kids everywhere, they don't really recognize limitations on their range of movement or the decibel level of their playful outcries. I love watching them streaming past on their mini-scooters weaving, mostly successfully, through the throngs on the sidewalk. Their parents nonchalantly follow behind unconcerned about whatever mischief their young ones might engage in. Perfect. If you should happen to be sitting at a café on a market street, like Rue Mouffetard, it brings a smile as you watch the interaction with customers and the animated, hand gesture-filled conversations taking place. It doesn't matter what they're saying; it's the visible tableau that your senses are responding to.

All in all, what passes in front of you while you casually sit back sipping your wine or coffee is nothing short of a cinematic landscape almost in slow motion, constantly changing, offering up a peaceful montage of life Parisian style. Lean back, take a deep breath, smile and forget whatever it is that might have been bothering you. In that moment, you are relaxing, and you are at peace.

The Lizard Whisperer

I'm thinking I may have missed my calling. Seriously. I'm not saying my career as an attorney was time squandered; I believe I did pretty well and I know I greatly enjoyed the experience. But, something happened today that made me think I might have this other skill set that maybe I haven't given enough thought to developing. To be specific, I'm wondering if maybe I should have been a therapist, or at least an animal therapist. And, you'll never guess how this occurred to me. I have a lizard to thank.

It was mid-day, and I was, as the phrase goes, minding my own business when I noticed an odd shape in silhouette form on the floor in the hallway just outside one of our bedrooms. Was this a large dust ball or just yet another aggregation of Mojo's shedded hairs that had finally achieved enough critical mass to attract my attention? When it moved a bit, my first impulse was that it was simply movement spurred by the nearby air conditioning vent. But, then its moves took on a much more animated, life-like aspect that no hair ball I had ever seen had ever indulged in. As I drew closer, I saw this dark form was alive. It was a creature. I stopped in my tracks. What am I dealing with here? How do I keep Mojo from messing with whatever this is? And, most importantly, is there a chance in hell that I can actually catch this thing?

Soon enough I came to realize I was staring at a gecko lizard. And, I could see it was staring back at me. My concerns here were fairly simple. I didn't want this guy or girl setting up shop in the house and launching the Gecko Hilton where hundreds or thousands of these seemingly harmless little creatures would take up residence and tell all their buddies about how great life is inside the Jeff and Lily residence. This was not the Party Central I envisioned for our place. Not unreasonable of me, right?

But, as you know, these little fellows are super fast. If you think you can chase one of them and catch them, you are seriously deluding yourself. And, not only are they fast, they are nimble. They can change course radically and in nanoseconds. Not only that, gravity is not their enemy. They can run swiftly not only on the horizontal plane (i.e., your floors), but on the vertical plane as well (i.e., your walls). Chasing them is an utter act in futility, especially since this guy had already noticed me tracking him. No, I said to myself, I need a different strategy here. So.....I decided to have a conversation with him.

I know what you're thinking. You did what?? You're engaging a reptile in an adult conversation? Have you lost your mind? Yeah, probably. I'm not suggesting this was a two way dialogue, mind you. I may be delusional, but I'm not a complete idiot. Yes, it was a monologue. First, I decided to give the little fellow a name. I called him Steve. People who know me are aware that I commonly name strange animals, whether they be burros, sea lions or monkeys as Steve. I can't explain that. But, Steve it was.

As Steve inched his way into the bedroom, I followed him very slowly ever so much not wanting him to take off where I would never be able to find him again or watch him slither into the air conditioning duct and forever be lost to me while he embarked on the initial staging for the Gecko Hilton. Fortunately, Steve moved about as slowly as I did and he kept looking back at me no doubt wondering what my next move would be. Rather than continuing to move forward, however, I stopped and crouched down and simply talked to Steve in a calm deliberate voice. I asked him about himself and his family and what his plans were. I assured him that I would keep Mojo at bay and that he had nothing to fear from me. In fact, I told him, if he worked with me I would help him find his way back to the out of doors which I assumed is what he really wanted anyway. In hushed tones, I described to Steve the beauty of the great outdoors, its tastes, fragrances and sights. Steve did not run away. He stopped, turned a bit, tilted his head and eyed me with what I will most foolishly describe as curiosity and perhaps a sprinkling of interest. I continued to talk in soothing tones ever so slowly inching closer. Steve, somewhat to my surprise, held his ground.

I know this sounds ludicrous, but I began to think that Steve was beginning to think that I was not the threat to him that he first contemplated. I was beginning to think that my calm, soothing demeanor and very slow movement were sending him a message that maybe this weird dude could help him. That maybe he could even trust me. As I got closer, I reached for a waste paper basket that had a plastic bag liner in it. I moved in uber slow motion. Steve barely budged, but we were moving, albeit achingly slowly, toward the back of the room where we would have our final showdown.

We were now inches from the window and mere inches from the air conditioning duct. I kept telling Steve in the softest tones that I could muster how this could really end well if he would only let me help him. He turned and now looked squarely at me, eyes tilting this way and that. I was now down on the floor as close to eye to eye level with him as I was apt to get. Ever so slowly I lowered the basket and encouraged Steve to get in. I did not reach out to him, confident that would only cause him to scurry down the duct or clamor up the wall. I knew I had to be patient. It was my only option, although Mojo was laying in the doorway his ears at red alert, his body ready to pounce. In what seemed like an eternity, Steve inched his way to the basket and jumped in! Of course, we'll never know whether Steve's decision was a leap of faith by him in trusting my constant pleas, or whether he wrongly assumed this basket was really just another escape route. But, allow me the indulgence to believe Steve and I had a moment of understanding there. In any event, in he went and I quickly took the top of the plastic bag and folded it on top keeping Steve inside for the few seconds it would take for me to escort him outside.

The interesting thing is that when I got Steve out on the deck and released him, he left the basket, but he did not run away. Instead, he turned around, cocked his head again and looked at me. I smiled and told him it was a pleasure working with him and that I'd see him around.

Back inside, I patted Mojo for his forbearance, and I patted myself on the back for tapping into a skill set I never knew I had: how to meaningfully communicate with a lizard! Who knew?!

And Along Came Owen

As any parent will tell you, the moment your child is born is like no other in your life. I mean, think of it. You have created a life. It is one of the few abilities that all humans -- no matter what their station in life or where they live or what their belief system might be -- share. And, while our lives are hopefully filled with an array of amazing adventures and colorful memories, there is nothing quite like being there at the moment your son or daughter arrives on planet earth and you are introduced for the first time.

In our case, the arrivals of Jesse and Alex are forever emblazoned in Lily's memory and mine although, obviously, from radically different perspectives. With Jesse, the drama was intense. Not only was this our first experience, but Jesse made a lasting impression by putting his mom through the ringer with a most stressful and rigorous labor experience. It turns out he decided to twist his body upside down at the last minute complicating delivery options, increasing pain levels for Lily and producing a meteoric rise in stress levels for his father as I helplessly looked on. I do vividly remember the hospital staff hurriedly whisking Lily down to the delivery room as I stumbled behind them ever so awkwardly trying to put on the surgical slippers over my flip flops as I frantically hopped down the hall trying to keep up with them. But when the delivery had concluded and when they handed Jesse to me to hold, and I gazed into that little face, there was no way to hold back the tears. There is no way to define the specialness of these moments or to adequately convey the depth of emotions that course through your veins.

With Alex, on the other hand, the labor and delivery were clearly choreographed by Walt Disney, I am quite certain. It was painless; it was peaceful. It was on schedule. I even had an opportunity to go to the cafeteria to get some breakfast! And, importantly, Lily's memories are not clouded by pain or stress. Once again, though, those first moments of holding Alex in my arms transcend everything. In those moments, the world stops spinning; there is nothing else happening. All that life is, all that it embraces, is staring right back at you, this little life you have created. Amazing. Overpowering. There are no other words for it.

We flash forward now more than three decades. While parenting never ends, grandparenting is about to begin. We have been anxiously awaiting the arrival of Alex and Katie's baby for months, and the time has come for us to visit and receive our formal introductions to our first grandchild. We now know his name to be Owen Michael Golland. Yes, that's OMG! As we take a seat on the living room couch, Katie hands Owen to Lily who cradles him in her arms while I gurgle some over the top emotional words that I'm sure made no sense as I take a spot right next to Lily. Both Lily and I start talking to Owen as if he's already quite conversant in English. When I get to hold Owen, I immediately tell him that over the next several days I'm going to tell him everything about his dad when he was a baby and beyond. No, there won't be any secrets here.

But, there's something else at play here. I realize it's the passage of time. As I stare into Owen's eyes, I feel like I'm looking at history. My mind flashes back to my parents and even my grandparents -- this chain of history that continues to unfold at a most personal level. To put a somewhat different spin on it, I see a passing of the torch. Here is the next generation, one that is likely to take us well into the next century. And, as I think back to my grandparents, whose roots date back well into the 19th century, the passage of time takes on a whole new dimension, one so much bigger than me. This perspective makes each of us seem so microscopic in significance. And part of me wishes that my parents and grandparents were here to share this moment with me. Oh well....much better to live in the moment, I conclude.

Maybe it's just me but I find it hard to look at Owen and not project more mature, well developed thoughts and reactions in him as I closely watch his every squirm and twitch. When he occasionally crinkles his nose or purses his lips, I can't help but wonder what he might be thinking. As I watch his eyes dart back and forth behind closed eyelids and those barely perceptible eyelashes, it is impossible not to ask what is he seeing? Is he dreaming? If so, what could possibly be on his mind? I mean, the little guy is only two weeks old. The same goes for his smiles, at least in the early days after our arrival. Is he actually pleased about something or is it just gas?

Then there's this issue with "the touch"? I seriously doubt that I have originated that term here, but what I am referring to is the ability to calm a baby once he or she becomes agitated or, worse, flat out screaming unhappy. It is undisputed that Katie has the touch. She is the master of the touch. When Owen gets beyond the second level of fussiness, Katie is there to magically and consistently bring serenity to the little guy. It may take the form of soothing words or the right bouncing motions, or the right stroking or body positioning. And, of course, feeding is always an option. We're talking an art form here not a science. If this were merely a function of arithmetic calculation, everyone would be good at it. But, no. Meme Lily, I must say, had an excellent touch. Most excellent calming abilities. And, new daddy, Alex, showed us his very impressive patience and equally impressive skills at using the large exercise ball to calmly bounce Owen into tranquility. Poppy Jeff, on the other hand, uh... not so much. Not that Owen would revolt whenever I would assume the babysitting duties. No, not at all. Owen and I definitely had a number of extended periods of time where he would either sleep in my arms or, if he were awake, I would fill his ears with stories of Alex as a young child as I had promised when we first arrived. But, when Owen did get fussy I cannot say I had "the touch" that Katie, Alex or Lily had to calm him down and bring him back to a calmer reality. I would shift the way I held him. I would endlessly stroke or pat him on the back. I would walk him around the house. I would bounce him on the big ball. I wanted desperately for one of these techniques to work if only to allow Katie to get some richly deserved sleep which she otherwise only got in sporadic stretches of about two hours or so. All the while I would whisper in a frenzy to Owen, "no, no, no, Owen. Please, please let mommy sleep." Not very effective. I guess it's a good thing I could do the food shopping, cooking and dog walking.

As the days wore on, we could actually see Owen develop some. Most memorably, as Owen's smiles developed, we knew them to be legitimate reflections of his happiness. Whether it was the touch or voice of one of us, or a response to music, or his sheer joy of stretching out on the couch and testing out his churning legs, there was little doubt there were stimuli that made the little guy happy. Think about it. There are few things that can make you smile so instinctively as seeing your own grandchild smile. I'm telling you, the kid is a charmer. Even his burps and farts are charming.

Yeah, we're over the moon alright. Isn't that where all grandparents belong?

Chaos x 2 = Nirvana

Chaos is a term we tend to throw around rather loosely. Even thoughtlessly, you might say. Just like I'm going to do right now. Normally, we use the term chaos to describe pandemonium or complete dishevelment, a situation so removed from our usual norms that we're at a loss as to how to cope with it. Lord knows, we can all conjure up situations around the globe that give chaos its truest meaning, and I know you know what I mean. But, in our own, mostly controlled, lives we very liberally call upon the term chaos to help describe hiccups in our normal life rhythms, although some hiccups are louder and more disruptive than others.

Lily and I are witnessing first-hand a world gone mad, or, as I've suggested, chaos, having visited the world of Jesse and Laura. Here are two absolutely wonderful people -- our older son and daughter-in-law -- who have been living fabulous lives and whose careers have taken them from Denver to Quito to Mexico City. Living the dream some might say. But, on December 19 they were presented with new additions to their lives, twin sons Oliver and Charlie! Yes, having children is something billions of us go through and not just survive but feel that it thoroughly embellishes our lives. It surely provides us with an unmatchable lifetime experience. But twins? Well...that poses a whole set of challenges most folks never have to face, doesn't it?

It's been decades, of course, since Lily and I had to deal with the dramatic nuances and roller coaster adventures of being parents for the first time. But, having been introduced to grandparenthood for the first time four months ago courtesy of Katie and Alex, those moments of drama, and more importantly, the stresses and rollicking emotions of those early experiences were re-awakened through baby Owen's introduction to life on planet earth. And, with Owen, we witnessed the dislocation of the otherwise established rhythms of daily living to which Alex and Katie had grown so accustomed. You know, the sleep deprivation, the diaper changing, the seemingly endless demands for new supplies and equipment, the disruption of work schedules. And, did I mention sleep deprivation?

So, the chaos (again, if I may use that term) that greets new parents has fondly reached out to Laura and Jesse. In spades. Let's start with the most obvious challenge: who is who? During the term of the pregnancy, Laura and Jesse regularly referred to "baby A" and "baby B." Not that they were abstractions, mind you. It's just that there was no need to tell them apart. But, once having entered the world, all that has changed. And, remember, Oliver and Charlie are identical! Before leaving the hospital, they had the wisdom to paint a couple of Oliver's toenails red which was a great way to distinguish the two little guys. However, 98% of the time the two of them are all swaddled up or, at a minimum, wearing socks, so you can never see their feet! They also had different colored knit caps for each of them but that pattern quickly got messed up as Oliver and Charlie got whatever cap was within arm's reach.

Okay then, so when you're holding one of the babies in your arms and you say, "how YOU doin'?" you really can't be all that certain who you're talking to. Even with Oliver and Charlie passing the one month landmark, both parents not infrequently would not be sure who they were holding. Charlie's head is a bit longer from front to back, but since most of the time the two boys are wearing knit caps that clue isn't all that helpful. Lily believed she saw discernible nuances in a curve in Charlie's nose and a wrinkle in his ear, and she was often right in her identifying guesses. But...not always. I can't wait to see how this mini-drama develops.

Then there's the challenge of keeping the little guys on the same schedule. You have to do this since the alternative means being deprived of any sleep for perhaps the next two years. Not really tenable, right? In the case of Oliver and Charlie, this means getting the little guys up every three hours to feed them regardless of whether they may think of themselves as being hungry or not. During daylight hours this may not seem like an overwhelming burden, but at night? Every night? And, of course, it's not just a matter of awakening the little sleepers and sticking a bottle in their adorable mouths. Oh no. There's the associated burping, soothing, applications of the burp rag, and, naturally, the diaper changing (which, judging from their most vociferous screams, do not appear to be either Oliver or Charlie's favorite pastimes). Then there's the bathing which brings out the kind of baby screams that can likely be heard in the next zip code. And, for poor Laura, she must add into this ritual time for the regular pumping of breast milk. What fun!

But, just when you think you've hit your limit and exhaustion is about to declare victory, there are these amazing moments of calm. The calm within the chaos. It is in these moments that the nirvana of it all can be seen and felt. Often, these occur while the boys are feeding or in the moments immediately following. They are at peace and so are you. It is then that you have the luxury of taking that deep breath and staring at their tiny but gorgeously precise features. Remember, these babies are preemies so whatever image you have of newborns back them up a few weeks. What you have are facial features, for example, that are exquisitely perfect but absolutely miniature in dimension. I know that I have never seen such small noses or eyelids, or such divinely pursed lips. Their fingers are so tiny that if the fingers of one hand could be stretched wide I doubt they could span the width of two piano keys. And, their toes seem like nothing more than adorable afterthoughts.

So, yes, there is much "chaos" at play here if I may use that term loosely. But, for the most part, it is a quiet chaos if that makes any sense. And, what a grand way to start a new stage in one's life!

Here's to Laura and Jesse! And, here's to Oliver and Charlie!

The Undoing of History

We tend to think of history as something that happens somewhere else, to someone else. To be sure, we feel deeply affected by worldly events no matter how far away they may occur, but history is, for the most part, something we unconsciously reserve to history books. We read about historical events and try to envision what it must have been like to be there, but notwithstanding our best efforts, we are dealing in abstractions here, not gut wrenching realities. Even with respect to current day events, we learn what we know through the TV screen or other forms of mass media. The images on the screen definitely bring these events to life in a way that no printed word can, but even here as you sit in the comfort of your home the reality of this history -- the feel, the smell, the immediacy of it -- are still several steps removed.

That all changed for Alex and me a couple of weeks ago in Paris. It was early evening and, as had had become our new pattern, Alex, Katie and Owen had settled in for a break at the apartment just as Lily and I had in our hotel room, all awaiting a meeting up for dinner once Owen fell asleep. But then Alex got in touch with me sending me urgent images of a cathedral on fire. To be honest, these images which were from a newsfeed, at first did not resonate with me. But, suddenly I realized these were images of the cathedral of Notre Dame. And, yet even in those moments I was somehow doubtful of their truthfulness. But Alex said he would be by in five minutes and said we had to go and witness this. I agreed.

When I went down to the hotel lobby, the desk clerk was unaware of the event. When I mentioned it to him, he frowned and tilted his head in disbelief but then did a quick search on his computer. When the images came up on his screen, he gasped and his hands went to his mouth in a pure statement of shock. Alex appeared and we took off.

As we raced through the narrow streets of the Left Bank and peered into bars along the way, the TVs were all blaring the news of the fire. But, here's where the reality set in. Navigating the narrow streets and heading downhill, the sky was filled with billowing smoke and then, depending on a break in the skyline of the buildings in front of us, the hot orange of flames shooting skyward could be seen. It looked like the whole city was on fire just blocks away. The crowds thickened and soon it became a lava flow as everyone headed for the river. The stress was palpable and contagious among the crowds the closer we got to ground zero.

As we neared the river, we could now see in full view the cathedral in flames. In my life I had never seen flames so large, so high, so sweeping. They were at least thirty to forty feet high and massive in width. They stretched from the back side of the magnificent two front towers to the rear section of the cathedral and its now clearly threatened spire wholly engulfed in flames licking at its very existence. Helicopters would occasionally swoop by. Sirens were the constant soundtrack. Police would be feverishly yelling at people to stand back in efforts to control the lava flow of the many, like Alex and me, wanting or needing to witness history. The gridlocked cars had windows opened, passengers with jaws agape or cameras flashing. The crowds were universally dumbstruck by what they were witnessing. And, many were either openly crying or quietly wiping away tears that just wouldn't stop.

As I stared in bewilderment, I kept wondering where were the fire fighters? All I saw were two streams of water, one near the front, the other near the back of the cathedral which seemed so utterly inadequate in the face of what might not unfairly be described as an Armageddon-like expression of fire. I expected helicopters dousing water from above and boats gorging water from the river. In the panic we were all feeling in those moments, we wanted water coming from every possible source and from every possible direction. No effort seemed sufficient.

The mammoth flames had now devoured enough of the roof to not only tumble the cathedral's beautiful spire, but to fully expose the skeletal timbers of the building's roof. All exposed, they were nothing now but mere kindling to some demonic bonfire and we knew it would only be moments before the entire roof collapsed. But, when it happened it was stunning. In a moment the roof was gone and it was only a question of where the flames would turn to feed their unending appetite. The gasps and moans from the crowd were penetrating to anyone with a soul.

It was just ninety minutes earlier that we had been finishing up our day's explorations when we decided to take a run past Notre Dame. Lily decided to take the stroller and sit in the small but fabulously charming park behind the cathedral while Katie, Alex, Owen and I walked an encircling route around the building taking in the towers, smiling at the gargoyles, dodging the long lines but, as always, taking in an iconic bit of world history. I mean, here is a building that has been with us for close to nine centuries surviving every monstrous act of man and nature that has dotted human history all these centuries. It is part of the reason that Notre Dame is such a world renowned landmark. And yet here it was, in front of our eyes, its existence actually threatened. In those moments, it felt like the undoing of history.

So, this is what experiencing history in the most real sense feels like. I cannot say that I physically felt the heat of those flames, but emotionally I most surely did.

With One Bite...

Vivid memories can be triggered by so many things, can't they? A random thought, a conversation with a family member or a good friend. Or, sometimes, they can be triggered by the senses, like a piece of music or a long forgotten fragrance or aroma. Or, perhaps, a familiar sight not seen in many years.

For me, though, my mind zoomed back decades not by any of these stimuli, but by my taste buds. With one bite, actually. We were out in San Diego visiting Alex, Katie and baby Owen when one morning I found myself driving Katie to a doctor's appointment. Katie had broken her ankle some weeks before and couldn't drive and I was happy to take on the job. When dropping her off, she suggested I might kill some time at a Jewish deli a few blocks down the street -- a place called D.Z. Akin's. Excellent idea, I thought.

I entered the mostly empty restaurant and sat in a booth beginning to peruse the menu. Frankly, I was expecting to order a bagel and lox. I mean, how can you not do that at a Jewish deli at breakfast time? But, as I gazed at the menu, I could not stop staring at one item: the potato knish. For those of you not familiar with this Eastern European culinary tidbit, imagine a filo dough stuffed with a seasoned mashed potato that's been baked to a crispy, hot, melt-in-your-mouth definition of comfort food. I knew I had to order this notwithstanding the fact that I hadn't tasted one in about sixty-five years, and I'll tell you why.

When I was a child, we lived in White Plains, New York, a Westchester suburb of New York City. Back then, my grandfather -- my father's father -- lived in a home for the aged in Brooklyn along the boardwalk at Coney Island. From time to time, we would get in the car and drive to Brooklyn to visit grandpa. I have to admit these visits were not my favorite outings. First, the road trips were long and boring. More importantly, while grandpa was most definitely a sweet man, communications with him were most difficult. He spoke very little English; Yiddish was his language of choice. Plus back then I was hopelessly shy and any effort at conversation by me with any adult was a challenge seldom overcome. The seemingly endless conversations between my father and grandpa were entirely in Yiddish which I understood as much as the squawking of the birds outside on the boardwalk. So -- I would sit there numbly squished between my father and my grandpa listening to words I did not understand, staring at old people who in my youthfulness all seemed like they were four hundred years old, wishing only for my exit visa.

At some point, my father would arise and declare the visit to be over and offered to go for a walk along the boardwalk. Freedom!! Getting out into the warming sun, feeling the sea breeze, watching the swooping seagulls, and watching other families enjoy the same panorama was hugely rewarding and more than made up for the almost claustrophobic-like feelings I had experienced earlier being trapped among the ancient beings where grandpa lived. But, the best was yet to come.

As we strolled up the boardwalk, we would always stop at a small eatery that offered, among other treats, knishes of all stripes. I only remember the one stuffed with kasha, which is like a buckwheat or barley filling. And, of course, the potato, my favorite. After experiencing the high of the boardwalk stroll, the potato knish brought it all home, so to speak. It finished the outing on a perfect note.

So, when the waitress brought my knish to my table in San Diego, I could only stare at it for a few moments and smile. This was not just a snack. For me, I was staring at history coming to life. And then I took a bite. As I bit through the crunch of the covering dough and sank my teeth into the savory warmth of the seasoned potatoes, I closed my eyes and allowed myself to travel back through time, through all those decades back to Brooklyn, back to those moments of happiness when the sun and sea air surrounded me and gave me a taste I will never forget. All with one bite.

CPSIA information can be obtained
at www.ICGtesting.com
Printed in the USA
LVHW070804010322
712279LV00040B/971

9 781638 372349